IMAGINING LOS ANGELES

# IMAGINING LOS ANGELES

*A City in Fiction*

## David Fine

University of New Mexico Press
Albuquerque

© 2000 by University of New Mexico Press
All rights reserved.
First Edition

Library of Congress Cataloging-in-Publication Data
Fine, David M., 1934–
Imagining Los Angeles: a city in fiction/David Fine—1ST ed.
p. cm.
Includes index.
ISBN 0-8263-2207-7 (cloth: alk. paper)
ISBN 0-8263-2208-5 (pbk: alk. paper)
1. American fiction—California—Los Angeles—History and criticism.
2. American fiction—20TH century—History and criticism.
3. American fiction—19TH century—History and criticism.
4. Los Angeles (California)—In literature.
5. City and town life in literature.
6. Cities and towns in literature.
I. Title.
PS374.L57 F56 2000
813.009'3279494—dc21
99-050717
CIP

Designed by Sue Niewiarowski

Photographs courtesy of University of Southern California,
on behalf of the USC Library Department of Special Collections.

# CONTENTS

# PREFACE AND ACKNOWLEDGMENTS

This history of narrative fiction about Los Angeles from the 1880s to the 1990s grows out of a long interest I have had in California, particularly Los Angeles, fiction, an interest that began some years ago when I taught a seminar on Nathanael West and F. Scott Fitzgerald that focused on their years in Hollywood. That experience led to several critical essays and reviews and the editing of three collections of essays on West Coast writing. Even before this interest emerged, I published a book (an expanded version of my dissertation) on fiction about European immigrants in the American city just before and after the turn of the century. What I came to discover was that the two subjects have considerable overlap. Not only do both deal with the subject of the city in literature, but with the notion of border crossings, geographic and cultural passages, representations of the process of entering one place and leaving another. Although the earlier book dealt chiefly with people who left Old World farms, slums, and shtetls for New World slums and ghettos and the present book deals with an essentially middle-class migration across a continent, by Pullman and not steerage, the migratory experiences have considerable parallels. The parallels have been even more noticeable in the past few decades, as immigration—from Latin America and Asia as well as from every other region of the globe—has all but replaced domestic migration as the chief source of population growth in Los Angeles. This shift is reflected in the strong presence of a vital multicultural, multiethnic fiction in Los Angeles today.

From its beginnings Los Angeles fiction has been a migrant fiction, constructed essentially—and until the past few decades almost exclusively—by men and women who left homes elsewhere, drawn to Los Angeles and Hollywood largely to work as screenwriters. Like immigrant fiction, Los Angeles fiction is double-edged: implicitly, at least, it is about both the place discovered and the place left behind, what is gained and lost in the process of extirpation and resettlement. In the migrant writers' imagination the past is an "elsewhere" that is never fully erased from memory. The dialectical interplay between past and present, then and now, East and West, is a recurring and significant feature in the fiction. Paradoxically, in the city located at the farthest edge of the continent and dedicated to new beginnings and liberation from the past (which lies in the East), history—the claim of the past—is never far away in consciousness, never escapable. This is a theme I return to again and again.

I approach the fiction in the contexts of both urban and regional literature. Both categories present problems—problems, though, that help to define the local tradition and distinguish it from literature produced elsewhere. First, in its low-density horizontal spread across a vast basin the city simply did not look like a city to the arriving writers—not like New York, Chicago, or San Francisco. It was a city that appeared to have no center and hence no periphery. It rambled on and on across a landscape that spread from mountain to ocean. Its pastiche of architectural styles, moreover, simulacra of every manner in architectural history, gave it the appearance of what the historian Carey McWilliams called "a giant improvisation." It seemed to the newly arrived writers like an "unreal" city—and was represented as such in their fiction—a fragile and temporary place that could be torn down at any moment if it didn't collapse first in an earthquake. Writers from James M. Cain and Nathanael West to Norman Mailer and Alison Lurie invoked the image of the movie studio itself: the city as giant annex to the back lot, a jumble of sets and props.

If placing Los Angeles fiction in an urban paradigm presents one kind of problem, though, situating it in a regional context offers another. As migrant fiction it undercuts the conventional wisdom of literary regionalism: that it is the product of writers intimately bound to the places about which they write, who have an abiding relationship with the land. In Los Angeles no such abiding relationship existed— not, that is, until very recent times when at least some of the fiction has been the work of native-born Angelenos who express a real connection with the place. In general, though, it is the migrant writers' sense of removal, of dis-placement, that gives the Los Angeles novel its distinctive and distinguishing qualities, qualities that persist in the fiction to the present day. Viewing the literature from both urban and regional perspectives—setting it against the conventions of both perspectives, that is—offers a useful opening to the literature.

My approach is to place the fiction in the contexts of Los Angeles's social and cultural history. I look at the writers who came, when and why they came, what they found, and how they responded to the city in their fiction. I am interested both in the way the place—in all its apparent oddity—shaped the writers' imaginations and how their imaginative renderings shaped the city, structured it in image and myth as the city of dream, desire, and deception.

Surprisingly, given the fact that Los Angeles has emerged as a major twentieth-century literary center, arguably *the* late twentieth-century American literary city, scant critical attention has been given to the extensive body of fiction produced in and about it. Franklin Walker's *A Literary History of Southern California*, the only full-length study, is now a half-century old and covers essentially the nineteenth century, barely getting into the twentieth. Walker leaves off with a few pages on the 1920s and 1930s—the very decades when Los Angeles fiction had its real beginnings. Since Walker there have been a number of studies, books and essays, focusing on specific authors or particular modes of Los Angeles writing, like the Hollywood novel, the tough-guy detective story, and the 1930s brand of hard-boiled crime fiction; and there have also been chapters in recent books—notably those of Mike Davis and Kevin Starr—that discuss aspects of Los Angeles fiction. My own edited collection of critical essays, by various hands, on Los Angeles writers, *Los Angeles in Fiction: A Collection of Essays* (published by the University of New Mexico Press in 1984 and reissued in an expanded second edition in 1994), remains, though a compilation of different voices, the only full-length study. To date there has been no comprehensive single-author book-length assessment of the city's rich fictional history. This book is an attempt to remedy that lack.

Los Angeles, America's second city, has come to mean different and opposite things in the national imagination: America's Utopia and Dystopia, the site of its national Heaven and Hell, the best and the worst place the country has to offer. It has come to be, if not a national obsession, a place to read the national pulse, a gauge to register its cultural possibilities and darkest apprehensions. Of late it has become the capital of American noir. The identification of the city with dark imaginings and violent endings began in earnest in the 1930s in the fiction of Raymond Chandler, James M. Cain, Horace McCoy, and Nathanael West. Today the ghosts of these writers are haunting the contemporary narrative landscape of the city—in both fiction and film, in recyclings and resurrections of the hard-boiled style, the tough-guy detective story, and the dark, satiric Hollywood narrative. If, though, the major tradition in the fiction runs to disaster and dark comedy, there has also been, in some recent novels I discuss in the final chapter, a countertrend toward affirmation; even in apocalyptic, millennial times writers, both Anglo and ethnic, have found reason to celebrate life lived at the edge.

Attempting to trace principal lines of Los Angeles fiction poses the inclusiveness/exclusiveness dilemma; thousands of novels have taken Los Angeles (or Hollywood) as their setting. Is the subject better served by citing as many novels as can be squeezed into a single volume or by focusing closely on the most significant, definitive works? To be "inclusive" would have run the risk of reducing the book to little more than an annotated bibliography; to be "exclusive," to focus narrowly and deeply on the "major" works only, would have the disadvantage of decontextualization, of failing to see the tradition whole— in its full literary, cultural, and historical context. There are obviously main highways and minor roads, red and blue lines, on the literary map of the city. I have tried to navigate the ground by taking into account, sometimes quite briefly, a large number of works that I found of some literary and cultural interest and treating in greater detail the works that lie on the main highway—"vintage" works, for instance, by Upton Sinclair, Raymond Chandler, Ross Macdonald, John Fante, Nathanael West, Aldous Huxley, and Budd Schulberg and, in more recent years, by Christopher Isherwood, Alison Lurie, Norman Mailer, Joan Didion, Thomas Pynchon, Walter Mosley, James Ellroy, Kate Braverman, and Carolyn See—works that merit detailed attention. In the end, though, it was the theme of each chapter that dictated the works chosen for inclusion. Obviously, my selection will not satisfy every reader. As I write this, I have before me the Sunday, April 25,

1999, issue of the *Los Angeles Times Book Review*, which is devoted to Los Angeles literature and cites a good number of contemporary novelists writing about Los Angeles who have not found a place in this book. The field is enormous, beyond the scope of a single book.

I am indebted to California State University, Long Beach, for a stipend in summer 1997 and a sabbatical leave in fall 1997 to pursue this study and to the John Randolph and Dora Haynes Foundation for a generous grant to work on the book in spring 1998. My gratitude also goes to several individuals: to Mark Laurila, who read many of these novels while I was preparing the manuscript and spent many hours with me discussing them, providing dozens of useful comments both on specific novels and on the structure of this book; to Elizabeth Young, whose sound literary judgment and expert editorial skills helped immeasurably in the book's final preparation; to David Peck, who carefully read the manuscript and made judicious comments throughout; and to Elizabeth C. Hadas, my editor at the University of New Mexico Press, for her encouragement and helpful suggestions. A further debt is owed to José Luis Matud, my computer wizard, for many hours of technical assistance.

# 1

## STARTING POINTS

*The Place and the Writers*

Hell, we threw the land in and sold 'em the climate.
ATTRIBUTED TO LAND DEVELOPER LUCKY BALDWIN

I should have stayed home.
HORACE McCOY, BOOK TITLE

Next day, we took a taxi to Hollywood. I was amazed at the sin
of the city, and at the lack of shape. There seemed no reason why
it should ever stop. Miles and miles of little houses, wooden or
stucco, under a technicolor sky. Miles of little gardens crowded
into blossoms and flowering bushes; the architecture is dominated
by the vegetation. A city without privacy . . . the only permanent
buildings were schools and the churches. On the hill giant letters
spell "Hollywoodland," but this is only another advertisement. It is
silly to say that Hollywood, or any other city is "unreal." But what
the arriving traveler first sees are merely advertisements for a city
which doesn't exist.
CHRISTOPHER ISHERWOOD, DIARIES, 1939–1960

Writing about San Francisco as a literary city more than a century ago (1897), Frank Norris had this to say:

> There is no great city to the north of us, to the south none nearer than Mexico, to the west the waste of the Pacific, to the east the wastes of the desert. Here we are set down as a pin point in a vast circle of solitude. Isolation produces individuality, originality. . . . We have time to develop unhampered types and characters unbiased by outside influences, types that are admirably adapted to fictitious treatment.[1]

Norris's essay, "An Opening for Novelists: Great Opportunities for Fiction Writers in San Francisco," pitched that city, not only as *the* West Coast metropolis, but also as the ideal setting for western local color fiction, a city that offered "types" one could not find elsewhere. San Francisco's isolation provided the opening, the opportunity, for a vigorous new literature uncontaminated by genteel East Coast conventions. It was an endlessly fascinating place for the Chicago-born Norris, a wayward, polyglot city at the end of the frontier that offered itself to storytellers in search of the exotic and the colorful. It possessed "a strange mixed life . . . an undefinable air suggestive of stories all at once." Its hybrid quality, its odd blend of racial and ethnic types, made for a splendid sideshow. Norris talks about a red-haired child "half Jew half Chinese" and of a dishwasher in a Portuguese wine shop with a Negro father and a mother who was a Chinese "slave girl."

These were the exotic "types" spawned by the city that came into being in the gold rush. Its migrants and drifters, outcasts and opportunists would be incorporated by Norris two years later in his novel *McTeague*. In constructing his wayward San Francisco of the nineties, Norris had earlier literary explorers of the city to draw on, a whole generation of journalists and storytellers who since the 1850s had been drifting in from somewhere else—Mark Twain, Bret Harte, Ambrose Bierce, Robert Louis Stevenson, and others—writers who had bestowed on early San Francisco its dual image of crowded, polyglot city and exotic frontier arena of oddballs whose stories cried out to be told. In the stories and sketches of Norris and his fellow visiting journalists in the second half of the nineteenth century, the city was an amalgam of the urban and the backwoods, the instant metropolis and "wild west" town, replete with the kind of frontier eccentricity and peculiarity demanded by local color writing.

What Norris did not know in 1897 — perhaps *could* not have known then — was that at that very time a new instant city was being manufactured, packaged, and promoted four hundred miles to the south, one that by the 1920s would reach and then surpass San Francisco in population. Los Angeles emerged as the consequence not of gold rush migration but of a land boom made possible by the convergence of two rail lines into Southern California — the Southern Pacific in 1876 and the Santa Fe in 1886 — and the aggressive promotion of land speculators, subdividers, city boosters, and railroad tycoons (who were given large land subsidies for bringing in the roads). The land south of the Tehachapi Mountains, the "cow counties" of Southern California, began filling up not with the kind of hardy adventurers who came to Northern California a generation earlier by ship or Conestoga wagon but with a more timid, gentler breed of migrants — largely white, middle class, and Protestant — lured by a national advertising campaign hawking consistently warm weather, open land, healthful dry air, and agricultural opportunity.

Boosted into existence, Los Angeles grew steadily, if unevenly, and sometimes spectacularly in the next several decades. In the 1880s the population went from 11,000 to 50,000. It doubled to 100,000 in the nineties, tripled in the first decade of the new century to 300,000, and by the early 1920s matched San Francisco's population of 575,000. After that it never had to look back — or north — to see who was gaining. Unlike San Francisco, hemmed in on the tip of a peninsula, Los Angeles had room to spread out across a vast land basin stretching from the San Gabriel Mountains to the Pacific Ocean. With a man-made harbor, imported water, oil reserves, a movie industry, aviation plants, wartime defense manufacturing, and a postwar aerospace industry, it has grown into a Pacific Rim metropolis of more than 3.5 million people.

Not only America's second most populous city, Los Angeles rivals, and may even surpass, New York City as its most culturally diverse. From a white Protestant city it has become in a hundred years a multiethnic enclave and immigrant destination where at least eighty languages are spoken and where today nonwhites constitute a decided majority. This is true not only of the city but of Los Angeles County and parts of surrounding counties in the basin. City limits have never really defined Los Angeles, a regional city-state stretching from Ventura County on the northwest to Orange County to the southeast, with a landmass comprising one-sixth of the state and a population of about fifteen million people, almost half the residents of the country's most populous state.

Back in the pre-railroad 1850s and 1860s, though, while San Francisco was shaping itself as *the* West Coast city (and today San Franciscans still refer to it as *the* city), Los Angeles was a small encampment of Mexicans, Indians (living in a kind of limbo after the abandonment of the Spanish missions), Anglos (both ex-miners and opportunistic "Yankee Dons" who married into prominent rancho families), and Chinese (some of whom drifted down from the mines). El Pueblo de la Reina de Los Angeles (the Town of the Queen of the Angels) was, despite its then-sparse population, like the San Francisco of Twain and Harte, a wayward frontier town, a maze of bordellos, gambling dens, and saloons radiating out a few blocks from a central plaza. It was a place of wooden huts and adobe haciendas, of dirt streets laced with *zanjas*, or irrigation ditches, and of gun-toting, knife-wielding toughs who roamed its muddy paths.

It was a zone of racial conflict too, conflict that intensified after California became part of the Union at midcentury. As the Anglos took control of the land, they saw the darker-skinned population — including those whose arrival predated theirs — as dangerous aliens, foreigners who stood as a threat to community and progress, to the Yankee imperative of Manifest Destiny. That many of the Anglo-Americans who arrived after the Civil War came from the Confederacy and brought their secessionist, pro-slavery sentiments didn't help in racial matters. Horace Bell, one of the early chroniclers of the period and a member of the Los Angeles Rangers, a self-appointed vigilante group that hunted down banditos like Joaquín Murieta, Juan Flores, and Tiburcio Vásquez and prepared them for the frontier justice of lynching, described the pueblo's notorious "Nigger Alley" — "niggers" being anyone not Anglo — in his book *Reminiscences of a Ranger:*

> Every few minutes a rush would be made, and maybe
> a pistol shot would be heard and when the confusion
> subsided . . . you would learn it was only a knife fight
> between two Mexicans, or a gambler had been caught
> by a bullet. Such things were a matter of course and no
> complaints or arrests were ever made.[2]

Violence in "Nigger Alley," a block that bordered the plaza, peaked in 1871 when an Anglo man was killed trying to stop a Chinese gang battle. In the ensuing retaliatory mob attack, nineteen Chinese were killed. Seven men were tried and convicted—of one hundred fifty who were arrested—but their convictions were subsequently overturned and they went free. Bell, an observer, noted that the massacre was not a spontaneous act but was incited by the new police department, whose chief had given orders "to shoot to death any Chinese who might stick a head out of or attempt to escape from [a] besieged building."[3]

The massacre, occurring shortly before the rail lines were built and the city boosters began their campaign to lure tourists and settlers to the region, stands as violent preamble to white hegemony. The process of Americanizing the city began in earnest in the 1880s and continued through the next several decades. A white middle-class population was thickly layered over an ethnically mixed frontier town. The competing rail lines were offering lower and lower fares for transit from the Midwest (dropping at one point to $1 a head in the competition), and a national advertising campaign hawking the magical curative properties of the climate brought hundreds of thousands of tourists and migrants who took up the railroads on their bargain fares. Those who stayed settled not just near the founding zone of the old downtown plaza but, abetted by a new interurban trolley network, were drawn into aggressively marketed new towns stretching across the basin. Greater Los Angeles, the basin, that is, emerged as an aggregation of distantly spaced settlements carved out of a coastal plain bordered by mountains, beyond which lay the desert. Rail magnates, city boosters, and land speculators (often the same people) were busy slicing up the old Spanish and Mexican land grants. The old Californios, the "first families" who held the land grants, were unable to defend their claims in Anglo courts—unable to pay the legal fees much less to understand the laws that were disenfranchising them—and so lost their lands, piece by piece, to Yankee speculators.

In the promotional literature Southern California was hailed as the New Italy, the New Spain, the New Athens—whatever Mediterranean identity helped to sell the land to sun-starved midwesterners. In more grandiose, biblical terms it was lauded as the latest version of the New World Garden, the New Eden (its latitudinal proximity to the Holy Land not lost on the city fathers) ready for occupation by a regenerate Anglo-Saxon population. Thus the booster construction of Southern California as an Anglo-Protestant paradise was superimposed on a place that had been for the past hundred years a Spanish and Mexican Catholic enclave. The Catholic/Mediterranean garden could be marketed as the appointed destination of the Anglo Protestant in search of a fresh start after the East had been spoiled by overcrowding and immigration. The conventional Anglo-Saxon racial linkage of the cooler north with Anglo vigor and productivity and the warmer south with enervation and laziness could be reconfigured. The Spanish and Indian past could be appropriated, idealized, and celebrated as epic and romantic history—ignoring the enslavement and decimation of the Indians in the mission system—while an Anglo-Protestant future could be conjured into existence on the land.

Above all, though, the land was hawked for its sunshine. Salutary properties were attributed to the Mediterranean climate. The railroads put on their payrolls journalists who lauded the miracle of year-round sunshine in promotional tracts. The Southern Pacific hired Charles Nordhoff, former managing editor of William Cullen Bryant's *New York Evening Post*, and Ben Truman, a former *New York Times* correspondent, as publicists. Nordhoff's influential *California for Health, Pleasure and Residence* was published in 1872 and Truman's *Semi-Tropical California* (confusing tropical with Mediterranean) came out two years later, both books significantly appearing just before the railroads entered Southern California.

The railroad publicists, working in tandem with city boosters like *Los Angeles Times* owner and open shop extremist Harrison Gray Otis, his son-in-law Harry Chandler, and his indefatigable city editor, Charles Fletcher Lummis—editor of his own journal, *Land of Sunshine*—together with the new chamber of commerce aggressively and relentlessly promoted the region. It was one of the biggest land

promotions in history. Rail cars were sent across the country filled
with local exhibits—agricultural products, photos, graphs, and statis-
tics. In the decade of the nineties the Santa Fe alone was carrying
three to four trainloads of visitors and potential settlers into Southern California every day. Those who did settle made the region the
destination of what the historian Carey McWilliams called "the largest
internal migration in United States history." It was also, he added,
citing Lummis as the source, "the least heroic."[4]

New towns appeared everywhere across the basin. Speculators
subdivided land into parcels, laid out a few streets, and built a few
hotels. They hounded potential buyers as they got off the trains, lur-
ing them to new town sites with brochures, banners, and free lunches.
Lumber was placed on unsold lots along with "sold" signs. The whole
basin was mustered, coaxed into existence as a vast commodity. By
the turn of the century more than a hundred town sites were on the
market. Some survived while others went bust, standing like ghost
towns among their flourishing neighbors.

With its forest of oil wells, a new deep-water harbor in San Pedro
(a site chosen over Santa Monica after a protracted battle between
General Otis and the chamber of commerce forces and Collis Huntington, whose Southern Pacific Railroad controlled access to Santa
Monica Bay), an aqueduct bringing water two hundred forty miles
across the mountain from Owens Valley, and a vast interurban rail
network with a thousand miles of track, Los Angeles, shortly after the
turn of the century, was poised for even more growth. The old city
limits were extended in every direction. The harbor site brought the
annexation of a long, narrow strip of land leading south to San Pedro
and Wilmington, and the aqueduct (completed in 1913) led to the
annexation of much of the San Fernando Valley, where the pipeline
terminated and where Otis and his cohorts had formed a syndicate
to take options on land in advance of the project. Eager to get a share
of the new water supply, dozens of towns throughout the basin joined
Los Angeles. In a period of less than half a century a small enclave
surrounding the plaza became a vast city of four hundred forty
square miles.

General Otis died in 1917, but in the hands of his son-in-law, the
*Times*, backed by an aggressive chamber of commerce and the All
Year Club, continued to hawk the bright future of Los Angeles as *the*
West Coast metropolis. And in the 1920s it became that. The popu-

lation of the city more than doubled to 1.2 million by the end of the decade, becoming the nation's fifth-largest city and covering an area larger than any other American city. Los Angeles County, too, more than doubled in population, growing from 900,000 in 1920 to 2.2 million in 1930. Big industry was booming. The movies had found a home in the then-suburban town of Hollywood in the 1910s and by the 1920s constituted the major industry of the city. Rich oil deposits, meanwhile, were discovered in Signal Hill, Huntington Beach, and Santa Fe Springs. Future-oriented Southern California also fostered the new aviation industry. The region hosted the first International Air Meet at Dominguez Field in 1910. In the 1920s and 1930s Glen Martin, the Laughead (Lockheed) brothers, Donald Douglas, and Howard Hughes began building and testing planes across the vast expanse from Santa Monica to Santa Barbara.

All of this meant more spread, more sprawl. The population, having gleefully appropriated the automobile, migrated west all the way to the ocean, north to the San Fernando Valley, and south all the way to the harbor, settling dozens of towns along the routes. The coming of the automobile was not in itself responsible for the sprawl within and beyond the expanding city limits. Horizontality was already in place, the product of the checkerboard pattern of town building established by real estate subdividers even before the turn of the century. Los Angeles emerged as a vast semiurban region (McWilliams called it "rurban"), growing less in the conventional urban way of expansion outward from a dense core than by the more or less simultaneous development of widely separated towns linked by the Pacific Electric rail lines. When the automobile came the city was clearly positioned for its arrival. A vast network of roads and highways, promoted by the new Auto Club and built alongside the trolley rights-of-way, crisscrossed the basin. People could move increasingly faster and farther, live at a greater distance from work and shopping. In 1925 there was an estimated one car per 1.6 residents. Interstate highways, too, were being built, and while the Southern Pacific and Santa Fe railroads made mass migration to Southern California possible in the early years, the new interstates offered an alternative route into the promised land. Automobility, in high gear in the 1920s, both responded to and created the demands of a mobile, fluid, post–World War I population. In contributing to the decentralization of the city, the automobile diminished the central city's hegemony.

In such a landscape where does downtown figure? Visiting British architectural critic Reyner Banham, who lamented that he had to learn how to drive in order to "read" Los Angeles, wrote in his 1971 *Los Angeles: The Architecture of Four Ecologies* that the city's downtown is irrelevant. It was never that. Despite the city's decentralization, downtown, with its beaux arts and art deco municipal buildings, its department stores on Broadway and Spring streets, functioned as a crowded, vital urban center. But as the "white flight" move into the suburbs and the emergence of self-contained edge cities intensified after World War II, downtown came to be associated more and more with urban blight. When Banham was writing at the end of the sixties, the massive Bunker Hill redevelopment project, an attempt to revive a dying downtown and attract Pacific Rim trade and finance, was underway. Among other things, this entailed the razing of the stately old houses on the hill and the forced relocation of its inhabitants, a matter that engendered considerable controversy and resentment. Over the last twenty-five years more than thirty skyscrapers (most foreign financed and owned), several apartment buildings, and a contemporary art museum have been set in place on the hill.

Whatever its future, downtown is not, and never has been, irrelevant. It exists today, as it did in the boom years, as a dramatic study in contrast—a microcosm of the city's multiethnic mix, a reflection of its extremes of wealth and poverty, its class and race conflict. Just to the east of the postmodern skyscrapers of the Figueroa/Flower highrise corridor lies the vital Broadway, once the city's theater district (its "Great White Way") and since the 1940s a crowded Mexican-American shopping zone. To the north a few blocks lies Chinatown, and to the east Little Tokyo and the East Los Angeles barrio.

Even before World War I the city began to spread west (Beverly Hills, for instance, was subdivided in 1907—in advance of, perhaps in anticipation of, its becoming the movie colony's favorite homesite), offering the first challenge to downtown hegemony. The march west picked up speed in the twenties. Wilshire Boulevard's "Miracle Mile" of zigzag art deco (and later rounded streamline moderne) commercial sites began the process of rivaling downtown as department store center, and Hollywood (meaning not just the town but, collectively, the whole movie studio constellation including Burbank, Universal City, and Culver City) offered another rival to downtown concentration. The move west not only enlarged the size of the city but altered its racial, ethnic, and class configuration. The important fact about the movie industry, Mike Davis has written, is "that it was headed by East European Jews who, despite their legendary wealth and conservative politics, could not play golf or send their kids to the same schools with the Chandlerian elite."[5] The Westside, from Hollywood to the ocean, emerged as the principal enclave of the at least partly Jewish, partially movie-dependent new middle- and upper-class population. From the twenties the ascendant Westside short-circuited the power lines of the old downtown/Pasadena elite; the city's power was thereafter to be split between Eastside and Westside, old and new money, and—with considerable generalization here—Protestant and Jew. When the Jews were unable to get into the Christian-only country clubs, they could, and did, build their own clubs on the Westside, defiantly preempting the established political bloc.

The eastern, earlier-settled regions of Los Angeles were composed of more than the downtown/Pasadena nexus of the Otis-Lummis crowd. They also included the territory east of the Los Angeles River— East Los Angeles—where the city's Jewish population was concentrated in the early years in the Boyle Heights district. With increasing affluence and the loosening of orthodox ties and practice, they migrated step by step west—first to the West Adams neighborhood, then to the Fairfax district (the "Borscht Belt"), and then to the suburban Westside (Beverly Hills, Brentwood, West Los Angeles). In the 1950s and 1960s Jewish migration was dominated by the move north into the San Fernando Valley and to some extent Orange County. East Los Angeles, including Boyle Heights, when abandoned by the Jews, became almost exclusively Mexican-American turf, the largest barrio in the city, harboring the greatest concentration of the largest ethnic group in the city.

African-Americans, meanwhile—many employed as dairy farmers, Pullman porters, and maids—had been settling in a neighborhood called Watts (originally the "Watts Junction" of the Pacific Electric line, running to Long Beach) south of downtown and now part of a larger area loosely called "South Central." Watts, or "Mudtown," as its earliest settlement was called, was annexed to Los Angeles in the twenties, largely as a means of absorbing and controlling the black vote. Arna Bontemps, contributor to the Harlem Renaissance but born and raised in Southern California, wrote of Mudtown in his 1931 novel, *God Sends Sundays*. "Here," he wrote, "removed from the influence of white folks, they [the inhabitants] did not acquire the inhibitions of their city brothers. Mudtown was like a tiny section of the deep south literally transplanted."[6] A half century later the novelist Walter Mosley, raised in South Central, would set his crime novels in a Watts of southern blacks who migrated during and after World War II. Today Watts is no longer an exclusively black community but a mixed zone of African-Americans, Latinos, and Asians.

Multiethnic from the beginning, but dominated by the Anglo-Protestant downtown plutocracy, Los Angeles in the 1920s was moving toward its present configuration—massive westward spread, Westside affluence, and increasing racial and class segregation along east-west lines. For the whites the journey west followed the two major east-west thoroughfares, Sunset and Wilshire boulevards (the latter developed and named for the flamboyant millionaire Gaylord Wilshire, utopian socialist, land developer, and friend of Upton Sinclair). Along Wilshire going west from downtown was the neon-lighted Wilshire district, a canyon of hotels (including the Ambassador with its cottages inhabited by the movie crowd), apartment and office buildings (prominently featured in Raymond Chandler's fiction), and department stores (including the impressive art deco Bullocks Wilshire). Traveling west along the parallel Sunset Boulevard to the north one reached Hollywood, West Hollywood, the Sunset Strip (then an unincorporated part of the city laced with nightclubs), and Santa Monica. Along the way were the new upscale hillside developments of Beverly Hills, Bel-Air, and Brentwood.

By the second decade of the new century, the movies found a permanent home in Los Angeles in the sleepy subdivision of Hollywood, engendering what was to be not only the city's most powerful industry and a magnet for thousands of dream-seekers but also the enduring concept of Los Angeles as American Dream Capital, keeper of our national fantasies. The movies came because the region had plenty of sunshine, open space for outdoor shooting, and a varied landscape (including mountains and desert for westerns). Not incidentally, the place also had the appeal of being three thousand miles away from the Edison patents the early moviemakers were seeking to escape.

In another, but less direct way, Los Angeles offered a congenial home for the making of fantasies: the city itself was beginning to look like a movie set, a resemblance that the city's novelists beginning in the 1920s were to exploit for satiric effect. Los Angeles as fantasy capital—as the "unreal city," the nation's consummate theme park, the repository of exotic, bizarre architecture—has been a theme played on by novelists and debunking journalists since the early years of the century. It has also been a significant part of the tourist hype since the booster years; Disneyland, Magic Mountain, Universal's City Walk, and the rest are more recent evocations of a propensity for fantasy creation that has gone on for a full century.

One manifestation of this propensity is the city builders' cultivation of the Mediterranean image—either Spanish or Italian. The romantic, nostalgic Spanish mission myth promoted by the city boosters as authentic, indigenous regional history found expression on the built landscape in elaborate renditions of what has been called mission revival architecture, a style carried to fantastic extreme in structures like Frank Miller's Mission Inn in Riverside and done with simpler, more graceful mission lines (fused with art deco/streamline moderne details) in the 1939 downtown Union Station, built on and forcing the relocation of the original Chinatown. There was also the consummate Italianate fantasy of the cigarette manufacturer Abbot Kinney's Venice-by-the-Sea, with its network of canals and bridges and its replica of the Palace of the Doges. For the tourist these were places to write home about, as were such other attractions as Olvera Street on the old plaza with its tourist-targeted Mexican shopping stalls, the funicular car to the top of Mount Lowe for a view of the basin, a trip to Catalina Island, a visit to Lucky Baldwin's spectacular ranch in Santa Anita or to Knott's Berry Farm, and a zoological spectacle of ostrich, alligator, and even lion farms. Forest Lawn, the statue- and chapel-studded Glendale cemetery that proved irresistible as metaphor to the British expatriate writers Aldous Huxley and Evelyn Waugh, has to be counted as still another major theme park.

The human landscape offered no less a spectacle. As what sustained the dream above everything else in Southern California was the supposed curative power of the climate, the landscape absorbed more than its fair share of the sick and feeble. And in their wake came a motley assortment of healers, spiritualists, psychics, and utopian schemers. Movements bearing such names as the Mighty I Am, Mankind United, Krotona, and Ham and Eggs flourished in the growth years of the city, and charismatic leaders like Katherine Tingley (the "Purple Mother" of Point Loma's Theosophy movement) and Sister Aimee Semple McPherson (of the Four Square Gospel) electrified the faithful. It was a spectacle not lost on the novelists. In Don Ryan's 1927 novel, *Angel's Flight*, we get this:

> Swamis stalked the streets wrapped in meditation and bedticks. Famous bunko men honored the city with permanent residence. Cults and creeds that had lain dormant since the time of Pythagoras springing to life to bloom exotically in the semi-tropical air. An alchemist hung out his sign on Sunset Boulevard, advertising to perform physical and spiritual transmutation. Holy men from the hills, barefooted, hairy bearded in simulation of the Nazarene, selling postcards on the corners.[7]

One would be hard-pressed to find a Los Angeles novel written between the 1920s and the 1960s without the inclusion of a bizarre cult, spiritualist, prophet, or medical quack. While it is tempting to exaggerate their significance in the city's history (as so many debunkers—who have written about the place as one vast loony bin—have), their centrality to the city's fiction cannot be denied. Spiritualists and "psychic consultants" (Raymond Chandler's term) have been permanent and conspicuous residents in the fiction about Los Angeles, from the 1920s novels of Don Ryan and Upton Sinclair, through the 1930s and 1940s fiction of Chandler, Nathanael West, Evelyn Waugh, Aldous Huxley, and Myron Brinig, and up to the more recent, postwar fiction of Ross Macdonald, Norman Mailer, Thomas Sanchez, Alison Lurie, and Joan Didion. In the literary construction of the city, the charlatans and cults signal the fusion, or confusion, of reality and illusion, fact and fantasy, that has been one of the recurring themes of Los Angeles fiction.

## II

As a literary city Los Angeles did not really exist until the 1920s. Frank Norris still would have been right if he made his 1897 remark about San Francisco as the only West Coast literary city twenty-five years after he did. While Norris, Jack London, and Gertrude Atherton, following in the wake of Twain, Harte, and Bierce, were placing turn-of-the century San Francisco on the literary map, it took another generation for Los Angeles to emerge as a literary territory. With the significant exceptions of Helen Hunt Jackson's myth-creating romance, *Ramona* (1884), and Mary Austin's novel about the stealing of Owens Valley water, *The Ford* (1917), neither of which was set in Los Angeles per se, there was little important fiction about the city before the 1920s. Harry Leon Wilson's *Merton of the Movies* (1923) and Mark Lee Luther's *The Boosters* (also 1923) introduced, if gently, the satiric tradition of writing about the city—the one about Hollywood, the other Los Angeles. Later in the decade Ryan's *Angel's Flight* and Sinclair's *Oil!* (both published in 1927) offered tougher indictments of the booster-hawked city. The four novels established the beginnings of the city's literary identity, an identity that the Hollywood novel, the hard-boiled crime fiction of the 1930s, and the tough-guy detective story would build on and which would persist to the present time.

What has to be remembered is that the writers—virtually all of them until the most recent few decades—were themselves outsiders, newcomers, visitors. This must be the starting point for any discussion of Los Angeles fiction. Literary regionalism, traditionally and almost by definition, is the work of writers born in, and nourished by, the regions about which they write. Midwestern writers like Mark Twain (who began his career in San Francisco) and Hamlin Garland and southern regionalists like Flannery O'Connor and Eudora Welty have stressed the sense of belonging, and love, as a requisite to regional writing. To Welty, place is "the heart's field."

In Los Angeles fiction place is anything but the "heart's field." The Los Angeles novel is not the work of those born to the manor but of visitors and outsiders, men and women who lived and worked for a time in the region—since the 1930s largely as screenwriters. Like almost everyone else in Los Angeles, they were strangers to the place. Los Angeles fiction is about the act of entry, about the discovery and the taking possession of a place that differed significantly from the place left behind. The distanced perspective of the outsider, marked by a sense of dislocation and estrangement, is the central and essential feature of the fiction of Los Angeles, distinguishing it from fiction about other American places. The writers came into an expansive landscape that appeared to them to have no discernible center, no reigning architectural style, and no sense of a regional past that, despite the mission and Spanish-derived buildings cropping up everywhere, could exert any local aesthetic authority or convince them that they had, in fact, arrived in a *place*.

The result was a fiction that played, at times obsessively, on themes of unreality, masquerade, and deception and that elicited these themes in image patterns that took in all of the landscape. I can think of no other regional fiction that so pervasively appropriates the built landscapes—the eclectic and bizarre architecture, the preponderance of roads and highways, the apparently centerless sprawl. This at times obsessive preoccupation with the built features of the land is one perhaps inevitable consequence of the outsider status of the writers: the look of the land offered, in contrast to remembered places, images of instability, fragility, unreality.

As the work of outsiders, Los Angeles fiction offers a sense of temporal as well as spatial dislocation. Traditionally, regions in literature contain, either explicitly or implicitly, the dimension of history: a region's present is played off against its past. One thinks of the contrast between Edith Wharton's old and new New York, Sherwood Anderson's pre- and postindustrialized Ohio Valley, and William Faulkner's ante- and postbellum Mississippi. These are places captured in the process of change, places that are situated in the historical context of modernization, urbanization, and the shifting demographics of race, class, and power. In Los Angeles fiction the counterpoint is not between the present and past of *a* place but between a Southern California present and a past carried from some *other* place. History is not so much absent as displaced; it exists as a different geography.

Immigrant fiction provides the analogy—both the turn-of-the-century fiction written by European immigrants (Ole Rolvaag, Abraham Cahan, Anzia Yeziersksa, as examples) and the more recent fiction of Asian and Latin American immigrants—fiction that centers on the disjunction of Old and New Worlds, lands left behind and lands found. The past is a remembered elsewhere, geographically and culturally dismembered from the present, but never far in memory. The present is always gauged against the past, the new country against the old. Immigrant (and migrant) fiction is the literature of crossings, of extirpation and transplantation. New settlers seek fresh starts but bring selves nurtured elsewhere. They remain painfully aware of what has been left behind even as they try to graft the old ways onto the new place (to wit: the ubiquitous California bungalow style with its nod *not* to the Hispanic past but to the Protestant Midwest). The graft doesn't always take; the gulf between East and West, past and present, is a recurring feature in the fiction. Nathanael West, in *The Day of the Locust* (1939), has his eastern-trained artist/protagonist, Tod Hackett, who has become a Hollywood set designer, muse ruefully, "He knew he would never again paint a fat old Nantucket barn, old stone wall, or sturdy Nantucket fisherman."[8]

Novels about the West are thus in some way also about the East— more precisely about the complicated and ambiguous interaction of East and West, past and present. Los Angeles fiction in this sense is biregional, or bicoastal, or in the case of British expatriate writers in Hollywood—Huxley, Waugh, Isherwood—binational. For such expatriates Los Angeles, or Hollywood, was about as far as one could get from London. The West Coast city is constructed in their Los Angeles/ Hollywood fiction in international terms, as a wholly different civilization. For Waugh, who was the most extreme exemplar of this tendency, Los Angeles stood as the marker of the end of Western, that is, British, civilization.

Joan Didion has written in an essay titled "Some Dreamers of the Golden Dream" that "the future always looks good in the golden land" because "no one remembers the past."[9] It is also true, though, in the fictional Los Angeles, that no one entirely forgets the past— or is allowed to forget it. Crime fiction is one place that foregrounds history. What makes the tough-guy detective stories of Chandler and Macdonald, and later John Gregory Dunne, James Ellroy, Michael Connelly, and *Chinatown* screenwriter Robert Towne, so central to the local tradition is that they focus on crimes committed and buried in past time, which the private eye or the police detective forces into present consciousness. Skeletons in the closet—or buried underground or encased in concrete—are not allowed to remain hidden. In the resurrection of noir fiction during the past few decades the focus is on historic crime—often, as in the fiction of Ellroy and Dunne, on actual local crimes committed in the past. The local detective story is about excavating the past, about recovering memory and past time. The American West, conventionally, mythologically, has meant, in Leslie Fiedler's words, the "stepping outside history," but the burden of the detective novel, the most characteristic Los Angeles story, is to reveal that history is not so easily outstepped.

Whatever power the old booster myth exerted in the early boom years, it gave way in the novelists' Los Angeles to darker visions. By the depression decade the landscape that greeted the writers was one that could no longer sustain the sunny version of new beginnings that lured the early settlers. It contained neither a sense of local history to which they could give allegiance nor an ordered sense of space. The only allusions to history they saw were in the romantic mission-style buildings that were cropping up everywhere, in the architec-tural parodies on the landscape aping every style in world history, and in the movie studio sets evoking images of histories that never were—history according to Cecil B. DeMille or David O. Selznick. History is rendered as simulacrum, like Disneyland's Main Street or Universal Studio's City Walk: matters of engineering and props in the service of historical mimicry.

The two realms—local architecture and movie set architecture—seemed hardly distinguishable. Some of the writers viewed Los An-geles as if it were a vast overflow of the studio back lots. Film histori-ans remind us that the colossal three-hundred-foot Babylon set for D. W. Griffith's *Intolerance* stood as an architectural monument on a Hollywood street corner for years after the completion of the film. To Aldous Huxley the studio-city connection was quite explicit; Holly-wood was a movie set, a point he drives home in his Hollywood novel, *After Many a Summer Dies the Swan* (1939). James M. Cain, two years after arriving, wrote home (to H. L. Mencken's *American Mercury*) about a landscape in which gas stations were built to look like the Taj Mahal and structures resembling giant oranges, windmills, mosques, and tea kettles were to be found everywhere. "There is no reward for aesthetic virtue here," he wrote, "no punishment for aesthetic crime."[10] This is the point. To the newly arrived writers, who measured the place against a remembered elsewhere, Los Angeles was more often than not rendered as an "aesthetic crime," an anarchic landscape set in a place that sprawled in every direction and lacked any governing architectural authority. All of this became the raw materials for a fic-tion preoccupied with defining a place that conveyed a sense of in-substantiality and unreality.

III

Richard Neutra, the Viennese-born architect who set up an office in Los Angeles in 1926, blamed the movies for the architectural eclecticism that provided the writers with the metaphors for cultural displacement and aesthetic confusion.

> Motion pictures have undoubtedly confused architectural tastes. They may be blamed for many phenomena on the landscape such as: Half-timber English peasant cottages, French Provincial and "mission bell" type adobes, Arabian minarets, Georgian mansions on 50x120 foot lots with "Mexican Ranchos" adjoining them on sites of the same size.[11]

It is of course simplistic to blame the movies for the city's eclectic architecture. It can be argued that the movie sets reflected, as well as influenced, architectural taste in the building boom of the twenties and thirties. The fact that many of the set designers, like the European émigré Kem Weber, were also practicing architects willing to execute any design a client desired and could pay for argues for a reciprocal relationship. In the absence of a reigning regional architectural style with which the new migrants from the East or Midwest could identify, together with the kind of climate that permitted the use of almost any building material and the desires of a fluid population, an "anything goes" attitude could easily take hold. Fantasy, of course, has freer reign in the West than in the East, where the burden of tradition curbs it. For the writers, though, the important thing was not which way the lines of influence ran but the fact that the city looked like a movie set, particularly in and around Hollywood. The spectacle proved, like the cults and cultists, irresistible to the novelists in their search for metaphors for cultural displacement and confusion, for the absence of tradition, order, and authority on the landscape.

Of course not all of the built landscape really looked like a movie set. In the absence of a dominant style, though, every style and manner found a place: downtown beaux arts and art nouveau; Greene Brothers craftsman bungalows, most notably in Pasadena but imitated everywhere; mission revival commercial buildings and their white-stucco-red-tile-roof domestic counterpart; Wilshire Boulevard art deco and its 1930s–1940s jazzed-up version, streamline moderne; and Bauhaus-inspired international modernism pioneered in Southern California by Neutra and Rudolph Schindler. What the writers appropriated in their fiction, though, is the kind of architecture variously called pop, fantasy, California kitsch, high/low camp, or surreal. The category, however labeled, was a catch-all for what are essentially three kinds of structures: (1) commercial buildings shaped like products they sell—tamale or orange juice stands shaped like tamales or oranges; here the message is direct: what you see is what you get; (2) designs, less direct, that offer a kind of symbolic or iconic relationship to their function—a restaurant in the shape of a derby hat or a tire factory shaped like an Assyrian Ziggurat; and (3) residential designs of the type Neutra excoriated, houses imitating, aping, parodying every style in architectural history. Struck by the eclectic, exotic fantasies, the writers appropriated them as images, exempla, of the absence of aesthetic control or cultural authority. Today many observers of the built landscape feel differently; groomed by an antielitist, postmodernist penchant for pop icons, and influenced by books like Banham's *Los Angeles: The Architecture of Four Ecologies* and Robert Venturi, Denise Scott Brown, and Steven Izenour's *Learning from Las Vegas*, they enjoy the play of signifiers such structures offer.

Not so with the 1930s migrant writers. West, in *The Day of the Locust*, has his protagonist/speaker remark, with a blend of amusement and derision, that only dynamite would be of any use against the eclectic facades—everything from Moorish to Tudor housing designs—that line the slopes of the canyons above Hollywood Boulevard. The line between movie set and city has been almost wholly obliterated. For West, as for Chandler and Huxley, and for virtually all the writers who followed in the next few decades, the region's fantasy architecture stood not only as the consummate image of *absence*—the absence of a dominant style, the erasure of an ordered sense of time and place—but also as projection, or externalization, of the compulsive role-playing of characters, their failure to distinguish real life and fantasy, living and performing. In West's novel virtually all the Hollywood characters are compulsive masqueraders, and the houses they inhabit are projections of their masquerades—an odd twist on the Emersonian/Thoreauvian organic notion of the "indweller."

The impression of removal from both a sense of time and a sense of place is central to a number of Los Angeles novels written in the decades after West's novel—in, to cite two examples that will be elaborated in later chapters, Norman Mailer's *The Deer Park* (1955), set in a desert resort frequented by the movie colony, and Alison Lurie's *The Nowhere City* (1965), an elaboration of a place that, like the hole in the giant revolving cement donut the heroine passes on her way from the airport, is a big advertisement for nothing. William Faulkner, the most successful of the movie-drawn writers, having scripted Ernest Hemingway's *To Have and Have Not* (for Howard Hawks), Chandler's *The Big Sleep* (also for Hawks), and *Strangers on a Train* (for Alfred Hitchcock), wrote little in the way of fiction about Los Angeles, only a single story, "Golden Land." Like the work of his Hollywood contemporaries, though, it is the story of a place that exists in a liminal zone, never quite real, inhabited by beings that seem to have come from some other planet. The central character has come to Los Angeles from Nebraska, made a fortune in that most characteristic local enterprise, real estate, and lives in a palatial home, but his life is collapsing around him. His marriage is in ruins, his children are aimless drifters, and he has become an alcoholic. Angry and bewildered, he sits on the beach watching the young tanned bodies that

> seemed to him to walk along the rim of the world as though they and their kind alone inhabited it and he with his forty-eight years was the forgotten last survivor of another race and kind, and they in turn precursors of a new race not yet seen on the earth: of men and women without age, beautiful as gods and goddesses, and with the minds of infants.[12]

The ocean, the "rim of the world" to Faulkner's protagonist, is the setting for the last act of a good number of Southern California protagonists. While the booster version of Los Angeles, constructed by a downtown/Pasadena coterie, oriented the city to the East, to the desert and the Spanish/Mexican/Indian Southwest, the generation of writers who came in the thirties and after, reflecting the westward shift of the city's power and population, positioned it to the West, facing the Pacific. The continental highway ended against the ocean, and the dream ended with it. It is at the ocean that one finds there is no more room to move. The California highway becomes a cul-de-sac carrying one back to the past, to beginnings, or downward to ex-haustion and death. In Cain's *The Postman Always Rings Twice* (1934) the first ringing is triggered by a murder committed on a cliff over-looking the ocean and the second by a fatal car crash on the Pacific Coast Highway. In Horace McCoy's *They Shoot Horses, Don't They?* (1935) a murder committed in a dance hall on a pier perched over the ocean puts an end to a dance marathon and leads to the hero-ine's murder at the very edge of the pier. In Chandler's novels, cars are run off piers, and houses cantilevered over the ocean on the Pa-cific Palisades threaten to drop into the sea.

Parallel to the cultural instability evoked in the novelist's Los An-geles is the instability of the land itself. Natural as well as man-made disasters have furnished the plot lines for much of the region's fic-tion, as they have for much of the city's history. The sun-drenched land that drew all the seekers is also the land of destructive earth-quakes, brush fires, floods, droughts, and mud slides. In F. Scott Fitz-gerald's Hollywood novel, *The Last Tycoon* (1940), and John Fante's *Ask the Dust* (1939), the 1933 Long Beach-centered quake marks a shift in a protagonist's consciousness and destiny—for Fitzgerald's Hollywood producer Monroe Stahr a tragic downward spiraling, for Fante's Arturo Bandini, a comic case of postcoital Catholic guilt. Los Angeles has often enough served as the site of apocalypse brought on by natural or man-made forces. The earthquake, coming as the Big One, the one that causes the city, or the whole Pacific coast, to slide into the sea, appears as finale in Myron Brinig's fantasy, *The Flutter of an Eyelid* (1933), as quasi-documentary account in Curt Gentry's *The Last Days of the Late, Great State of California* (1968), and in films like the 1974 disaster epic *Earthquake* and the 1996 futuristic *Escape from L.A.* Armageddon in the form of mankind's atomic or nuclear madness appears in fiction ranging from Aldous Huxley's fu-turistic *Ape and Essence* (1948) to Carolyn See's *Golden Days* (1987); in the former Los Angeles is rendered as a wasteland of grotesquely maimed survivors under the heel of a ruling class of fascist sadists, and in the latter the apocalyptic city perched at the edge of the ocean is a testing ground for the human will to survive and endure.

Other kinds of disasters, natural and man-made, provide mate-rial for the writers. Every year hot, dry Santa Ana winds (the kind of weather in which, Chandler tells us, meek housewives sharpen kitchen knives while eyeing their husbands' necks) race from the desert through the canyons on the way to the ocean, firing not only tempers but the dry mountain and canyon chaparral into flame. The hills, no longer covered by protective brush, erode, becoming rivers of mud when the heavy winter rains come. Cliffs give way, dumping tons of mud onto houses and the coastal highway. The title story of Gavin Lambert's story collection, *The Slide Area* (1951), gives some sense of the encounter between cliff and ocean:

> High lurching cliffs confront the ocean, and are just
> beginning to fall apart. Signs have been posted along the
> highway, DRIVE CAREFULLY and SLIDE AREA. Lumps
> of earth and stone fall down. The land is restless here, restless
> and sliding. . . . The land is falling. Rocks fall down all over.
> The cliffs called Pacific Palisades are crumbling slowly down
> to the ocean.[13]

The menace of the ocean recurs in the fiction, signaling the fragility of life at its edge. In Macdonald's crime novels, set along the coast running from Santa Monica to Santa Barbara, tidal waves, oil spills, and forest fires—the kind that denude the hillsides and precipitate the landslides—are linked with crimes committed and hidden by the rich, who live luxuriously in the hills along, and above, the ocean. Ecological disasters are encountered as responses to greed—the responses of an angry God to the kind of greed that permitted a vast coastal basin lying on unsettled land to be heedlessly exploited for profit, a process of relentless commodification that had been going on since the building booms of the 1880s.

Fire is the consummate image of apocalypse in the fiction. "The city burning," Didion has written, "is Los Angeles' deepest image of itself."[14] A fire in the coastal hills rages out of control in Macdonald's *The Underground Man* (1971) as detective Lew Archer digs up corpses and family secrets. The centerpiece of West's *The Day of the Locust* is Tod Hackett's painting of Los Angeles in flames, a prophetic visionary piece that is realized symbolically in the movie premiere conflagration at the novel's end. But Hackett's painting is just that—a painting, a metaphor within the larger metaphor for the dream's end that is the novel itself. The betrayer of the dream is not nature's burning but man's.

The collapse of high hopes is rendered by the writers less often in

images of natural disaster than in episodes of man-made violence—
the violence of the gun and, even more appropriately for the locale,
of the automobile. Ever since the city emerged in the 1920s and 1930s
as the city on wheels, the car has offered itself to the novelist as either
death instrument or metaphor for the illusory promise of mobility.
The fast car on the coast highway represents in much of the fiction
the betrayed promise of West Coast freedom. The illusion is given
special intensity in Cain's Los Angeles novels, particularly *The Postman Always Rings Twice* and *Mildred Pierce*. In the latter the heroine's futile attempts to elevate her status and lifestyle are represented
by her failed attempts to navigate the highway between middle-class
Glendale and upper-class Pasadena. For a character like Mildred
Pierce social mobility is equated with geographic mobility, personal
power and control over one's destiny with the presence of the highway. Chandler's Philip Marlowe, the first motorized private eye, uses
the highway not to attain personal power or autonomy but to solve
crimes. Crime is everywhere on the landscape, and the car enables
him to traverse the whole basin in search of clues. In Didion's 1970
novel, *Play It as It Lays*, Maria Wyeth, the heroine, witnessing the
unraveling of her life, tries to give some order to her existence by
speeding, without destination, on the freeways. And in See's *Making
History* (1991) two horrible automobile crashes on Pacific Coast Highway frame the narrative. From Cain, writing in the 1930s, to See, writing in the 1990s, the California highway running along the coast marks
the end of the line.

One wonders what the early city boosters would have made of
such jeremiads about Los Angeles as the place at the end of the line.
In the full century since the boosting era, the city has undergone an
unimaginable metamorphosis—phenomenal growth; water, oil, government, police, and movieland scandals; earthquakes and destructive fires; smog and an oil-polluted ocean; serial killers and freeway
snipers; race riots and gang wars. In the collective national imagination, fueled by movies, television programs, novels, and newspapers,
the city has come to represent a dream gone haywire. Yet it is still a
destination for resettlement. The Mediterranean climate, economic
opportunity, the lure of the global economy, and the ongoing development of new suburban and edge cities still draw migrants and immigrants to the basin. Among them are the estimated 1.2 million

illegal immigrants, most from Mexico and Latin America, most con-
fined to barrios, ghettos, and working-class zones in the inner city
that reproduce the very conditions from which they have fled—a
spectacle that offers an ironic spin on the global economy theme.

Los Angeles is a city, Chandler wrote long ago, that is "lost and
beaten" but, he added, "no worse than other cities." Twentieth-century
fiction about Los Angeles is less a collection of hate mail to a belea-
guered city than an expression of anxiety about the modern condition. For a look at how far imaginings of the city have evolved in a
hundred years, I turn now to the old booster vision.

# 2

## BOOSTERS AND BOASTERS

### *The Making and Unmaking of a Myth*

L.A. is probably the most mediated town in America, nearly
unviewable save through the fictive scrim of its mythologizers.
MICHAEL SORKIN, "EXPLAINING LOS ANGELES"

Los Angeles is the richest and best educated city in the Union . . .
a standing riddle to the cooped East, which cannot yet conceive
how a city so cultured and so beautiful can have sprung up so
swiftly here upon the very brink of the Jumping-off Place.
CHARLES FLETCHER LUMMIS, IN *LAND OF SUNSHINE*

The myth centered on the old missions. Except for the one in Santa Barbara, Southern California's missions, ignored and neglected after the Yankees took over the land, had fallen into a state of decay. Roofs had collapsed, adobe walls had crumbled, and gardens, orchards, and grape tracts had become fields of weeds. With the booms of the 1880s and 1890s, though, all this was to change. Suddenly the missions became capital. To Charles Fletcher Lummis, dean of the early boosters, and to his fellow spirits—an amalgam of railroad tycoons and their hired publicists, real estate speculators and land developers, and soldiers of the new chamber of commerce—the epic story of the missions and the Spanish adventure in the American Southwest could be turned into a commodity, appropriated as vital myth to lure tourists and settlers. In a land hyped for its future promise, for its prospect of new beginnings in a new land, the Spanish conquest and the religious and secular culture it had imposed on Indian lands a century earlier could be offered as historical counterweight, a necessary fiction that would link the region to a past evoking Old World grace and charm, moral earnestness, and heroism.

Never mind that it was not *their* history, neither the history of the city boosters nor that of the Protestant migrants they were trying to attract; it was a usable past, a marketable past. It was the odd case of a group of Anglo-Protestant boosters selling the land to Anglo-Protestant buyers by hawking a Spanish Catholic past, offering an ersatz history, a nostalgic reverence for a past neither they nor anyone else ever knew, one that never existed in the way it was represented. History here is a text, a fiction, a deliberate construct to serve real estate interests. Thus the Yankee settlers, who justified their own claims to the land by excoriating the old Spanish/Mexican Catholic rule and then confiscating Hispanic land grants, became in the 1880s and 1890s suddenly enamored of the life under that earlier rule. The place at the edge of the West that was promoted for its newness was also advertised, paradoxically, as the site of a romantic, pastoral sombrero and fandango myth. The boosters worked it both ways, proffering the opposing visions of progress and nostalgia, future possibilities and historic charm, as enticements for tourism and settlement. The forced enclosure of the mission Indians and their consequent decimation 29 by cultural uprooting and European disease found no place, of course, in this mythic reconstruction of history, which centered on the image of the humble, godly, kneeling countenance of the Spanish padre ministering to the needs of the ignorant, helpless aborigines, lifting them from savagery and ignorance and instructing them in the civilization of Christianity and agriculture.[1] In the secular terms of the myth the city fathers called into being images of shady verandas and courtyards, olive and fig trees, the plaintive strumming of guitars and mandolins, and the good, simple, unhurried life of people who knew both hard work and leisure.

In the act of engendering the mission myth the boosters had to do an end run around the discomfiting issue of Spanish mistreatment of the mission Indians—let alone their own mistreatment of the Indians still afloat in the city of the 1880s and 1890s and the racial assumptions that justified their land-grabbing. It was a matter, as the historian Kevin Starr has noted, of "Americans promoting their growth in Southern California via a mythic perception of a time and place that had been destroyed by the arrival of the Americans."[2] In Mike Davis's words, the myth was one that "not only sublimated contemporary class struggle, but also censored and repressed from view, the actual plight of Alta California's descendants."[3] Carey McWilliams spoke of the "masochism" inherent in the mythmaking, finding it "astonishing" that the Anglo city boosters who created the myth assumed full responsibility for the historical mistreatment of the Indians, letting the Franciscans off the hook.[4]

## II

This mythic construct owes its genesis, essentially, to a single writer, Helen Hunt Jackson, and to one novel, *Ramona* (1884), which appeared just as the booster movement was born, just as the nascent tourist industry was getting off the ground, and just as the first trainloads of migrants were disembarking. The timing couldn't have been better. The region needed a myth, a historical narrative that would connect it with a past, provide it with a sense of historical continuity. Appropriately for the Los Angeles of the 1880s, it was a newcomer, a visitor, who provided the narrative. It was a "goggle-eyed, umbrella-packing tourist," wrote McWilliams, "who first discovered the past of

Southern California and peopled it with curious creatures of her own invention." (71)

Jackson was born in Amherst, Massachusetts, in 1830, the daughter of a Calvinist theologian. She had been writing sentimental verse (so different from that of her Amherst neighbor, Emily Dickinson) and nourishing her interest in American Indians. Between 1872 and 1883 she made three journeys to Southern California, first when *Century Magazine* commissioned her to do a series of articles on the neglected missions and the plight of the deracinated mission Indians. She fell under the romantic sway of Spanish California and particularly of Father Junípero Serra, who established the first nine of the string of missions along coastal California. The publication of *A Century of Dishonor* (1881) and a *Century* article, "Father Junípero and the Indians," led to her appointment by the Department of the Interior to investigate the conditions of the former mission Indians. She was accompanied in her journeys to Indian villages in San Diego County by Abbot Kinney, prominent booster figure, southwestern desert enthusiast, and, as noted earlier, fabulator of that consummate early-twentieth-century Los Angeles fantasy theme park, Venice-by-the-Sea. The report they issued was never acted on, but her explorations of Indian settlements take up the second part of her novel, the whole of which was written in a New York hotel room after her return east.

*Ramona* extols life on the ranchos and haciendas in the 1870s, just as that life was drawing to an end with the invasion of Yankees and the theft of Mexican and Indian lands. Intended both as critique of Yankee imperialism and defense of Indian land rights, it was appropriated by the boosters for a far different end: the representation of romantic and gracious Hispanic Southern California in its waning years. It provided instant, employable history to promote the region. The villain of the piece is the invading Anglo, but Jackson's Anglo readers, caught up in the romance of rancho life, failed to take much notice of this. The novel, enmeshed in the conventions of 1880s sentimental, domestic, and local color fiction, was taken by its contemporary audience as a dramatic, yet realistic, narrative about ill-fated lovers in a land that still had its storied charm. The sentimentalization of Alta California is laid bare on the opening pages:

It was a picturesque life with more of sentiment and gayety
in it, more also that was truly dramatic, more romance than
will ever be seen again on these sunny shores. The aroma
of it still lingers; industries and inventions have not yet slain
it; it will last out its century, — in fact it can never be quite
lost, so long as there is left one such home as the Señora
Moreno's.[5]

All of Jackson's old Californians are swathed in such sentiment.
Señora Moreno, who epitomizes the best spirit of Spanish/Mexican
California, has heroically survived the American invasion, lost her
husband in the Mexican War, and lost much of her rancho (bequeathed by Governor Pio Pico himself) to the conquerors. Stoic
and kind, she ministers to her Indian sheep shearers (the old Spanish obligation), her sickly son, Felipe, and Ramona, the "daughter"
left in her charge. Ramona Ortega and Allesandro Assis, Jackson's
doomed-lover protagonists, are Indians, McWilliams has written,
"surely never seen on this earth." (75) Ramona is a half-breed (her
father a Scottish seaman, her mother a full-blooded Indian), who has
been left as an infant in the keeping of Señora Moreno. The portrait
of Ramona, half daughter, half servant, is that of a lovely and genteel
señorita, seemingly more Spanish than Indian. Alessandro Assis, the
full-breed Luiseño Indian with whom she falls in love and elopes, is
not only literate but spiritual and artistic as well. A fiddler, he is summoned frequently to the rancho to soothe Felipe with his music. He
appears to have stepped out of an English public school rather than
an unsettled, racist frontier. Alessandro (whose name has an Italianate
ring to it) possesses an inborn sense of virtue — a kind of territory's-
end Huckleberry Finn.

The second part of the novel, following the elopement of Ramona
and Alessandro, traces their journey south in an attempt to find a home
together in Luiseño villages near San Diego. The advancing Yankees
are pillaging and burning the villages, and the pair is forced to move
from one settlement to another — Soboba Springs, Temecula, and the
Cahuilla Valley, places that Jackson, accompanied by Abbot Kinney,
visited on their investigative trips. The climax occurs when Alessandro is shot by a Yankee as a horse thief when, in a fit of distraction
brought on by the illness of their infant daughter and the refusal of

a doctor to come to their mountaintop hideout, he takes the wrong horse in his rush to get home.

Setting aside the anti-Yankee sentiments such passages were clearly meant to elicit, the city fathers made this story of courageous, noble peasant history into grist for the booster mill. They read it less as an attack on Yankee imperialism and cruelty than as a "real life" account of life on the old ranchos and as an authentic portrait of the "noble Indian." It offered the kind of myth, the kind of history, and the kind of Indian that the boosters wanted and needed. The story of the star-crossed lovers became the centerpiece of mythic Southern California. Through the sleight-of-hand of the mythmakers, the story was taken as history, as fact. Tourists were taken to the places the allegedly real Ramona and Alessandro courted, married, lived, and journeyed as they searched for a home to raise their daughter. Ramona tours became a major Southern California tourist industry. Postcards and Ramona curios awaited tourists as they stepped off the Southern Pacific or Santa Fe trains.

The novel, which went through 135 printings in the first fifty years after its publication, has spun off historical sagas, dramatic presentations, at least three movies, and an annual pageant in Hemet, in the heart of "Ramona Country." Books appeared bearing such titles as *The True Story of Ramona* and *Ramona's Homeland*. George Wharton James, the most indefatigable booster writer in Southern California (some forty books), assumed the role of chief propagandist for the missions, the desert, and the Ramona story, issuing such titles as *In and Out of California's Missions* (1905), *The Wonders of the Colorado Desert* (1906), and *Through Ramona's Country* (1908). Another of the tireless boosters, John Steven McGroarty, for forty years a *Los Angeles Times* correspondent, made what amounted almost to a career of tracing the footsteps of Ramona and Alessandro. His dramatic work, *The Mission Play*, was staged at a specially built theater near the San Gabriel Mission from 1912 to 1929. The production, which cost $1.5 million to mount, drew some 2.5 million patrons in its seventeen-year life. Predictably, in the evolution of Ramona spinoffs, the Anglos were given less and less of the blame for the plight of the Indians—and the Mexicans more and more. Today the legacy of Ramona—the freight it has carried into the twentieth century—manifests itself in Southland pageants and costumed fiestas and pervasively in the exploitation of mission design elements in commercial and domestic architecture. The so-called mission revival style became such a craze in the early years of the twentieth century that it provoked the derision of modernists like Frank Lloyd Wright, who saw mission architecture as "flatulent and fraudulent with a cheap opulent taste for the tawdry," and Irving Gill, who held that "more architectural crimes have been committed in the name of the missions than any other unless it be the Grecian temple."[6]

*Ramona*, though pure invention, drew on events Jackson heard about when she visited Rancho Camulos in the Santa Clara Valley in Ventura County. Managed by the del Valle family, it was one of the land grants still in Mexican hands. The novel's Señora Moreno was modeled on Doña Ysabel del Valle, mistress of the rancho. The novel's two priests who minister to the rancho, the wholly idealized Fathers Salvierderro and Gaspara, are based on Franciscan priests from Santa Barbara. The removal of Indians from Temecula Village and the killing of an Indian horse thief are events Jackson heard about in her travels to Indian lands. Whatever critique of Yankee imperialism the novel contains is undercut by its slick philo-Hispanic veneer, which played perfectly into the hands of the land developers. The most enduringly popular (and still in print) piece of fiction about Southern California, *Ramona* does for the region what *Gone with the Wind* did for the South: provide a comforting reconstruction of history, confer a reassuring sense of a noble past. It was a narrative that could be manipulated for promotional interests — ersatz history posing as regional history.

## III

It was to Rancho Camulos, some forty years after Jackson's stay, that Charles Fletcher Lummis, six years before his death, went to recuperate from one of the illnesses that plagued him throughout his life. Like so many of Southern California's other early settlers, including fellow boosters Abbot Kinney, George Wharton James, and Joseph P. Widney, Lummis came west to regain his health and soon "went native," cultivating a fascination that became an obsession with all things Californian — the missions, the Hispanic and Indian cultures of the Southwest, and the desert. Here was another New England-born Yankee who fell into the romantic arms of the Hispanic West (although he balked at the inflated, overly romantic rhetoric of Jackson). "Don Carlos," as he liked to call himself, swapped his eastern clothes for a corduroy suit, broad, brightly colored cummerbund, wide-brimmed hat, and Navajo jewelry. Unremittingly histrionic, he switched among the roles of Navajo chieftain, western Thoreauvian individualist, Teddy Roosevelt vitalist, and majestic Spanish Don.

As city editor of Otis's new *Los Angeles Daily Times,* editor of the journal *Land of Sunshine* (later *Out West*), president of the Landmarks Club (dedicated to the preservation of the missions) and of the Sequoia League (which had as its slogan "To make better Indians by treating them better"), city librarian, and prolific author of books and pamphlets on the Southwest, Lummis focused on the two principal booster themes: Los Angeles as locus of the Anglo-American future and as inheritor and preserver of a long Hispanic and Indian history. Southern California was both the happy destination of the future-oriented Anglo settler and the legatee of the "sun, silence, and adobe" culture of the Hispanic Southwest. With no small measure of booster hyperbole and historical distortion, he wrote from the editorial desk of *Land of Sunshine,* soon after assuming it, that "Southern California has a million square miles, a thousand years of legend, three hundred years of history, God's own sample-case of physical geography and scenery."[7] "History" in Southern California begins, it would seem from such a passage, with Spanish discovery; the "thousand years" of pre-Spanish Indian habitation is "legend."

As history or only legend, the Indian past was an essential part of the local story to Lummis. Influenced by his reading of Jackson's *A Century of Dishonor,* he became an ardent supporter of Indian land rights, arguing in *Land of Sunshine* for the Indian claims to Warner's Ranch in San Diego County in the protracted battle between Indians and the federal government over that land. A desert enthusiast, he retreated to the Colorado and Mojave deserts, collecting Indian artifacts, whenever his body, ravaged by heavy drinking and smoking and long workdays, broke down. In 1888, following a stroke, he went to New Mexico, there regaining his mobility by strenuous walking and horseback riding.

Lummis was both an ardent lifelong collector of southwestern Indian artifacts and the master of ceremonies of one of the earliest literary salons in Southern California. His collection of artifacts forms the basis of the Southwest Museum, which he helped found near his stone house, El Alisal (the Alder Tree), in Arroyo Seco. Lummis's Saturday night, quasi-bohemian gatherings at El Alisal—his "noises," as he called them—became the meeting ground of neighboring and visiting writers, artists, and actors, the guest list including such literary and theatrical luminaries as John Muir (the naturalist from Yosemite), Mary Austin (the desert writer/naturalist), Sarah Bernhardt (the actress), Madame Helena Modjeska (the Polish expatriate actress), Will Rogers (the comedian), Douglas Fairbanks (the movie actor), and Eugene Manlove Rhodes (the cowboy novelist).

The son of an itinerant Methodist minister, Lummis was born in Lynn, Massachusetts, in 1859 and attended (but didn't graduate from) Harvard, where he urged his frail body on through a regimen of boxing, wrestling, and running. An older classmate and, later, friend was Theodore Roosevelt, whose advocacy of physical culture influenced Lummis in his Harvard years. This cultivation of strenuous physicality, the life of manly adventure, athletics, and risk-taking, was a significant strain in late-nineteenth-century and early-twentieth-century American life. One thinks of the cult of the physical as practiced by such outdoor-adventure contemporaries as George Sterling, Jack London, Richard Harding Davis, and Stephen Crane. After leaving Harvard, Lummis moved to Ohio, where he ran a farm (owned by his wife's family) and edited a rural newspaper. Then on September 12, 1884, just as Helen Hunt Jackson was creating mythic Southern California in *Ramona*, the twenty-five-year-old Lummis left on a journey from Cincinnati to Los Angeles—on foot.

No other Los Angeles migrant had done that before. He had been in correspondence with Harrison Gray Otis, who had just taken over as editor/publisher of the new *Los Angeles Daily Times*, and offered to write weekly dispatches along the way. The boom was on in Southern California, and Otis, recognizing a salable idea, agreed. When Lummis arrived, 143 days later, having logged 3,705 footsore miles through seven states and two territories, he was met by Otis near the San Gabriel Mission and offered a job on the paper's city desk. Together, the story goes, the two men walked from the mission to downtown Los Angeles.

Otis, too, had drifted west from Ohio, arriving in Los Angeles three

years earlier, in 1882. Born in a log house in Marietta, he worked as
an apprentice printer and became a delegate to the Republican convention that nominated Lincoln for president. During the Civil War,
Colonel Otis, serving in an Ohio volunteer brigade, was wounded
twice. (He would be promoted from colonel to general in the Spanish-
American War, leaving his post on the paper to fight in the Philip-
pines.) He went west in 1874, settling in Santa Barbara and then migrating north to Alaska. Returning to Southern California in 1882, he
put up $6,000 (mostly borrowed) for a chunk of the new *Los Ange-
les Daily Times*, which he ruled autocratically under the banners of
hard work and an open shop. Lummis, looking back on Los Angeles
forty-four years after he went to work for Otis, remarked that the city
"owes no other man so much as this rough old soldier."

Otis not only turned the *Times* into a major newspaper but also
built an empire in landholding. Along with the railroad magnates
E. H. Harriman and Henry Huntington and other city oligarchs, he
formed a syndicate, Los Angeles Suburban Homes, which bought,
or took options on, much of the San Fernando Valley. They got the
parched land at bargain basement prices, and Otis coaxed *Times* readers into floating a bond to build an aqueduct to carry water to the
growing city of Los Angeles from the Owens River on the east side
of the Sierra range—a distance of 240 miles. Between 1907 and 1913
that aqueduct, with the water engineer William Mulholland in charge
of construction, was completed. Its terminus was the northern edge
of the San Fernando Valley—land the syndicate controlled. A hot,
dry agricultural region now had a plentiful water source, and the
land Otis and his collaborators had been secretly acquiring suddenly
became a bonanza. Not surprisingly Otis became a multimillionaire.
Two years later most of the valley was annexed to Los Angeles, eager
to get the water. With the water diverted to Los Angeles, the Owens
Valley reverted to a desert, but Los Angeles was able to grow into a
metropolis.

The aqueduct has been a source of controversy ever since. Was
the whole enterprise just sound business—a group of visionary city
fathers recognizing the imperatives of an emergent metropolis as prior
to those of a thinly populated rural area—or was it, as one of the early
critics, Morrow Mayo, termed it, the "rape" of Owens Valley and "a
colossal swindle." The criminal conspiracy version of the water proj-

ect, taken up by McWilliams in his 1946 *Southern California: An Island on the Land*, is the basis for Robert Towne's script for the 1974 film *Chinatown*.[8] In the film the city engineer Hollis Mulwray (a slight variation on Mulholland) is portrayed wholly as a victim, killed by the water swindlers (headed by one Noah Cross, a composite figure representing the real-life conspirators) when he discovers that water is being dumped into the ocean to create an artificial drought. He knows too much. So does the private eye Jake Gittes, and the conspirators try to kill him, too. Noah Cross's primal crime, the rape of his daughter, who later marries Mulwray, becomes the film's principal metaphor, or synecdoche: the personal defilement representing, and intensifying, the public defilement.

One of those who protested the scheme to divert water from the Owens Valley was Wallace Stafford Austin, who was registrar of the U.S. Land Office in the valley and husband of writer Mary Austin. Wallace Austin knew at first hand what the water diversion would mean to the valley ranchers. Mary, estranged from her husband and about to move north, to Carmel, nonetheless sided with the ranchers in the valley she had come to revere (the setting of her most famous book, *The Land of Little Rain*, 1903). Born in Illinois, she settled in 1888 with her mother and brother, after her father's death, on a homestead in the southern San Joaquin Valley, cattle country near the Tejon Ranch in the Tehachapi foothills, and moved to Lone Pine in the Owens Valley after her marriage. In 1899 she lived briefly in Los Angeles, where she became affiliated with the Arroyo Seco/*Land of Sunshine* group that hovered around Lummis. She returned for a time to Lone Pine, but in 1906, the marriage in ruins, she settled in Carmel, where she became part of the bohemian colony there. It was in Carmel that she became a full-time writer and wrote the majority of the thirty-one volumes she produced—collections of essays and sketches focusing on the natural landscape of the high desert Owens Valley, novels, and an autobiography. Between 1912 and 1917 she did most of her fiction writing, culminating in a novel about the water grab, *The Ford*.

Drawing on memories of three California places Austin lived— the San Joaquin Valley, the Owens Valley, and Carmel—*The Ford* is an expansive, panoramic novel that, like Jackson's *Ramona* a generation earlier, cuts across broad reaches of the state and combines several stories. The novel includes a romantic plot, a theatrical plot focused on Austin's activities at Carmel's Forest Grove Theater, and a political plot centered on the theft of California land and water. Although the three strands never quite come together, the novel achieves power in its depiction of the water scheme. The principal setting, a cattle-raising region she calls Tierra Longa in the southern San Joaquin Valley, appears to be a composite of that region and the Owens Valley to the east. Oil has been discovered and a boom is on; at the same time a group of entrepreneurs hatch a scheme to buy up ranchlands and water rights for the purpose of diverting water to San Francisco (not, in Austin's fictional displacement, Los Angeles). Kenneth Brent, a young lawyer born to a local ranching family, goes to work for one of the schemers, Rickhart, but when he finds out (like the fictionalized Mulholland in Robert Towne's screenplay) how the ranchers are being robbed of their land, he rebels (unlike Mulwray in *Chinatown*, who gets murdered for what he knows) and tries to organize the ranchers to defend their lands. The events in the novel, though geographically relocated by Austin, occurred in 1905, when a federal water reclamation agent named Lippincott went to the Owens Valley to explore the possibilities of an irrigation project, one that would allegedly benefit local ranchers, but which led to the diversion of valley water to Los Angeles.

In 1905 Austin was spending time both in Lone Pine and Los Angeles. Her association with Lummis began in 1889 when she showed up at El Alisal. Lummis had already published some of her poems, and she sought him out for advice on becoming a writer. He found a house for her and her daughter in the arroyo, and she soon became a regular at his Saturday night "noises." The relationship, though, got less and less cordial. She found in him something of a bamboozler and dissembler. Her feminist side objected to what she saw as his obsessive womanizing and the mistreatment of both his former and present wives. (She got to know both, and liked them.) She felt there was something phony about his desert enthusiasm, as, unlike her, he had never had to scrape out a living in the desert. She also held against him his close connection with Otis, who spearheaded the Owens Valley water diversion, which ruined the valley. Lummis was to her a city booster and not a real lover of the land, as he claimed to be. In his desert enthusiasm, his Southwest caballero role-playing, he was to her a consummate poseur.

Lummis epitomized to her the urban, bigger-is-better, boosting

mentality, a man aligned more closely to the Otis gang of city oligarchs than to the landscape. For Otis, the consummate city booster,
Los Angeles was destined to grow, and bigger was definitely better.
All the city needed was water, and once it had the water, its growth
rate accelerated. For Otis the Manifest Destiny imperative of the city
would be achievable only through a cheap workforce. His antiunion-
ism came to a crisis in 1910, when a dynamite bomb exploded in the
*Times* building. Twenty employees were killed, and the McNamara
brothers, active unionists, were arrested. Job Harriman, a socialist,
was running for mayor that year. The bombing occurred as the aqueduct was being built and Harriman was asserting that the aqueduct
was for the benefit of the land syndicate. Clarence Darrow defended
the McNamaras, but a deal was cut. The brothers avoided the death
penalty by pleading guilty. Harriman went on to defeat, and unionism in Los Angeles suffered a setback from which it took a long time
to recover.

In the years ahead very little happened in Los Angeles without
the aggressive push of the dynasty Otis founded (and passed on to his
son-in-law, Harry Chandler): the incorporation of most of the San
Fernando Valley and the annexation of a long strip of land leading
south to San Pedro and the new harbor, downtown development and
Bunker Hill redevelopment, the Coliseum (built for the 1932 Olympics), the Hollywood Bowl, the Music Center (with its flagship Dorothy
Chandler Pavilion), and even, a dozen years after Otis died, the freeways—the first of which, the Arroyo Seco, cut north from Los Angeles to Pasadena, alongside Lummis's house. Today the Times Mirror
Company, the house that Otis built, is one of the world's biggest and
richest media monopolies with holdings all over the world.

## IV

Lummis didn't stay long with the *Times*. After his first New Mexico
stay he returned to Los Angeles and in 1895 took on the editorship of
the promotional journal *Land of Sunshine*, begun the previous year
by Charles Dwight Willard. As secretary of the new chamber of commerce, Willard, who had also edited the short-lived *Pacific Monthly*,
simply didn't have time for the journal. Lummis took it on with the
enthusiasm of a zealot, making of it (and its successor *Out West*) both

a booster magazine and a full-fledged journal of Southern California and Southwest culture. The two interests were in fact linked in Lummis's mind: Los Angeles, the city, was the capital (or destined capital) of the Southwest, oriented not west to the ocean but east to the desert. The journal, under Lummis and his successor, George Wharton James, featured articles on art, archaeology, and regional history. It included poetry and local color fiction and was illustrated with photographs (some by Lummis) and reproductions of California and Southwest paintings, including those of William Keith (who painted all the missions), Maynard Dixon, and Gutzon Borglum (the sculptor of Mount Rushmore). Among the literary and cultural voices heard in the journal before it folded in 1917 were those of Stewart Edward White, Mary Hallock Foote, Nora May French, Edwin Markham, Grace Ellery Channing, Joaquin Miller, Charles Dudley Warner, and Robinson Jeffers, who over the next two decades was to emerge as California's finest poet.

While the roster of writers was impressive, most of them contributed only occasionally. No literary stable attached itself to the journal as it did to San Francisco's *Overland Monthly*. Lummis himself, the most prolific contributor, was given more to booster bombast than insightful commentary. Second to Lummis was one William Smythe, an irrigation expert (author of *The Conquest of Arid America*, 1899), who wrote the column "Twentieth Century West." Another frequent voice was that of Sharlot Hall, who wrote sentimental verse and stories about the hardships of women's lives in the Southwest and articles on desert Indian cultures. Mary Austin contributed four short stories and a novelette set in the Southwest desert. Nebraska-born Eugene Manlove Rhodes, vernacular teller of cowboy stories, appeared fairly often, providing some of the livelier writing. While Lummis positioned the magazine against San Francisco's *Argonaut* and *Overland Monthly*, which he saw as effete, overly intellectual journals, out of touch with the everyday, he nonetheless saw *Land of Sunshine* as a magazine that would show that the region "grows brains as well as oranges."

Still it was the oranges that got most of the attention. Boosting the region was clearly the editorial priority. The early issues are filled with celebrations of the sunshine, citrus crops, and health benefits that Southern California offered. In his monthly column, "In the Lion's

Den," Lummis ranted euphorically about the God-given natural wealth of the region. "One thing makes Southern California unique," he wrote—and the rhetoric is typical—"its wealth is intrinsic and not epiphytic. Its future rests on the guarantee of the Almighty—not upon the activity of earthworms."[9] In Southern California, he happily predicted, there would be no slums or tenements like those in the East, for the simple reason that the poor would be kept out by rising real estate prices, $300 an acre being "as tall a fence as is needed around any community."[10]

The key to rising real estate prices was of course climate. To the argument made by unenlightened Old Guard easterners like Harvard's Charles Eliot that too much sunshine is enervating and that productive work demands the bracing climate of the Northeast, Lummis replied that Eliot failed to understand the corresponding "Puritan conviction that whom the Lord loveth, He giveth pneumonia."[11] Charles Dudley Warner, who collaborated with Mark Twain on *The Gilded Age* and wrote *Our Italy*, a celebration of Southern California's fortunate similarity to Italy, addressed the climate and race issue in *Land of Sunshine* in 1895. In Southern California Warner saw the prospect of melding Anglo vigor and Mediterranean grace. "The Anglo Saxon energy and spirit in the setting of the peculiar climate of Southern California," he wrote, "will produce a new sort of community, in which the vital forces of modern life are not enervated, but have added to them something of the charm of a less anxious and more contented spirit."[12]

Comparisons of Southern California to Italy, Spain, and Greece dominated the pages of *Land of Sunshine*. The Italianizing spirit in Southern California had a powerful voice in Grace Ellery Channing, daughter of the New England Unitarian-Transcendentalist family, who in Los Angeles became Lummis's associate editor. Channing, enchanted with Italy (as were so many American writers before and after the turn of the century—Howells, James, and Warner among them), urged Angelenos to do as the Romans do: spend time outdoors in the sun, and live in houses with large patios and courtyards. Charlotte Perkins Gilman, another celebrated New Englander (related to Lyman Beecher and his daughter, Harriet Beecher Stowe), settled for a time in Pasadena after a nervous breakdown in the East (which led later to her story, "The Yellow Wallpaper," the most famous

breakdown story in American literature as well as one of its most celebrated feminist parables). She was, like Channing, an Italophile, envisioning a Southern California that would be the nexus of Anglo-
Saxon and Mediterranean cultures. Abbot Kinney was still another
of the New World Italy spirits, his re-creation of Venice standing as
an icon of the Italian/Mediterranean vision of Southern California.
In time the Mediterranean motif so central to the booster program
would become an object of satire—early and notably in a piece by
Willard Huntington Wright in *Smart Set* in 1913—but the romantic
Mediterranean linkage, whether the model was Greece, Italy, or Spain,
formed an essential component of the selling of Southern California
at the end of the nineteenth and beginning of the twentieth century.
Thus while well-heeled Americans were making the fin-de-siècle
"grand tour" of Europe, city boosters were promoting a new sunny
southern Europe on America's West Coast.

Joseph Pomeroy Widney, another migrant who came for his health,
made explicit the Anglo-Saxon racism implicit in the Southern California Mediterranean vision. Widney arrived from Ohio in 1868, before the boom, with his brother Robert. A medical doctor and physical educator, he went on to help found the University of Southern
California as a Methodist college, write one of the earliest booster
tracts, *California of the South* (1888), and offer in *The Race Life of the
Aryan People* (1907) a fulsome account of the race destiny of the Anglo-
Saxon in Southern California. What he called the "Engle" people
(linked to terms like Aryan and Nordic and, as cognate, to Anglo)
were destined to thrive in the region. The North Sea people go west,
following the sun, and are reinvigorated. The movement away from
the American East, where the cities have been blighted by the in-
undation of hordes of clannish and unassimilable immigrants from
southern and eastern Europe, is movement toward freedom, toward
regeneration and racial destiny.

The identification of the West with Anglo-Saxon racial health is
a familiar enough theme in late-nineteenth- and early-twentieth-
century western writing. One finds it (and its obverse: the fear of a
foreign presence in the West) in, among other western writers, Owen
Wister (for whom the West was "the last outpost of the Anglo Saxon"),
Jack London, Frank Norris, and Gertrude Atherton. Such voices gave
a distinctly West Coast sound to the Anglo-Saxon racism of turn-of-

the-century East Coast writers, politicians, and race theorists—men like Henry Cabot Lodge, Lothrop Stoddard, and Madison Grant, who sought to curb immigration by demonizing southern and eastern Europeans. That the same sunny Italy that offered the model of gracious living in Southern California for Warner, Gilman, and Channing was also the largest source of southern and eastern European immigrants—the stiletto-bearing "wops" who were pouring into and supposedly contributing to the blight of the eastern cities—is not just a paradox but another example of cultural schizophrenia in fin-de-siècle America. Still another example of this split personality is the case of the California Indians: their population uprooted and decimated first by the Spanish and then the Anglos, they were nonetheless idealized as the true exemplars of desert spirituality—a model of what regenerate Anglos could learn from close contact with the primitive.

For Widney the proximity of the desert was the key to the Anglo-Saxon reclamation project. The desert would improve the racial stock by putting the right kind of people in close contact and harmony with natural, and spiritual, forces—as the immigrant-infested eastern city could not. Physical and spiritual health were linked to the desert, which evoked the sublime in the effects of light, the unbroken vista of sky, and the eternal stillness of a landscape that transcended history and change. It bespoke the enduring, the immortal, and the simple, natural lives of the primordial population—that is to say, before those same idealized Indians were extirpated, their cultures erased, and their numbers decimated. To Lummis's editorial successor, George Wharton James, a defrocked, expatriate minister from England, who was a cultural liaison between the British Arts and Crafts movement and the American Southwest, the desert was God's "health-giving laboratory." In Mary Austin it inspired the mystic. "Great souls" go to the desert, she wrote, and come out saints and prophets. To her thinking, however, Lummis was not one of them. Nor was Helen Hunt Jackson. In her 1932 autobiography, *Earth Horizon*, Austin complained about "the factitious effort" to invoke a romantic history out of old missions, out of *Ramona* in particular, which she found to be a second-rate romance.

Factitious or not, an obsessive interest in the desert runs rampant in the early-twentieth-century literature of Southern California. There were John Van Dyke's *The Desert* in 1901, Mary Austin's *Land of Little Rain* in 1903, George Wharton James's *The Wonders of the Colorado Desert* in 1906, A. J. Burdick's *The Mystic Mid-Region* in 1907, and J. Smeaton Chase's *California Desert Trails* in 1913. It was a recurring subject in Lummis's *Land of Sunshine*. The vast wastes of desert that kindled terror in the hearts of the early western pioneers became for the Southern California boosters and Southwest enthusiasts the zone of enchantment and spirituality, the place in which to lose oneself in order to find oneself. What has to be kept in mind is that when Lummis and the others were writing about the Mojave and Colorado, the deserts were being crossed daily by thousands of California tourists and migrants in comfortable Pullman cars. It was no longer a terrifying terra incognita, at least those stretches of the desert visible from the club cars of the Santa Fe.

In the years to come the desert would continue to carry for some people the meanings Lummis, Austin, James, and the others gave to it, but today, as the Mojave has come to be the new frontier of tract housing, discount warehouses, malls, and country clubs (in a kind of reverse westward migration—West to East—back over the mountains), the view is less awe-inspiring. As places like Palm Springs, Rancho Mirage, Las Vegas, and Laughlin have emerged as sprawling, over-populated, and overbuilt pleasure domes—as the outstretched arms of imperial Los Angeles—Southern Californians are less and less in touch with the older meanings. One has to go farther and farther into the Mojave to find the sublimity the early desert enthusiasts found.

The role of the railroad in domesticating the desert appears in an early novel about Los Angeles, Mark Lee Luther's *The Boosters* (1923). For the migrating architect George Hammond the desert is just a place to cross, to get through, in a comfortable train on the way to the promised land, rendered as an urban, paved paradise. As the train rolls past the Colorado River, entering California, Hammond is assailed by a fellow passenger, a booster and boaster whose vision is pointed not toward the desert in front of him but toward the city to the West:

It's the garden spot of the globe, and Los Angeles is the pick of the garden. . . . There she sits on her rolling hills—

Our Lady, Queen of the Angels—the Sierra Madre at her back, the blue Pacific at her feet, the wonder city of the world.[13]

The desert takes on other meanings in other novels. In John Fante's 1939 *Ask the Dust*, set on Bunker Hill, in the very center of the city, the empty waste of the desert corresponds to the emptiness at the core of the protagonist's heart. The Mojave is a metaphor for Arturo Bandini's sense of waste and futility: at the novel's end he chases the drug-addicted Mexican woman he loves out into the desert where she disappears, and all he can do in the face of her disappearance is hurl his just-published novel out after her into the sand—as Fante himself hurls his novel into the world. In a more recent novel, Norman Mailer's 1955 *The Deer Park*, the Mojave has turned into a movie-colony watering hole, a desert in which the light and space celebrated by earlier desert enthusiasts become irrelevant because life is lived indoors, in casinos, bars, and hotels, and where the very distinction between day and night, between the seasons themselves, has all but been obliterated. In other novels set at least partly in the Mojave—Joan Didion's *Play It as It Lays* (1970) and Leo Wurlitzer's *Slow Fade* (1984) are examples—the desert becomes the wasteland refuge of outcasts, derelicts, and escapists, along with the occasional western moviemaker and an assortment of health cultists.

V

By the early twenties, a period of mass migration, the booster myth was barely hanging on. Harrison Gray Otis died in 1917, George Wharton James in 1923, and Charles Fletcher Lummis in 1928. *Out West* folded in 1917, although it reappeared for a time as a joint venture with *Overland Monthly*. Even before that, though, the booster myth was becoming an object of satire. In 1913 Willard Huntington Wright (brother of modernist painter Stanton MacDonald-Wright), author of the Philo Vance mysteries (under the name S. S. Van Dine) and editor of *Smart Set*, hammered one of the early nails in the booster coffin in an article for that magazine called "Los Angeles—the Chemically Pure." That year the chamber of commerce was still hyping Ramona, sunshine, and oranges, James was at the helm of

*Out West,* and General Otis, having survived the *Times* bombing, the unionist scare, and the threat of Job Harriman's mayoral campaign, was still in command of the paper—and the city. Wright, meanwhile, from the editor's desk at *Smart Set* (a desk H. L. Mencken would assume the next year), found laughable hypocrisy in the Hispanic touting of the region:

> The Spanish civilization breathed its last, and its influence,
> too, passed out with the desecration of the Franciscan
> missions. Only the upholstered Spanish names remain
> to remind us that Los Angeles indeed has a past. The
> Americano brought with him his own clothes, foods,
> habits and liquors. He built on the ruins of Spain, but he
> might as well have built on a virgin desert for all the effect
> those ruins had upon him. And today the average citizen
> of Los Angeles, far from being influenced by a Spanish
> heritage, knows nothing of California's history prior to 1890,
> and more than likely is unable to pronounce the name of his
> own street. Scratch any native and you'll find an Iowan.[14]

The booster attempt to graft onto Los Angeles a Spanish heritage simply didn't take, according to Wright. The Los Angeles he delineates with loving hate is a village of misplaced, displaced midwesterners, a place "whose personality is that of the rural pietist, of the rigid and uncompromising Puritan," (90) a city that rolls up its sidewalks at midnight and where it is hard to find a decent meal, let alone a cocktail. Of Angelenos, "the spirit of cosmopolitanism has not yet ravished their minds or inflamed their blood." (93) In their uprooted state, their quest for a sense of belonging to something, they have turned to "faddists and mountebanks—spiritualists, mediums, astrologers, phrenologists, palmists and all other breeds of esoteric windjammers." (96) Among other things Wright here is anticipating the literary preoccupation with cults that would run through the fiction of the 1920s and 1930s.

He is also anticipating the "revolt from the village" theme of midwestern fiction in the years ahead, rendering Los Angeles an overgrown Gopher Prairie, Spoon River, or Winesburg, Ohio. Oddly enough the piece ends on a more melioristic note, as if he needed to say something nice about the place he has just scorched. Given its "embryonic condition," he predicts, it has the means of becoming in the years ahead "a metropolis wealthy and diverse, commercially powerful and artistically wise." (102)

The myth died hard. Booster narratives—fiction and reportage—continued to be produced in the twenties and thirties. Typical of them is Katherine Ames Taylor's *The Los Angeles Trip Book*, published in 1928, which, in the aggressive city-building spirit of the 1920s, is a paean not to the Lummis/James Hispanic and/or Southwest desert legacy but to the go-getter Otis spirit of urban enterprise, the model for which she saw in the Midwest. Los Angeles, she wrote, "threw off its Spanish mantle, sombrero, and lazy slouch and donned instead the manners of the enterprising Middle West. New hands began shaping the destiny of the city." The city, she went on, has become one of "the most romantic and amazing tales of civic achievement."[15] Going even further in lauding the Anglo destiny of the city, Harry Carr, longtime *Times* writer and crony of Harry Chandler, wrote in *Los Angeles: City of Dreams* in 1935 that "Los Angeles is an epic—one of the greatest and most significant migrations in the long saga of the Aryan people." The passage could have come directly from the pages of one of H. P. Widney's racist tracts. Carr tells us that the "Aryan tribes took boats and crossed the sea. The last trek was across the American prairies in covered wagons to the Pacific Coast—to California."[16]

Mark Lee Luther's 1923 novel, *The Boosters*, referred to earlier, complicates the booster vision, offering a gloss on both the hype and anti-hype. It comes to rest on an optimistic vision of future possibilities in the city but at the same time complains about its huckster qualities, its sham architecture, its ruthless acquisitiveness. George Hammond, a down-on-his-luck Boston architect, is persuaded to seek a fresh start in Los Angeles, where his wife's brother has already made a fortune in real estate. Mrs. Hammond, the daughter of a forty-niner, encourages the voyage as a nostalgic retracing of her father's path across the desert; the retracing, of course, is by Pullman train. The entry into the city is disastrous for Hammond, who only wants to build beautiful buildings. The August sky is overcast, and the landscape is dominated by junkyards and orange juice stands (looking like giant oranges). Everywhere he sees parking lots and souvenir shops. The house of Mrs. Hammond's wealthy brother is described as looking like a battleship—a mammoth, graceless rectangle. "The faults of structure," Hammond concludes, "were surpassed only by the sins of decoration." (21) He has brought New England with him, and nothing pleases him. He loathes the ubiquitous oil wells (which by the early twenties were sprouting up everywhere in the city), the ever-present spiky (and imported, like everything else) palm trees, and the tasteless, imitative architecture aping every conceivable style.

The drift of the novel is to modify Hammond's initial distaste for the city. The task is achieved largely through the offices of a good woman—not his wife but the estranged wife of his brother-in-law, the go-getter real estate capitalist Spencer Ward, who is his nemesis. The opposition between Ward, the Yankee booster, hell-bent on exploiting the land for all it can bear, staking his claim on it as his father had done on the Mother Lode, and Anita, the true Californio, daughter of the mixed Anglo/Spanish past (Ramona in urban dress), frames the narrative. Both are stereotypes—broadly drawn opposites who represent the poles of California's possibilities: Anita, the claims of history, preservation, and living in harmony with the land; Spencer, the claims of city building and the bigger-is-better future. Hammond, trapped between the two, establishes by the novel's end his own relationship to the land. He throws his energies in the path Anita has shown him, devoting his architectural skills to the planning of houses that combine his eastern legacy with a distinctively Hispanic-California flair, much in the manner of the architect Irving Gill—on whom Hammond may well have been based.[17] Hammond finds himself at the end comfortably situated in a house in the Hollywood Hills and at work on the design for a model community in which every house is to be "the best of its type."

Luther's Los Angeles emerges as both the best and the worst of places, the land of the fast buck promoter and the bigoted, race-conscious civic booster (anti-Japanese sentiment runs high among the novel's city builders), but also the land that holds out the redemptive possibility of a new American landscape and identity forged by the impact of East and West. For Willard Huntington Wright the graft didn't take. Luther is more sanguine about the possibility. In a scene near the end of the novel the Hammonds stumble on a New York State picnic (of displaced New Yorkers) in a park and see sheets of paper bearing the names of people hoping to locate East Coast neighbors. The names suggest to Hammond the diversity of the Southern California population (though one wonders how diverse that population of uprooted New Yorkers was). To Hammond the names offer the image of a new melting pot on the West Coast, a region that was blending the groups "triumphantly . . . into a single type." (346) The novel is no unadulterated booster manifesto in the ebullient manner of Lummis, James, and Carr, or a savaging of the place in the vein of Willard Huntington Wright. Set against the Los Angeles fiction that began to appear a few years later — novels by Upton Sinclair, Don Ryan, Carl Van Vechten, the Graham brothers, and others — it is an elegy to a dying vision. By the end of the twenties the booster vision, though capable still of an occasional last flicker, was effectively dead. And Los Angeles fiction was born.

# 3

## THE TWENTIES AND BEYOND

### *Oil, Movies, and Salvation*

Los Angeles is a middle-aged obese woman from somewhere else in the Middle West, lying naked in the sun. As she sips from a glass of buttermilk and bites off chunks of hamburger sandwich, she reads Tagore to the music of Carrie Jacobs Bond.
MYRON BRINIG, *THE FLUTTER OF AN EYELID*

All visitors from the East know the strange spell of unreality which seems to make human experience as hollow as the life of a trollnest where everything is out in the open instead of being underground.
EDMUND WILSON, "THE BOYS IN THE BACK ROOM"

Fiction came to Los Angeles in the 1920s not by the route of literary modernists like Eliot, Joyce, or Hemingway but via the satirists and debunkers like Willard Huntington Wright, Sinclair Lewis, Louis Adamic, and H. L. Mencken. The booster-bloated city was ripe for deflation. Mark Lee Luther may have fired the first satirical shot at the booster mentality, but his 1923 novel concluded more like a booster than an antibooster work, coming to rest with its architect-protagonist's happy accommodation with Los Angeles and his determination to make it the City Beautiful. As the twenties progressed, and the population reached the million mark, the city's booster energies went into promoting it less as Mediterranean Garden than as West Coast Metropolis—an industrial and commercial arena of unlimited potential. In fiction and debunking journalism, though, Los Angeles was neither Garden nor Metropolis. Instead it was an overgrown Small Town, portrayed increasingly in the second half of the decade as the West Coast seat of unadulterated Babbittry—Zenith writ large. It offered itself to satirists as a sprawling town of wandering philistines and prudes from Iowa or Kansas, preyed on by an army of fly-by-night promoters, spiritual healers, medical quacks, and get-rich-quick schemers—each offering his or her panacea to an uprooted, unsettled, migrant population. The city was, in the words of one of the debunkers, Louis Adamic, a Yugoslav writer who settled in Los Angeles in the twenties, "the enormous village." Adamic characterized the population of Los Angeles in 1925 as an amalgam of boosters and Babbitts, small-time promoters and con men, cultists and health-seekers, and retired midwestern farmers in search of sunshine:

> The people on the top in Los Angeles, the big men, are
> the businessmen, the Babbitts. They are the promoters, who
> are blowing down the city's windpipe with all their might,
> hoping to inflate the place to a size that will be reckoned the
> largest city in the country. . . . And trailing after the big boys
> is a mob of lesser fellows . . . thousands of minor realtors,
> boomers, promoters, contractors, agents, salesmen, bunko-
> men, office-holders, lawyers, and preachers—all driven by
> the same motive of wealth, power, and personal glory. . . .

They exploit the "come-ons" and one another, envy the big
boys, their wives gather in women's clubs, listen to swamis
and yogis and English lecturers, join "love cults" and Coue
clubs in Hollywood and Pasadena. . . . Then there are the
Folks . . . they are the retired farmers, grocers, Ford agents,
hardware merchants, and shoe merchants from the Middle
West. . . . They sold out their farms and businesses . . . and
now they are here in California—sunny California—to rest
and regain their vigor, enjoy climate, look at pretty scenery,
live in little bungalows with a palm tree or banana plant in
front, and eat in cafeterias.[1]

II

In the city's cultural landscape two 1920s migrants—one in the religion of business, the other in the business of religion—stand out as
representative figures, symbols of the aggressive new, up-for-grabs city
in the post-Otis years, and exemplars of the big city/overgrown village dualism: oil speculator Chauncy (C. C.) Julian and evangelist
Aimee Semple McPherson. Their careers ran parallel courses. Each
was born in Canada, drifted into Los Angeles in the postwar years,
amassed a fortune in a very brief time as a consummate promoter—
the one as fast-buck oil stock promoter, the other as spiritual healer
with a flair for salesmanship and attracting big donations. Each was
run aground in a scandal in the mid-twenties, and each ended by
committing suicide. Each tells the quintessential Southern California
narrative of the new beginning followed by the calamitous end. And,
most appropriate to the scope of this book, each figures prominently
as a fictional character in the novels of the twenties and thirties.

Julian was among the first of the independent oil men to stake his
claim in the oil booms of the early 1920s. Thirty years after E. L.
Doheny's wells began pumping beneath the city streets near Echo
Park, large oil deposits were discovered in Huntington Beach, Signal
Hill, and Santa Fe Springs. The Signal Hill strike furnished the principal story line for Upton Sinclair's 1927 novel *Oil!* about the rise and
fall of an independent oil tycoon. The real-life Julian speculated on
oil leases, as did Sinclair's protagonist, J. Arnold Ross, and then formed
his own company to produce, refine, and distribute oil—selling his

"Julian Pete" stock to some forty thousand people for about $11 million. He oversold the certificates, though, and was forced to sell out to a pair of even wilier speculators who proceeded to issue $150 million in fraudulent stock, fleecing thousands of investors of their life savings. In 1927 (just as Sinclair was completing his novel) the courts stopped the trading of Julian stock, and Julian himself, not prosecuted (his company was still solvent when he sold out), fled to China, where in 1934 he took his life in a Shanghai hotel. Sinclair, who studied the Julian fiasco as well as the Teapot Dome scandals of the Harding administration, drew on the events of the 1920s oil scandals in his portrait of the rise and fall of J. Arnold Ross.

Sister Aimee's story is no less a story of meteoric rise and early collapse. She arrived in Los Angeles in 1918 (via a stay in San Diego), a divorced mother with a budding career as a tent evangelist. Five years later she dedicated her Angelus Temple near Echo Park. She was drawn to the site providentially, she claimed—a site appropriately, if coincidentally, very close to that of Doheny's 1892 oil strike. Her Four Square Gospel was a dazzling show business approach to preaching and healing, combining costume drama (she dressed as everything from George Washington to a football player to a motorcycle cop—in which costume she intoned, "Stop, you're speeding to ruin"), an orchestra, tear-jerking sermons, and a radio station (the "Glory Station of the Pacific Coast"). What could be more apt, more effective, than such spectacle as an approach to salvation in a city set down in the land of movies, exotic fantasy architecture, and theme parks?

Carey McWilliams, who arrived in Los Angeles in 1921, was fascinated with McPherson's show biz approach to things of the spirit, what he called her "theological entertainment." In an essay called "Sunlight in My Soul," he described a visit to the tabernacle where he witnessed "a memorable dramatization of the triumph of Good over Evil":

> On the stage was an illuminated scoreboard. As the lights
> dimmed in the auditorium, one could see the forces of Good
> advancing on the citadels of Evil, stalking up ravines, scaling
> mountains, jumping precipices. To the flash of godly gunfire
> and the blaze of holy artillery, the forces of General Evil
> began to retreat. Then a miniature blimp came floating over

the scoreboard terrain. A soldier of Good fired a single shot, exploded the blimp, and an ugly grimacing Devil landed on the stage with a thud as the spotlight centered on an unfurled American flag.[2]

Not long after McWilliams witnessed Sister Aimee's dazzling histrionic flight, the evangelist "disappeared" in the surf at Ocean Park, presumably drowned. It was 1926 and she was at the height of her career. Happily for her minions, she resurfaced a month later in Douglas, Arizona, claiming to have been kidnapped and taken over the border into Mexico. Back in Los Angeles one hundred thousand of the faithful greeted her as she passed in parade in a rose-colored Cadillac. It turned out that she had been holed up in a love nest— actually a series of love nests—with her radio technician. She was later indicted for providing false information but was released, having committed no real crime. She returned to the temple, continued her razzle-dazzle performances, but suffered a series of nervous break- downs and took her own life in 1944.

Another observer of Sister Aimee in the 1920s was H. L. Mencken, who visited her tabernacle in 1926, just after her return from "drown- ing." Mencken, who had no love for Los Angeles, found the church too tempting a target to resist. His *American Mercury* had been pub- lishing satiric, debunking pieces on the city by young writers on the coast in the twenties and would continue to do so in the thirties— among them Adamic, Jim Tully, an Ohio-born hobo-turned-prize- fighter-turned-screenwriter, McWilliams, a young journalist, and in the 1930s, James M. Cain, a journalist-turned-screenwriter who had been with Mencken on the *Baltimore Sun* before coming to Holly- wood. Mencken visited Los Angeles only once. Following his break with George Jean Nathan, he came by train across the South, his "Sahara of the Bozart," arriving in Hollywood just as Valentino died, prompting his characteristic remark, "[The death] throws a heavy re- sponsibility on me. I am now the most powerful aphrodisiac in the western world." He debated socialism with Upton Sinclair, dined at Metro-Goldwyn-Mayer with Louis B. Mayer and Irving Thalberg, and paid tribute to McPherson's Four Square Gospel. He wrote in a letter home that he sat in her "evangelical bull ring," listening to hymns "to brass band and ukulele accompaniment" and observing the evangelist "in her long white robe with very low cut collar and the fixed smile and self-possession of a fancy-house madam . . . caress the anthropoids of this dusty, forbidding region with her lubricious coos." Los Angeles, he concluded, after his two-week visit, was "an inconceivably shoddy place . . . a pasture for the cow-town evangelism of a former sideshow wriggler."[3]

This kind of send-up typified the response of the sneering journalists. Sister Aimee emerged as the emblem of everything that was fatuous about Los Angeles. Her career came to be identified with the charlatanism endemic in the city. She was an easy, highly visible target. Like the characters who came to inhabit the Hollywood novel from the late 1920s through the 1930s and 1940s, her story served as metaphor for the pervasive role-playing bred in the movie capital, the performative display of a self-constructed identity. And what could be more Hollywood than the roller coaster rise and fall of a star? Her disappearance/reappearance was her most histrionic act, her consummate Hollywood masquerade performance, ready-made for novelistic representation. At the same time it anticipated the Los Angeles detective story that would be Raymond Chandler's and Ross Macdonald's stock-in-trade over the next few decades: the kidnapping, the search for the missing woman, the invention of a new identity, the lurid details of secret meetings in different hotels in different cities.

Because she epitomized, personified, the city of illusion and deception, Sister Aimee, in one form or another, has appeared more frequently in fiction than any other real-life figure of her time (C. C. Julian and Valentino included). Hers was the archetypal local story, and she emerged as *the* local cult figure of her time. Her appearance in the fiction—in one incarnation or another—is more the rule than the exception. She, or someone very much like her, makes at least a cameo appearance in Don Ryan's *Angel's Flight* (1927), Carl Van Vechten's *Spider Boy* (1927), Myron Brinig's *The Flutter of an Eyelid* (1933), Richard Hallas's [Eric Knight] *You Play the Black and the Red Comes Up* (1938), and even Sinclair's *Oil!*, where she appears in drag as the evangelist brother of the political radical Paul Watkins. Her recurring appearance, along with that of her minions, in the fiction of the late twenties and early thirties serves as a kind of shorthand both for the show biz, theme park approach to life in Los Angeles and the obsessive concern in the fiction for delineating "the folk"—their desperate migrant quest for the transcendental quick fix, for the healing of body and spirit. She offered the miraculous cure, the magical makeover—or, if nothing more, at least a sense of belonging in the city of strangers. Although there have been other popular evangelists (e.g., the powerful Robert "Fighting Bob" Schuler, Sister Aimee's nemesis), she was by far the most successful and magnetic of them, precursor to a host of radio preachers and televangelists of the following decades. (At its peak the Four Square Gospel had four hundred branch churches, far-flung radio broadcasts, and a vast overseas network of missions.)

Although it would be wrong to call the Four Square Gospel a cult, it functions as such in the novelists' imagination, as the representation of a form of collective hysteria engendered by a charismatic leader. Surprisingly, while Nathanael West, in the most extravagant Hollywood satire ever written, *The Day of the Locust*, has his protagonist Tod Hackett comb Hollywood's cultist sanctuaries in search of material for his painting "The Burning of Los Angeles" (finding a host of them, like the Church of Christ Physical, the Tabernacle of the Third Coming, and the Temple Moderne), he doesn't include a McPherson stand-in in the novel. John Schlesinger, however, couldn't resist inserting her into his 1975 film version in a scene in which the dying Harry Greener is carried into Angelus Temple to be touched—to little avail—by the Sister, resplendent in her flowing robe. Sinclair's novel, written just after McPherson's triumphal, headlined return, represents the Sister Aimee figure as a consummate and dangerous quack. Eli Watkins, prophet of the Third Revelation, practices the Four Square Gospel, where "the Holy Spirit comes down to you and makes you jump," speaks in tongues, faints, foams at the mouth, and even, McPherson-fashion, fakes his own drowning.

But Sinclair's novel, more than a lampoon of religious charlatanism, is a long piece of documentary realism, a muckraking exposé of industrial corruption, municipal graft, and political chicanery. It is the most wide-reaching, most ambitious novel about Los Angeles in the 1920s by the most prominent American novelist to settle in the region at the time. Sinclair's centerpiece is the oil bonanza, but the novel goes far beyond the crude-oil boom to the anatomy of the social, economic, and political forces at work in the city. As a novel about power—those who seize it and how they seize it—it excludes blacks, Hispanics, and women, except in supporting roles, and, for the most part, the white middle class. The world of the novel is divided into the proletariat class—the working poor and the radical reformers among them—and the oil entrepreneurs and their collusion with government and powerful money interests. There is little in between.

Sinclair had been thinking about writing a novel about the Teapot Dome oil theft, but as with his earlier novel about Chicago's meatpacking industry, *The Jungle*, this six-hundred-page book spread beyond his original intentions. He had been in Southern California since 1915, lured to the coast by his friends Lincoln Steffens and George Sterling. He spent time in Carmel, home of Sterling and the Seacoast of Bohemia group, and then in 1916 settled with his second wife, Mary Craig Kimbrough, in a two-story house in Pasadena, overlooking the Arroyo Seco. It was the old home territory of the Lummis and James booster set and home, too, of his close friend, the millionaire socialist Gaylord Wilshire. Later the Sinclairs bought a second house on Long Beach's Alamitos Bay, not far from where Mary owned several lots on Signal Hill. It was when he witnessed oil men bargaining for leases on the hill in the boom of 1921 that he saw the real germ of his narrative. "Here were a score of 'little people,'" he wrote, "suddenly seized by the vision of becoming 'big people,' driven half crazy with a mixture of greed and fear."[4] He wrote feverishly, completing the book in 1927.

The story of the empire building and ultimate collapse of J. Arnold Ross (a composite of the oil barons of the twenties—including C. C. Julian) is told from the point of view of his son, Bunny, torn between loyalty to his father—pictured not simply as a ruthless tycoon but also as a loving, generous parent—and to the ideals of Paul Watkins, the son of poor ranchers on whose property Ross has finagled his oil leases. The brothers Eli and Paul Watkins represent opposing forms of idealism—the one a religious fanatic, the other a social reformer. At the end Paul, whose labor sympathy and frustration have drawn him to communism, is killed by a right-wing mob, his sister Ruth, haunted by the specter of a worker killed in the field, has committed suicide, and the elder Ross has died of a heart attack. Bunny, after a fling with a Hollywood starlet, marries a Jewish immigrant girl and contemplates starting a utopian workers' school, a commune where pacifistic socialism, the kind Sinclair professed, can be studied.

Before this, though, the novel takes us through the tumultuous period from World War I to the Coolidge years. Its documentary scope is immense, covering the oil boom and the rise of wildcat speculators (including more than most readers ever wanted to know about the mechanics of drilling), Tea Pot Dome and the Julian fiasco, the conniving of oil leases on residential property, the suburban real estate boom, Wilson's armistice betrayals, the buying of the 1920 Republican convention by Ross and his confederates, Harding and the "Ohio Gang," Hollywood and the star system, red-baiting and red-beating, college life, fast cars and high-speed highways, the sexual mores of the rich—petting parties, gold diggers, flappers, and Prohibition drinking—and even postwar Paris with its jazz and idealization of Negroes.

The opening of the novel offers a vivid picture of the fluid boom-time city as it is approached by car. Ross is driving with Bunny in a new roadster south across the Tehachapis on the way to Signal Hill to buy oil leases. The car offers the image of power, control, and progress, as "Dad" Ross, driving at fifty miles per hour, smoking a cigar at the wheel, maneuvers dangerous curves, skillfully avoiding speed cops. They enter Los Angeles through vast subdivisions and acreage for sale. Flags and banners announce the new tracts: "Gas? Yes," "Water? Best Ever," "Lights? Right," "Restrictions? You Bet," "Schools? Under Construction," "Scenery? Beats the Alps." The city is a maze of trolley tracks and roads and "thousands of speeding cars, and more subdivisions and suburban home-sites, with endless ingenious advertisements designed to catch the fancy of the motorist, and cause him to put on brakes."[5]

This opening lays the foundation for everything that follows: Los Angeles is the still-Protestant-ruled, ruthlessly promoted city on the make, the city that speculators like Ross can make their own through every kind of opportunism, including bribery. When he wants roads built to haul in oil rigs, he simply pays off city officials. Everything is for sale. During the war he sells oil to both the Allies and the Central Powers and justifies it as good business sense. He joins a federation of independent producers, and despite his own sympathy for labor and Bunny's urging, he is prevented by the federation from raising wages and reducing the workday to eight hours, resulting in a strike. He reminds Bunny that this is an "open shop" town and to argue about unions is about as useful as "butt[ing] your head against a wall." Strikebreakers ("guards") are brought in to provoke violence among the workers, and the industry's spin doctors spread the word that German agents and Bolsheviks are behind the violence.

At the University of Southern California Bunny comes to learn from a history professor that America has been carving up Europe for its own economic interests and that President Wilson and other heads of state have violated the self-determination agreements of the armistice. The professor is summarily fired. Founded by a Methodist minister and oil baron (an allusion to the racist ideologue and minister J. P. Widney), USC is represented as a bastion of reactionary politics. Only athletics count; sports bring in money. Bunny is increasingly drawn, as the novel closes, toward the socialist ideals of his boyhood friend Paul Watkins and away from the capitalist ideology of his father, who by the end of the work is a broken man, forced to flee the country to avoid prosecution (not exactly, but close to, the fate of C. C. Julian). However much it is an exposé of capitalism run amok, the novel generally avoids the preachy quality that mars much of Sinclair's fiction. It is not, though, without its authorial pronouncements—lest we miss the point—like this from the last paragraph:

> Some day all those unlovely derricks will be gone, and so will the picket fence and the graves. . . . [I]f men can find some way to chain the black and cruel demon which killed Ruth Watkins and her brother—yes, and Dad too: an evil power which roams the earth, crippling the bodies of men and women, and luring nations to destruction by visions of unearned wealth, and the opportunity to enslave and exploit labor. (526–27)

Ahead of Sinclair in California was his 1934 campaign for governor under the EPIC banner, his pamphlet "End Poverty in California," and his fanciful, utopian, prophesy, *I, Candidate for Governor, and How I Ended Poverty: A True Story of the Future*—followed by *I, Candidate for Governor: And How I Got Licked*. In 1934 an estimated three hundred thousand were out of work in the basin. Eight hundred EPIC clubs were formed throughout the state. When Sinclair won the Democratic nomination, a vicious countercampaign of vilification was unleashed, one that raised the specter of communism and the massive importation of homeless migrants. The attack on Sinclair was spearheaded by Harry Chandler and the *Times*. Kyle Palmer, a *Times* political writer, offered his services to Louis B. Mayer, who proceeded to produce fake newsreels showing bums (played by Hollywood extras) getting off trains in Southern California. A conservative antiunion politician, Frank Merriam, defeated Sinclair in the general election, although Sinclair got a more than respectable 45 percent of the vote.

The battle between Sinclair and the *Times* was long-standing and mutually vicious. In his exposé of American journalism, *The Brass Check* (1919), Sinclair attacked Otis, barely in his grave, as "one of the most corrupt and most violent old men that ever appeared in American public life," a man with "complete disregard for truth, and with abusiveness which seems almost insane." For his part Otis, a year before his death, responded in the *Times* to a speech Sinclair, just arrived in Pasadena, had given at an exclusive ladies' club. Sinclair, the general reported, was the friend of murderers and dynamiters (a reference, perhaps, to Sinclair's friendship with Clarence Darrow, who defended the McNamara brothers), adding that "never before an audience of red-blooded men could Upton Sinclair have voiced his weak, pernicious, vicious doctrines. His naïve, fatuous smile alone would have aroused the ire before he opened his vainglorious mouth."[6] Sinclair opened his mouth again and again in the years ahead; at a "Wobbly" protest for free speech in San Pedro in 1923 he was arrested while reciting the Declaration of Independence and the First Amendment.

## III

As the thirties approached, Sinclair got involved in film through his friendship with Charlie Chaplin, who put him in touch with Sergei Eisenstein. Their collaboration on the epic film *Thunder over Mexico* was never completed, and Sinclair, who bankrolled most of the project, was left with an enormous debt. In introducing Bunny Ross in *Oil!* to the world of Hollywood (an affair with a starlet), Sinclair touched on a subject that had already found its way into the regional fiction. While Hollywood fiction—as satire, exposé, and American

Dream critique—did not reach a mature and masterful level until West's *The Day of the Locust*, published in 1939, the 1920s saw a proliferation of novels about Hollywood. In fact, if one can count the dozens of juvenile books of Victor Appleton—all the Tom Swift, "Movie Chums," and "Motion Picture Boys" books (which had their girls' book version in Bobbsey Twins creator Laura Lee Hope's "Motion Picture Girls" series)—one can date the beginnings of the genre to the early teens, the years the movies first came to Hollywood. The genre took hold first in lightweight satires, frothy comedies, and rags-to-riches melodramas like Harry Leon Wilson's *Merton of the Movies* (1922), Anita Loos's *But Gentlemen Marry Brunettes* (1928—her sequel to *Gentlemen Prefer Blondes*), and Phyllis Gordon Demerest's *Children of Hollywood* (1929). In Rupert Hughes's *Souls for Sale* (1922), Edgar Rice Burroughs's *The Girl from Hollywood* (1923), Carl Van Vechten's *Spider Boy* (1928), Carroll Graham and Garrett Graham's *Queer People* (1930), and Myron Brinig's *The Flutter of an Eyelid* (1933), Hollywood fiction reached deeper levels of satire and dark comedy.[7]

Hollywood was rocked in the 1920s by a number of headlined scandals—among them the drug addiction of actor Wallace Reid, the murder of womanizing director William Desmond Taylor and his involvement with leading ladies Mabel Normand and Mary Miles Minter, and the San Francisco hotel "rape" and "murder" trial of Fatty Arbuckle. "Hollywood Babylon" was born. In 1924 the industry, fearing government censorship, established the Hayes Commission to monitor its activities—on and off the screen. While little of the scandalous side of Hollywood appeared in the early novels, those of the twenties, two exceptions should be cited—Hughes's *Souls for Sale* and Burroughs's *The Girl from Hollywood*, both novels about young women in the film capital. The former touches on the Arbuckle case, its heroine and her mother defending Arbuckle, noting that the crime, if it were one, was no worse than crimes committed elsewhere, while the latter, alluding to various scandals, offers, by way of contrast (in a plot so convoluted as to defy summary), a scathing indictment of Hollywood morality, focusing on alcoholism, drug trafficking, and murder. By the beginning of the thirties this lurid thread would be picked up, notably in the Grahams' *Queer People*.

Hughes and Burroughs aside, the Hollywood story through the first half of the twenties tended either toward inoffensive satires on the pretensions and masquerading of the movie crowd, "inside dope" stories (like the fan mags, voyeuristic peeps into the behind-the-scenes life of movie makers), picaresque tales of a young man's or woman's fabulous adventures in the Magic Kingdom of Movieland, or local color stories that exploited the place for the appeal of its otherness, the oddball, eccentric, antic qualities it offered to eastern readers, who were already convinced that Hollywood was an asylum. The categories of representation are overlapping and interconnected. The plots are often contrived as fabulous, fantasy-like adventures and sudden, magical transformations. One day you are a nobody, the next a star—or vice versa; one is on the way up or down. In a variation of the Horatio Alger story fame and fortune are gained—and lost just as easily.

Typically the tales center on the fortunes of a dream seeker from the Midwest who drifts into Hollywood looking for stardom—a version of the traditional American tale of the country bumpkin adrift in the Big City. Hollywood, though, in the twenties was not a big city but a village of stucco bungalows, orange groves, and improvised, hastily erected studios. Founded by the Kansas prohibitionist Horace W. Wilcox, the town was a bastion of conservative politics, puritanical respectability, and booster pietism when the movie industry invaded the place with its on-street filming, its legions of movie hopefuls, and its hordes of extras renting rooms in boardinghouses and private homes. The good folks of Hollywood opposed the invasion at first, but as the industry succeeded beyond anyone's expectations (by 1915 the annual payroll was $20 million and national box office receipts reached $1 billion a year in the twenties), the citizens joined the bandwagon. They came to regard its major figures—DeMille, Mary Pickford, Douglas Fairbanks, and others—as revered public citizens, particularly when the new industry supported the war effort with big bucks and benefits.

Harry Leon Wilson's genial and gentle 1922 satire, *Merton of the Movies*, offers one version of the Hollywood success story. Wilson, a prolific author of some twenty-four books and plays (most in collaboration with Booth Tarkington), creator of the enormously popular *Ruggles of Red Gap* (filmed twice and adapted for stage by George S. Kaufman and Marc Connelly), editor of the journal *Punch*, and high-paid contributor to the *Saturday Evening Post*, arrived in Southern California, like Sinclair, via Carmel, spending only a few months in Hollywood. As outsider he tells the story of another outsider, the young Hollywood-hopeful Merton Gill, who, after some madcap adventures and misunderstandings, becomes an insider, a star. Much of Wilson's novel is taken up with local color, an "inside dope" foray into the making of movies. In the early days of the studios, before sound stages and sophisticated lighting, indoor scenes were shot in two-walled rooms scattered across improvised "camps," and much of Wilson's novel centers on his curious hero's wandering from set to set, observing one, then another film being shot. In a kind of meta-fictional way we watch the star-struck Gill watch the movies being made. Meanwhile his own movie transformation is taking place, though not in the way his dreams have dictated. The twenty-two-year-old Gill is a humorless innocent who has come to Hollywood from the Midwest with the dream of becoming a serious actor, a matinee idol in silent melodrama, but winds up as a slapstick comedy star, unaware at first that his role as a western adventure hero is being played as pure burlesque, as parody, in Mack Sennet fashion. But success is success, and Merton accepts it, set straight by the worldly wise "Montague girl" who has engineered the transformation and whom he marries.

The "Montague girl" represents a type that recurs in Hollywood fiction—the smart, no-nonsense studio woman (often a script reader) who knows the ropes and has no illusions to be shattered. She functions as a "helper" to the befuddled hero adrift in Hollywood. In his 1928 Hollywood novel, *Spider Boy*, Carl Van Vechten gives us the type in Capa Nolin, a screenwriter who knows that what she is doing is a kind of prostitution of her talent but does what she is paid to do. She tells the confused, diffident screenwriter Ambrose Deacon, "Like the stucco houses, you can kick your foot through everything else here too. Nothing is real, except the police dogs and the automobiles, and usually they aren't paid for."[8] An opposite Hollywood female type, the vamp, appears in Van Vechten's novel as Imperia Starling, queen of Invincible Films, who lives life as elaborate masquerade, faking a European accent (à la Garbo or maybe Nazimova), inhabiting a twenty-seven-room "bungalow" in Beverly Hills done up in a combination of Tuscan, Spanish, Tudor, and Early American architecture, surrounded by cactus, palms in tubs, and a twelve-car garage. Van Vechten's novel is a Hollywood version of the captivity story:

the sensitive artist imprisoned by and cast among the philistines, a theme that would recur in later Hollywood fiction and film, as in, for instance, Budd Schulberg's novel *What Makes Sammy Run?* and films like Billy Wilder's *Sunset Boulevard* and Joel Coen and Ethan Coen's *Barton Fink.* Ambrose Deacon in Van Vechten's novel is a shy midwestern short story writer whose stories about the deprivations of small-town life resemble those of Sherwood Anderson (in fact one of them, as described, sounds very much like Anderson's "Death in the Woods"). When a play he has written becomes a Broadway hit and he becomes an overnight celebrity, he tries to escape the publicity by taking a train to New Mexico to visit a friend. On board are the imperious star and her director, Herbert Ringrose (whose name at least hints at his Jewishness, anticipating the stereotype of the despotic Jewish studio head in the years ahead), and the diffident writer is shanghaied to Hollywood. When he tells Imperia he is getting off in Albuquerque, she responds: "If you want mountains, we have them in California. If you want Indians there is a whole encampment near Culver City. There are orange groves and balmy breezes and acacias." (51)

Imprisoned in Imperia's Beverly Hills mansion, Deacon is assigned scripts but never asked to produce them. Unlike Merton Gill, who dreams of stardom, pores over fan magazines, and watches movies being made, Deacon is an unwilling captive, true hater of Hollywood, its people, and its product. Like Joe Gillies in *Sunset Boulevard,* he is literally a hostage in a Hollywood of decadent luxury. Deacon is unable to break away, not simply because his bedroom door is locked at night, but because the diffident man is incapable of making any move in defiance of dominating personalities; his protestations are taken as modesty.

In the novel's most interesting segment he manages one night to sneak out (climbing out his window) and board a train to New Mexico, where he meets a New England woman, a poet living with an Indian and devoted to Indian causes—Van Vechten's appropriation here of his friend Mabel Dodge Luhan—but is soon "rescued" and back in Hollywood. His one script idea—about his own misadventures in Hollywood—undergoes one transformation after another, becoming in turn a Persian drama, a circus melodrama, and a Russian spy thriller. What the studios want is his name, not his script;

even his script's title, *Spider Boy*, is changed to *Love and Danger* as it premieres at Girstein's Byzantine Theater. (Sid Grauman's Chinese Theater had just opened when Van Vechten completed his novel; his Egyptian Theater opened six years earlier, in 1922.)

Like Sinclair, Loos, Wilson, and Burroughs, Van Vechten arrived in 1920s Los Angeles a well-known author. An essayist, journalist, music and drama critic, and novelist, he had just completed his best-known piece of fiction, *Nigger Heaven*, which Langston Hughes praised as a major document in the Harlem Renaissance. His was only a brief visit. He spent the winter of 1926–27 in Hollywood, at the Ambassador Hotel in an adjoining bungalow to the Fitzgeralds, with whom he became friends. (Among his other Hollywood friends were Lois Moran and Greta Garbo.) In 1927 he wrote four articles on Hollywood for *Vanity Fair*, apprenticeship work for his Hollywood novel. As satire *Spider Boy* has more bite than any of the Hollywood novels that preceded it, and more of the dark comedy one finds in the Graham brothers' *Queer People* five years later and West's *The Day of the Locust* just over a decade later. The reviewers, though, were not sure what to make of *Spider Boy*. One called it, oddly, a "cream puff satire," and another, preferring the New Mexico scenes, lamented that "one almost wishes that Ambrose Dean had taken a later train out of New York so that his tale could have been told in the setting of its original destination."[9]

In its use of the fantasy/reality confusion theme, its comic portraiture of the sensitive-artist-adrift-among-the-philistines, and its anticipatory appropriation of the star as screen goddess and the studio head as know-nothing despot, the novel is a step in the evolution of Hollywood fiction, establishing some of the principal themes, metaphors, and character types that would constitute the genre. It is a better book than critics have acknowledged, despite its uncertain tone, its hovering between satire and farce, Hollywood invective and lampoon. It is tempting to think that West read the novel—certainly Van Vechten's name was known to West in New York—but West's novel is superior in its relentlessness, its thoroughly consistent tone, its clear target.

Another novel West may well have read is the Grahams' *Queer People*, which offers a still different version of the Hollywood migrant—the fast-talking, opportunistic, irrepressible rogue-hero. Theodore

Anthony "Whitey" White, a newspaperman who seems to have come right from Ben Hecht and Charles MacArthur's 1928 Broadway hit about tough, wise-cracking reporters, *The Front Page*, is a likable enough foil both to Wilson's naif Merton Gill and Van Vechten's shy, sensitive, Hollywood-hating midwesterner Ambrose Deacon. With the bluster of Budd Schulberg's Sammy Slick, Whitey fakes his way onto the *Examiner* staff as a gossip columnist, sneaks into movie star homes to get inside dope stories, and talks his way into the industry as a studio writer. A few weeks later the bubble bursts and he winds up as a press agent and then a cathouse pianist.

Whitey's transformation from screenwriter to bordello pianist, though, may not represent, in the novel's terms, so much a downward trajectory as a metonymic substitution, a lateral move from one commercial site to another. The linkage of studio and whorehouse is a recurring motif in the novel; a running gag in the work is the line that studios are like whorehouses: a decent man wouldn't be caught in either, but at least whorehouses don't make a pretense about what they are doing. Selling movies is like selling sex, and the commodification of desire that both represent is here and will be in later Hollywood fiction a persistent motif. Looking ahead to West's *The Day of the Locust* at the end of the thirties, one thinks of Audrey Jennings's opulent Hollywood bordello where the movie people go not to have sex but to watch people having sex—on film. When the film breaks, it is experienced as coitus interruptus.

Coming in the wake of several sensationalized 1920s sex and murder scandals in Hollywood, the Graham brothers' novel constructs the film capital as an arena of sex, violence, and betrayal, and Whitey—both innocent adventurer and irredeemable opportunist—is implicated in a series of lurid encounters. The novel is layered with stories within stories, each a violent tale of Hollywood betrayal. In one episode the young starlet Dorothy Irving, fresh from the Midwest, murders a studio head, an Irishman named Blynn, after he hooks her on cocaine and turns her into a sex slave. A parallel story reverses the gender roles: a beautiful but ruthless actress contrives her rise to the top by sleeping with studio heads, driving her husband to alcoholism and madness. Ultimately he leaves her, then kills himself—and she exploits his death for its publicity value. Although there are significant differences in the plot, this tale of the rising star and her defeated, self-destructive husband hints at the 1937 film *A Star Is Born* (with Janet Gaynor and Frederick March, the first and best of three screen versions of the story).

In *Queer People* the Graham brothers extend the range, if not the complexity, of Hollywood female representation, going beyond the binary opposition of the no-nonsense "Montague girl" of Harry Leon Wilson and the life-lived-as-performance actress of Carl Van Vechten. They offer another binary opposition: the Hollywood actress as used and abused victim of powerful men and the ruthless, casting-couch vixen who uses men to get to the top. Both types, after the Graham brothers, become staples in Hollywood folklore, fiction, and film. One looks in vain for something more than one-dimensional female types in early Hollywood fiction. But then one looks in vain for something more in male portraiture as well, particularly when it comes to the representation of Jewish studio heads.

*Queer People* is rife with anti-Semitism. If the Jews invented Hollywood (to quote the subtitle of Neal Gabler's book, *An Empire of Their Own: How the Jews Invented Hollywood*), the Graham brothers invented the most despicable Jews imaginable. The people in charge of "Colossal Studios," essentially the relatives of "Papa Jake" (part father figure, part despot, deriving perhaps from Carl Laemmle of Universal Studios), have nothing to do, and if they did they wouldn't have the competence to do it. With names like Moe Fishbein, Israel Hofburger, Sam Sniffler, and Jacob Schmaltz, they constitute a Dickensian rogues' gallery of stereotyped Jewish greed and vulgarity. Clearly the Graham brothers' anti-Semitic assault was a response—part of a collective response—to the domination of the film industry by Jews. According to figures cited by Gabler, 53 of the 85 prominent studio executives in 1936 were Jews.[10] Their hegemony in Hollywood rekindled the anti-Semitism that, a generation earlier, met the waves of Central and East European immigrants that swept over American cities. Hollywood's Jews absorbed conventional anti-Semitic demonology: they were, alternatively, Reds and un-American, greedy capitalists, or clannish vulgarians incapable of Americanization. The Graham brothers cast their studio Jews essentially in this latter role. The barbarians were not simply at the gate but inside the gate, running the show, interpreting the national dream in image and sound.

IV

Hollywood novels are not always about, or even set in, Hollywood—place or business.[11] Sometimes the business of moviemaking exists only peripherally, on the edges of the texts, but the works reveal the influence of Hollywood in the antics of the characters who behave performatively, as if they are acting in a movie. Hollywood in such works is a state of mind, an absent present, less a place than a textual site for the self-construction of identity. In Ryan's *Angel's Flight* and Brinig's *The Flutter of an Eyelid* the movie world per se exists only marginally, but the locales (downtown in Ryan, with the last sections in Hollywood; Laguna Beach in Brinig) are saturated with the influence of Hollywood. *Angel's Flight* is less a novel than a series of satirical and cynical set pieces on Los Angeles—its Midwest-imported village mentality, its Chautauqua preachers and inspirational healers, its downtown civic boosters and Babbitts, its Jazz Age immersion in bootlegging, drugs, and crime. Ohio-born Ryan worked in Los Angeles as a reporter (for the Los Angeles *Record*), scriptwriter, and actor. *Angel's Flight* reads like a series of debunking newspaper or magazine pieces he might have written (clearly not for the *Times*), a collection of city vignettes with reappearing characters. Angel's Flight, the funicular car running to the top of Bunker Hill, doesn't figure literally in the pieces, but the hilltop provides a vantage point for Ryan to look down cynically on a city of boosters, bums, and crooks. "His method," Carey McWilliams wrote in a review for *Overland Monthly*, "is not labored analysis or even successful narration, but the short vicious cuts of the columnist. Ryan batters away at the crust of Los Angeles in a relentless manner, and when he is through the place stands out in all its gaudiness and vulgarity. . . ."[12] The city he gives us is one of downtown invalids and old people, who become prey to a host of healers, among them Elsie Lincoln Benedict, inspirational speaker at Trinity Auditorium, and Mrs. Laura Hackensorter (perhaps modeled on Gene Stratton-Porter), whose uplifting books and puritanical diatribes attack such pessimistic, immoral writers as Sherwood Anderson, Theodore Dreiser, and Joseph Hergesheimer. While the inspirational speakers speak of morality and the city's bright future, downtown benches are "filled with grotesque cripples, abandoned hulks of men, gray invalids, impish hobo anarchists who taunt the furious apostles of fundamentalism."[13] As city boosters and chamber of commerce speakers applaud Los Angeles's bright future, Ryan writes, "swamis stalked the streets wrapped in meditation and bedticks" and at the harbor in San Pedro gin is being smuggled in while competing gangs are shooting one another for liquor monopolies. Ryan's narrator, cynical and detached, watches and records in a Mencken-like voice:

> . . . it was the greatest sideshow on earth. The city booming.
> Enriched by post-war food prices, the American peasantry
> with money to spend flocking to Los Angeles as to a country
> fair. Hither likewise came the variegated hordes to prey upon
> them. (62)

By the end of the work Ryan's cynical newspaperman has, somehow, become a Hollywood writer, but Hollywood is more an afterthought than a focus of the book; the real focus is on the pretense and fraudulence of the city that makes it an analogue to Hollywood. Looked at from a different angle, *Angel's Flight* may be Los Angeles's first hard-boiled novel, anticipating in its tough, detached, first-person narration the fiction of 1930s novelists like James M. Cain, Horace McCoy, and Raymond Chandler.

Another non-Hollywood Hollywood novel, no less cynical in its telling, but far more fantastical and whimsical, is Myron Brinig's *The Flutter of an Eyelid*, a bizarre, absurdist portrait of a colony of Southern California beach revelers, with their immersion in hedonism, body consciousness, sex, and drink. The group and their antics constitute a Seacoast of Bohemia South—a Southern California relocation of the Carmel colony that clustered around George Sterling earlier in the century—with that group's penchant for nude swimming and physical culture, but utterly without its creativity and art. Here there is only a quasi-chic bohemianism and hedonism set in a landscape of strange and exotic houses perched at the edge of cliffs, ready at any moment to nose-dive into the ocean below. And at the end this is precisely what happens: the coast slides into the sea in a surreal apocalypse dreamed up by the narrator.

The novel, in fact, *is* the fantasy of its narrator Caslon Roanoke, a New England writer, author of colorless New England novels ("gray words," he calls them) who has come to Southern California (Laguna Beach, called Alta Vista in the novel) for his health. The dour author (whose improbable name suggests his bluestocking eastern character) is captivated immediately by the luxuriant color and pleasure-seeking life of the colony at the same time that he is repelled, as a puritanical New Englander would be, by the mindless hedonism. This is the conflicted narrative stance a number of migrant Hollywood writers would take in the years ahead: a blend of fascination, amusement, and derision. Echoing Mencken, Roanoke says the revelers were an example of

> what happened when Homo-Americanus left the cool rigidities of New England, the flat, tedious moralities of the Middle-West, and the pseudo-gentilities of the South. Here in Southern California, all the people could act themselves out, reveal their intimate emotions of delight and despair, holding them in their upturned hands under the brilliant sun and clear moon for all to see.[14]

What Roanoke sees too much of is the beautiful Sylvia Prowse, who drives everyone, male and female, crazy with lust. She represents California yearning, its dream life, the unattainable, sensuous center of the land's desire. She is a combination Helen of Troy and siren. Captured by her eroticism after swimming nude with her (it is she whose "flutter of an eyelid" drives him to distraction), but unable to capture her in person, the straitlaced, frustrated Roanoke sets to work on a novel, compelled in an almost trancelike state to write the lives of these people, and in doing so, constructing, determining, their lives as he writes. Life follows script, obeys the pages as he hammers them out on his typewriter in a kind of exercise in automatic, and prophetic, writing. Roanoke's novel as it gets written *in* Brinig's novel *is* Brinig's novel. And vice versa. Roanoke is simultaneously his own invented character and Brinig's. He functions both as participant in the beach revels and as writer, the man who stands outside the group, observing, registering, and ultimately determining their lives when he sits at his typewriter. And after he leaves Southern California for the "rigidities" of the East, he constructs his final condemnatory chapter in which, in apocalyptic fashion that anticipates other Los Angeles/ Hollywood novels, he has the region dropping into the sea.

Among the characters who constitute the beach community is Angela Flower, the most overdetermined Sister Aimee figure to appear in the era's fiction. Prophet of the "Ten Million Dollar Heavenly Temple" in Echo Park, Angela is both evangelist to lost souls and a semialcoholic pleasure seeker who lays on hands, then comes down to the beach to drink and play, proclaiming that Jesus is everywhere: "Jesus is sex," and "Jesus is even in the scotch." In her most outlandish performance she costumes a semiliterate sailor, a Jesus look-alike, as the son of God, announces the arrival of the savior in Southern California, and sets out to have him walk on water in front of thousands of the faithful, a scenario that offers a bizarre twist to Sister Aimee's disappearance in the Pacific. The man manages to keep afloat for a while, but when the awestruck Sylvia, witnessing the miracle, swims nude out to him, the poor man gets aroused and drowns. Meanwhile dozens of others leap into the sea after him and drown.[15]

Brinig/Roanoke's gallery of grotesques contains other exhibits. Among them is Sol Mosier, a self-loathing Jewish antique dealer who leaves house and wife behind as he tries to discover himself by journeying on foot down the coast. Discovering that he cannot do without creature comforts (thus discovering the self he didn't expect to find), he turns back.[16] Another is the dowager Mrs. Forgate, who has poisoned a series of former husbands and reads Proust wrapped in a flowing robe. Mrs. Forgate, cultivator of exotic poisons (in a gothic subplot), is, among other roles, a caricature of the old Californio, descendant of a Spanish family that owned, she claims, one-fourth of Southern California. Nostalgic for the good old days of bucolic Hispanic California, she rants endlessly about the "the thousands of acres of ranchos, flocks of sheep, miles and miles of fertile land, oranges and lemons," adding that now the land is "motion picture studios, those hideous oil wells that disfigure even the sea . . . [and] monstrosities of architecture." (224–25) Here Charles Fletcher Lummis and Helen Hunt Jackson meet James M. Cain; the myth meets its countermyth, the idyllic version of the land its 1930s dark representation.

Brinig—a Jewish migrant from Montana—is himself, of course, more in the James M. Cain camp, but his novel, unlike Cain's, is not a work of 1930s hard-boiled or noir fiction (despite the region's sinking into the sea at the end) but a wicked satire on the antics of Southern California hedonists. *The Flutter of an Eyelid* may well be the strangest novel to come out of the territory—a novel not set in Hollywood or dealing with the making of movies, but saturated with every fantasy and dream associated with the region. As well, it is a prophecy of doom—anticipating the apocalyptic visions of Los Angeles/Hollywood fiction that would appear with increasing frequency in the years ahead.

## V

The 1930s, the first decade of sound movies, brought an avalanche of migrant writers and Hollywood novels. Austrian-born Vickie Baum came to Hollywood in 1931, following the success of her novel *Grand Hotel* (which she helped to adapt for the screen; the resultant 1932 MGM film had an all-star cast that included Greta Garbo, Wallace Beery, John Barrymore, and Lionel Barrymore). In Hollywood she wrote the novel *Falling Star* (1934), which, despite its melodramatic plot centering on a Rumanian-born silent screen star trying to make it in the talkies and her love affair with a dying alcoholic actor, offers an evocative glimpse of moviemaking in the 1930s: the studio and star system, script development, and movie premieres. In a subplot that echoes the one in *Queer People*, a small-town girl comes to Hollywood, takes to the casting couch, and ends up a prostitute. Like *Grand Hotel* it is both a cynical and a sentimental evocation of a world of faded glamour and defeated hope.

McCoy and Cain, both relatively unknown, came to Hollywood to work as screenwriters in the early thirties—the one an actor, playwright, and journalist from Dallas, the other a Baltimore newspaper man who worked for H. L. Mencken on *American Mercury* and the *Sun*. While neither wrote novels directly about filmmaking, McCoy's two Los Angeles novels, *They Shoot Horses, Don't They?* and *I Should Have Stayed Home*—which I examine in more detail in the next chapter—focus, like Cain's fiction, on the desperation of dream seekers who are chewed up and disgorged by the system. Although only the latter of the two is set in Hollywood, both portray the destroyed dreams of those who, fed back home on Hollywood fan magazines, have come west seeking stardom. Two other novels published in 1938, the year of McCoy's *I Should Have Stayed Home*, focus on Hollywood but deal only marginally with the making of movies, John O'Hara's *Hope of Heaven* and Cedric Belfrage's *Promised Land*.

O'Hara was another of the successful American writers who found himself in Los Angeles in the 1930s. Having worked as a movie critic for the *New York Morning Telegraph* and as the New York-office publicist for Warner Bros. and RKO, he took screen assignments in Hollywood with Paramount, RKO, and MGM throughout the thirties. He lived for a time in the Garden of Allah on Sunset Boulevard, where Robert Benchley and his migratory crowd held court in an "Algonquin West," and frequented Stanley Rose's bookshop on Hollywood Boulevard, hangout for Faulkner, Saroyan, Fitzgerald, and other disgruntled captives of the movie industry. *Hope of Heaven*, one of O'Hara's most plotless and aimless novels, is a Hollywood novel only in the sense that its protagonist, James Malloy, is a screenwriter. The novel's only excursions into Hollywood local color are the restaurants and nightclubs (the Brown Derby and Trocadero) frequented by stars and the endless cruising in cars as Malloy courts a young woman with a shady past. Of some interest is the woman Peggy's involvement in leftist politics. She attends antifascist meetings (backed by the Communists, we are led to believe), but the political issue is never developed.

In Belfrage's *Promised Land* leftist politics play a larger role—more, though, on a local than on a national or international level. The novel, which traces the destruction of two branches of the Laurie family—one in the Owens Valley, the other in Hollywood—reads as a quasi-Marxist critique of city building, the real estate and water greed that turned a semirural agricultural community into a big city laced with graft and corruption. Like Upton Sinclair's *Oil!* Belfrage's novel (subtitled *Notes for a History*) is immense in scope, tracing through the histories of the two sides of the family almost every headlined event in a period stretching from the 1860s to the 1930s: the booster years and the real estate boom in Hollywood, the rise of the movies, the citrus industry, the Owens Valley water "rape," the Fatty Arbuckle "rape" case, the collapse of the Saint Francis Dam. In one way or another the family is involved in, and victimized by, all of these events. The Laurie family are less characters in a novel than abstract, representative figures through whom the reader witnesses defining events in Los Angeles history. Although Belfrage tries to individualize his characters by having them tell their own stories and register their responses to events in personal terms, they remain stick figures. Ed and "Ma" Laurie, Hollywood pioneers, are cheated right and left by a host of schemers and then lose their Hollywood Boulevard property in the bank failures during the crash. Si Laurie, an Owens Valley rancher (whose journalist son becomes late in the novel the spokesman for the leftist position the book takes), loses his land in the city water grab and ends a victim of the collapse of city engineer William Mulholland's Saint Francis Dam—one of the four hundred killed in the actual disaster.

Belfrage, an English newspaperman, was London representative for Samuel Goldwyn, then came to Los Angeles in the late 1930s to help Theodore Dreiser piece together an antiwar book called *America Is Worth Saving*. Subsequently (in 1953), he was called by the House Un-American Activities Committee. He pleaded the Fifth Amendment and was deported. To the extent that the novel is so broad in scope and inclusive (if not always accurate) in its depiction of the rise of Hollywood, one can call it, as Budd Schulberg did, a "definitive" regional novel, a wide-angle panoramic view of the troubled growth not only of Hollywood but also of all of Southern California. It is the story of the unhampered capitalistic greed that turned a dream of paradise into a nightmare. As a novel, though, it lacks any dramatic coherence. It has a large cast of characters, some without any reason for being in the text (including a half dozen or so movie extras who, usually drunk, float in and out of the narrative) and others are not adequately developed. The characters in fact serve little purpose other than to play their roles as witnesses and victims of the city's anarchic growth. The novel, if it can even be called one, is a sociological and historical account of the city in which the characters play minor roles, the roles of extras, to the real drama of the promise gone awry.

Neither O'Hara's *Hope of Heaven* nor Belfrage's *Promised Land*, written just a year before West's *The Day of the Locust*, provide close antecedents to that novel or to the Hollywood novels that were to follow it. The true antecedents are found in satirical works like Wilson's *Merton of the Movies* and more emphatically in Van Vechten's *Spider Boy*, the Graham brothers' *Queer People*, and Brinig's *The Flutter of an Eyelid*. In these precursors the Hollywood novel with its fantasy/

reality confusion and its pervasive sense of masquerade, pretense, and deception has its genesis. Meanwhile Ryan's *Angel's Flight* offered near the end of the twenties a preamble to the hard-boiled Los Angeles narrative that flourished in the depression decade with writers like Paul Cain, James M. Cain, Horace McCoy, and Raymond Chandler.

# 4

# VIEW FROM THE BACK ROOM

## The Hard-Boiled Thirties

Something happened in Southern California in the 1930s. Some
new vision of evil rushed in upon the American consciousness.
Roman Polanski has of late caught that '30s feeling of moral
depravity in the film *Chinatown:* a sense of brooding evil just
beneath the movie-tone of Southern California life . . . . In Los
Angeles during those years death seemed everywhere, and a
mood of excess and disaster, strange and sinister, like flowers
rotting from too much sunshine, pervaded the city.
KEVIN STARR, *AMERICANS AND THE CALIFORNIA DREAM, 1860–1915*

These Depression-crazed middle classes of Southern California
became, in one mode or another, the original protagonists of that
great anti-myth usually known as *noir*. Beginning in 1934, with
James M. Cain's *The Postman Always Rings Twice*, a succession
of through-the-glass-darkly novels . . . repainted the image of
Los Angeles as a deracinated urban hell.
MIKE DAVIS, *CITY OF QUARTZ*

I

My chapter title is from Edmund Wilson's "The Boys in the Back Room" (from the old saying, "Set 'em up for the boys in the back room"), a 1940 essay delineating the tough stance and proletarian vision of California writers of the 1930s, among whom he includes not only John Steinbeck, William Saroyan, and Hans Otto Storm but also Southern California writers like James M. Cain, Horace McCoy, and George Hallas. The first of the two quotations I use as epigraphs is from Kevin Starr's 1975 piece in the New Republic, "It's Chinatown," which was occasioned by the appearance of the Roman Polanski/ Robert Towne film, Chinatown, that year, but which provides at the same time a reminder of the indelible imprint 1930s and 1940s Los Angeles-centered film noir and noir fiction have made on our collective movie and book consciousness. Since around 1970 Hollywood has found the 1930s and 1940s hard-boiled genre a marketable commodity, resurrecting it in original scripts like Chinatown and in screen adaptations of novels like Curt Hansen's L.A. Confidential (based on the James Ellroy novel and set in 1950) and Carl Franklin's Devil in a Blue Dress (based on the Walter Mosley novel set in the late 1940s). The resurgence of interest in the hard-boiled crime story evinces the hold that the tough, fast-paced, violent, underclass narratives of the thirties and forties have on us today.[1] James M. Cain and Raymond Chandler are the most direct authorial fathers of the mode, but the sources, as I attempt to show in the first part of this chapter, go back to earlier American prototypes.[2] My second epigraph, drawn from Mike Davis's "Sunshine or Noir" chapter of his 1990 book, City of Quartz: Excavating the Future of Los Angeles, suggests how the cynical brand of hard-boiled Los Angeles fiction of the 1930s and 1940s functioned as an "antimyth" to the old optimistic booster myth of the city, offering, in Davis's words, "a transformational grammar turning each charming ingredient of the boosters' arcadia into a sinister equivalent."[3]

The three comments, written decades apart—1940, 1975, and 1990—provide a framework for examining depression-era Los Angeles fiction, a gauge for measuring the distance the dark novels of the period traveled from the optimistic, sunny promotional literature of the Lummis-James-Otis era. The Janus-faced booster vision—directed both to the hyping of future urban possibilities and to the nostalgic yearning to preserve the old Spanish/mission legacy—had essentially run its course by the 1930s, despite the attempts of the *Times*, the All Year Club, and the chamber of commerce to keep it alive, particularly as the city was preparing to host the 1932 Olympics. Whatever regenerative possibilities Los Angeles offered in its first spectacular growth period from the 1880s to the 1920s, those possibilities could not be sustained during the depression.

At least not in the novelist's imagination. The satirical fiction of the 1920s described in chapter 3 began the process of demolishing the optimistic myth. With the novels of Paul Cain [George Sims], James M. Cain (not related), Horace McCoy, and George Hallas [Eric Knight] in the thirties—writers drawn to the film capital to write scripts in the new age of sound movies—the sunny myth was fully eclipsed. The dream, if it once had potency, was behind them. Writing against the fable of El Dorado, they replaced it with a counter-fable: that of the dream running out along the California shore. The novels were cynical in mood, fast in pace (reading almost like movie scripts), unsentimental in tone (not, though, without some lapses into the sentimental), violent in action, and often narrated as vernacular, direct, first-person confessionals with minimal background or character development. The tales told of migrant hopes dashed against the shore in a glaring sunlight. The land of the fresh start was transformed into the land of the disastrous ending, an ending played out, appropriately and frequently, at the very site of the myth's greatest allure—the edge of the ocean. In the iconography of hard-boiled depression fiction, the end of the American highway was also the end of the dream. Where the continent runs out, the dream runs out with it.

The kind of hard-boiled crime fiction that emerged in 1930s Los Angeles derives (in part) from gangster novels of the late 1920s and early 1930s set in other cities, novels like Dashiell Hammett's *Red Harvest* (1929), *The Maltese Falcon* (1930), and *The Glass Key* (1931) and W. R. Burnett's *Little Caesar* (1929). It has antecedents, too, in gangster films like Mervyn Leroy's adaptation of Burnett's novel (1930), William Wellman's *The Public Enemy* (1931), and Howard Hawks's *Scarface* (1932). The American stage in the 1920s also provided sources for Los Angeles hard-boiled fiction—plays like Eugene O'Neill's dark

expressionistic drama, *The Hairy Ape* (1922), and Hecht and Macarthur's tough newspaper saga, *The Front Page* (1928). In the popular culture of the thirties the gangster fully entered the national folklore. He became the consummate image of the urban rebel, serving
not only as a sign of the breakdown of American society and law enforcement, but as the hero who could master—if only temporarily—
a depression environment in which most Americans saw themselves
as victims. The gangster genre, in fiction and film, was a class
tragedy: the tale of the little guy who makes it big and then is brought
down. He was both a hero of protest and a threat to society. For
Robert Warshow in his essay "The Gangster as Tragic Hero," the
gangster represented to 1930s audiences a part of the national psyche
that rejected, or fantasized about rejecting, the strictures of conventional society. Audience identification could be so strong that gangster
films were sometimes prefaced with "crime doesn't pay" warning
labels printed across the screen. Such labels, of course, complicated
the challenge these films presented to ordered society, constituting
the very values (i.e., of a law-abiding society) the films themselves
were rejecting.

1930s hard-boiled fiction can be traced to other sources as well.
Edmund Wilson thought the presence of Hollywood and its pervasive
sense of unreality encouraged the hard-boiled stance. Alfred Kazin,
taking a different position in *On Native Ground* (1942), traced parallels to the proletarian fiction of the thirties, works like Edward Dahlberg's *Bottom Dogs* and Mike Gold's *Jews without Money* (both 1930).
In still another etymology, Frederick Hoffman, in *The Modern Novel
in America* (1951), saw the naturalism of Zola, Dreiser, London, and
Crane as influences. To one degree or another, Los Angeles hard-
boiled fiction can be linked to all these sources. The depression
decade activated, and encouraged, both proletarian and naturalistic
fiction, and Hollywood, as a mecca of temptation, greed, and deception, played as well into the cynical, hard-boiled rendition of Los
Angeles.

A less direct source of 1930s hard-boiled fiction, but one more
deeply rooted in American fiction and folklore, is the long tradition
of the American hero as outsider. The rugged frontiersman, the self-
reliant western hero, and the hobo each offers a version of the American hero as the man who has turned his back on society, acts in defi-

ance of its norms, and affirms his own individualistic code of behavior. From dime novel adventure tales to James Fenimore Cooper's Leatherstocking tales, Mark Twain's *The Adventures of Huckleberry Finn*, Owen Wister's *The Virginian* (the archetypal western novel), and Jack London's tramp narrative, *The Road*—and in dozens of other examples—American literature has given us the story of the disaffiliated man or boy on the road—explorer, adventurer, rebel, and seeker. The tradition of the American hero as loner, Melville's "isolato," without home or possessions and dependent only on his resourcefulness, has a long lineage in American letters and has fed, if indirectly, into hard-boiled depression-era Los Angeles fiction. One close link is Jim Tully—farm laborer, tramp, boxer, and eventually screenwriter and director in Hollywood—whose autobiographical novel, *Beggars of Life* (1924, dramatized the following year by Maxwell Anderson as *Outside Looking In*), his novel, *Jarnegan* (1925, about a boxer who kills his opponent), and his prison sketches, *Shadows of Men* (1929), turned him into something of a 1930s Los Angeles cult hero. All these antecedents contributed to the 1930s Los Angeles hard-boiled narrative and to the engendering of a mode that persists to the present time under the rubric "L.A. Noir."

## II

Los Angeles, the new up-for-grabs city given to big thinking and big ideas, was by the thirties riddled with crackpot fast-buck schemes, sensational murders (like the bizarre Winnie Judd trunk murders that opened the decade), and organized crime. The continuing influx of desperate migrants (the city grew to 1.5 million people in the thirties) made the city ripe for exploitation by oil, water, real estate, bootlegging, gambling, protection rackets, and crooked pension schemes. Added to this were the geographic opportunities provided by the vast terrain of the extended city, its long coastline ideal for liquor smuggling and for sheltering offshore gambling ships, its proximity to the Mexican border convenient for trucking illegal alcohol and drugs.

The corruption was there from the beginning of the city's growth, but given the power of Harry Chandler's *Times* and its tie-ins with big business and municipal government, little of it found its way into that paper's headlines. Bad news was bad for business, bad for enticing migrants and attracting investment. The reputation of the boosters' "white city," refuge from the urban corruption in the East, had to be protected. Some things could not be hidden, though, like the gangland assassination of gambling kingpin Charlie Crawford, which made headlines in May 1931, adding to the sensational headlines a few months earlier when the dismembered remains of Winnie Judd's victims were discovered in a trunk at the train station. With the election of the corrupt Frank Shaw as mayor in 1933, gangs and government reached new degrees of accommodation.

Not all Angelenos were taken in by the cover-ups. The reform-minded cafeteria owner Clifford Clinton, for one, wanted answers. He went after the mob, seeking evidence of the protection racket run by the police and the mayor's office. He hired a crusty ex-cop named Harry Raymond, a man with a disreputable law enforcement record himself, as a private investigator. The police kept Raymond's activities under surveillance, and in 1938, in the most headlined crime event of the decade, Raymond's car was dynamited. He survived to testify in court with one hundred fifty pieces of shrapnel in his body. Police lieutenant Earle Kynette, who headed the police department's Intelligence Squad, was sentenced to a term in San Quentin, Mayor Shaw was recalled, and Police Chief James Edgar ("Two Gun") Davis was forced to resign. That same year, under orders from state attorney general Earl Warren, the *Rex*, an offshore gambling ship commandeered by Tony Cornero Stralla, was raided and shut down. Los Angeles, under Shaw's successor, Fletcher Bowron, was at least going through the motions of cleaning itself up.

At the same time the stage was being set for the next gangster-run gambling mecca, postwar Las Vegas, just over the Nevada border. Thus the Mojave, idealized as the place of spiritual regeneration in the romantic desert evocations of an earlier, booster-inspired generation of sunshine-and-health writers, was transformed into the new suburban playground of both the high-roller and weekend low-roller gambler. Bugsy Siegel and Meyer Lansky staked their claim early, building the Flamingo Resort on the new "Strip" just after World War II. The desert city, with its legalized gambling and prostitution, its blurring of day and night in the nonstop twenty-four-hour casinos, and its celebrity lounge shows, became another suburb and proto-theme park, an extension of Los Angeles stretching along the highway into the Mojave— six hours away by car.

Although most of these events occurred after the earliest of the

1930s hard-boiled Los Angeles novels appeared, the atmosphere of the city's underworld of gambling, protection rackets, civic corruption, and gangland violence was there. A sinister mood descended on crime-blackened Los Angeles in the thirties, and the Hollywood-drawn 1930s authors, writing against the grain of city optimism, were quick to reflect this mood in their fiction.

*Black Mask*, the most enduring and influential of the pulp adventure magazines, provided the real apprenticeship for many of the writers. Founded by H. L. Mencken (who disliked mystery stories as much as he disliked Los Angeles) and George Jean Nathan—largely as a way to float *Vanity Fair* financially—*Black Mask* was the premier writing school for tough-guy storytellers like Paul Cain, George Hallas, Dashiell Hammett, Raymond Chandler, Horace McCoy, Erle Stanley Gardner, Raoul Whitfield, and Carroll John Daly. The magazine, which survived for more than thirty years (1920–51) and had a circulation that reached 250,000 in the early twenties, offered not only a venue but a style as well. Joseph T. Shaw, its exacting editor for a full decade (1926–36), encouraged the production of fast-paced adventure stories told in the slangy, racy (and often racist) language of the streets. The style, which has too often been attributed to Hemingway (ignoring the fact that many *Black Mask* stories predated Hemingway's early stories), was spare, lean, and minimal; background, character development, and analysis were sacrificed to action—brutal present-tense action, most often told as first-person narratives of men caught up in violent kill-or-be-killed adventure.

Westerns appeared alongside urban crime and detective stories on the pages of *Black Mask*. In fact the two genres, save the setting, were not all that different. As John Cawelti has reminded us in *Adventure, Mystery, Romance: Formula Stories as Art and Popular Culture* (1976), hard-boiled fiction owes a lot to the western story with its resourceful lone-wolf hero who obeys a personal code that places him in opposition to conventional law enforcement—often enough part of the corruption. The Virginian metamorphosed into Sam Spade, Gary Cooper into Humphrey Bogart. The six-shooter became the .45, the horse the fast car. But while the western's open spaces posited a fluid, future-oriented agrarian or town-building vision of America, the crime narrative as it emerged in Los Angeles, despite the continued optimism of the *Times* and its die-hard booster cronies, offered little sense of progressive town building on an open frontier but rather a sense of being at the last stop on the continental frontier, the place where the road to the future ends.

Among the *Black Mask* writers, Raoul Whitfield, Carroll John Daly, Dashiell Hammett, and Paul Cain set the tone for the Southern California brand of hard-boiled fiction. Whitfield's novel *Death in a Bowl* (1931), serialized in *Black Mask* in 1930, is probably the first of the hard-boiled Los Angeles private eye novels. Like a number of Los Angeles narratives to follow in the thirties and forties—among them Richard Hallas's *You Play the Black and the Red Turns Up*, Horace McCoy's *They Shoot Horses, Don't They?* and Raymond Chandler's *The Little Sister*—Whitfield links Hollywood and the film industry to crime-riddled Los Angeles, pointing to similar forms of deception and corruption in both arenas. The links were there in, for instance, the International Alliance of Theatrical Staff Employees and Moving Picture Operators (IATSE), controlled by gangsters Willie Bioff and George Brown, who extorted huge sums from the studios in exchange for no-strike guarantees. Ben Jardinn, Whitfield's tough, cynical, violent private eye, has his office on Hollywood Boulevard, near Grauman's Chinese Theater. Hollywood is offered as a sinister landscape: at a Hollywood Bowl concert (the bowl, to which the title refers, is the just-completed Hollywood Bowl) a guest conductor is killed onstage.

Daly's *Black Mask* stories featured another private eye, Race Williams, prototype, like Jardinn, of the tough detective who, trusting no one, is feared because he is capable of violence in his quest for justice. The line between the agents of justice and the criminal underworld blurs in *Black Mask* fiction. Daly's Race Williams calls himself a middleman between the cops and the crooks. He is the rugged, ruthless individualist, fighting for what he believes—justice but on his own terms. Hammett's unnamed Continental Op, precursor of Sam Spade, appears in dozens of stories as the fat, unglamorous hero, just doing his job, speaking in the street lingo of his environment. Like his later incarnations as Spade and, a decade later, Raymond Chandler's Philip Marlowe, he trusts only himself, a self that contains a social conscience and a sometimes chivalric attitude toward women, but he can also be a killer and a man who sets traps to get killers to kill other killers—as the Op does in *Red Harvest*. *Black Mask* was the original venue for Hammett's *Red Harvest*, as it was for Whit-field's *Death in a Bowl*, Paul Cain's *Fast One* (published as a book in 1933), and much of Chandler's fiction.

Introducing *Fast One* to its *Black Mask* audience in 1931, Shaw used the term "the New Wild West" to announce the migration of hard-boiled crime fiction to Southern California. Appropriate to its Los Angeles setting, *Fast One* doesn't obey the gangster formula of the local boy growing up on the wrong side of the city tracks. Like almost everyone else in the city, Kells, its gangster hero, is a migrant. He arrives in a city already sodden with corruption, a world in which he has to define himself, stake out his territory, find his loyalties, his boundaries, his friends and enemies. Cain arrived in Los Angeles in 1923 and worked as a freelance short story writer and screenwriter (scripting *The Black Cat*, based on the Poe story, for Universal in 1934). *Fast One* was his only novel, an episodic series of violent encounters — and a natural for *Black Mask*.

*Fast One* is the most relentlessly brutal of the Los Angeles hard-boiled crime narratives, a bloodbath rivaling Hammett's *Red Harvest* and Burnett's *Little Caesar*, and a novel that lies at the beginning of the road that leads to the brutal crime fiction of James Ellroy. Like the Continental Op stories of Hammett, the rapid-paced narrative deals with the manipulation of power, pitting (like the Continental Op stories of Hammett) crooked politicians, urban reformers, and competing gangs against one another in a war to control gambling, boxing, drugs, prostitution, and the protection racket. "Fast one" means the lie or cover-up — as in "pulling a fast one" — and the novel is a series of betrayals, double crosses, and ambushes. But the term has a second meaning with particular relevance to Los Angeles: fast movement by car across a seemingly endless landscape. The novel is about pursuing and being pursued, tailing and being tailed. While much of the novel takes place indoors — in grungy hotel rooms and cheap flats — it is also about the road. Kells knows the town, knows it well, as he pursues his nemesis Rose. He knows the streets, neighborhoods, apartment buildings, hotels, restaurants, suburbs, and the highways up and down the coast. By the 1920s the private auto altered the notion of distance in Los Angeles, and Kells, anticipating James M. Cain's protagonists, who equate fast driving with freedom, and Chandler's private eye, who spends most of his time following leads on the road, takes us across the whole terrain in his quest for knowledge and power: "They went out Sunset at about seventy miles an hour, went on through Beverly Hills, out Beverly Boulevard. At the ocean they turned north. The road was being repaired for a half-mile or so. Kells slowed to thirty-five."[4]

But the coastal highway ultimately is a cul-de-sac, a dead end. High-speed travel along the ocean leads not to power or domination over the environment but to the violent finish. Kells and Grandquist (his girlfriend known only by her last name) are killed when their car crashes in the rain and fog near Ventura. For Kells, as Paul Skenazy has put it, "the meeting of ocean and road confirms that there is no turning back. Maybe this is part of the lesson of cars in a California story: the faster one travels, the more one realizes there is nowhere to go."[5]

## III

In the Los Angeles brand of crime fiction that followed in the wake of Paul Cain's *Fast One*, the meeting place of ocean and highway is the recurring site of murder, suicide, and accidental death. The menace of the ocean recurs as a motif, signaling the fragility of life at its edge. The seacoast—the landscape of the dream, the place where the dream offered its most seductive image—is transformed in the fiction into the landscape of death. The last act for many a Los Angeles character is played against the ocean: in coastal canyons, on rickety piers, on fog-shrouded bluffs, on winding, rain-slicked highways.

After Paul Cain, though, violent crime and violent endings are not so much consequences of organized or syndicated crime but of personal crime—individuals acting alone or in collusion with a lover. The city's gangland crime provided the atmosphere, the backdrop, the fascination with criminal activity, but in the California brand of hard-boiled crime fiction, beginning with James M. Cain, violent acts are most often linked to, and motivated by, personal ambition, greed, and lust, not a desire to manipulate or control the city. The genre is less about corporate than familial crime, less about public than private acts. The California promise—transformation, the chance to start a new life—feeds the desire, the motive, the act: getting the woman and the money and then protecting oneself against those (like the blackmailer) who know the secret history. Even in Raymond Chandler's detective stories, where mobsters and gamblers like Eddy Mars in *The Big Sleep* play a central role, the primal source of crime is not in gangland activity but in families—in jealousy, lust, greed, or vengeance.

The hard-boiled crime story, like the gangster story, reflects the collective desires—as well as collective fears—of the depression decade. The stories express the rage and frustration of the decade as well as the desperation to succeed, against the odds, in an America that was grinding people down. Gangster movies were one school for the fiction, tales of the little man's revenge on society, his quest to have the commodified goods—money, power, and beautiful women— that consumer culture, including the movies, dangled before him. In much of the hard-boiled fiction, Hollywood, as neighborhood, industry, or construct, plays a significant role.

Richard Hallas's *You Play the Black and the Red Turns Up* (1938) is a semi-hard-boiled—call it medium-boiled—novel that fuses the Hollywood image with the Southern California crime story, a commingling of the murder tale (featuring two killings), satire (of Hollywood pretense), and parody (of the James M. Cain, Horace McCoy violent dream-become-nightmare novels). It is an odd blend: brutality played as comedy or comedy played as brutality. Like Cain's and McCoy's early fiction, which it succeeded only by a few years, it is told as the first-person confession of a killer, a man who has come to California, meets the woman who shares his dream of love and money, rides (in this case literally) to the top of the Ferris wheel, then comes crashing down. Like a James M. Cain novel, too, it is also a book about the California road, which promises so much and gives so little; its narrator, Richard Dempsey, speeds up and down the coast with his lover, equating the fast car and the open road with winning the girl:

> . . . . I drove up the shore and then turned right and went
> over Topanga, swinging the car round the curves where it
> drops off straight down at the edge. Then I kept on across
> the San Fernando Valley and on until we got to the San
> Fernando mission with all the long arches by the *Camino
> Real*.[6]

After hopping a freight from Oklahoma to Los Angeles on the trail of his estranged wife and son, Dempsey finds himself, purely by chance, living in a coastal town (which could be either San Pedro or Long Beach), working, appropriately to his sense of the place, on an amusement park ride, a loop-the-loop, that careens over the ocean, and living with an alcoholic divorcée. He witnesses one murder in which the wrong man is arrested, falls in love with another woman, tries to kill the first woman, and ends up killing the woman he loves when she shows up at the wrong time. The wrong man, the wrong woman, the wrong time: You play the black and the red turns up. The odds don't operate in spin-the-wheel Southern California; Dempsey even tries to lose at the roulette wheel (in an attempt to put back money that would implicate him in a robbery) but keeps winning. The only odds worth betting on are the unexpected, the unplanned, the inexplicable.

Meanwhile Hallas satirically takes on the worlds of Hollywood and local cults in a subplot focusing on a semimad, satanic, bisexual movie director and a revolving pension scheme called the Ecanaanomic Party, a blend of Aimee Semple McPherson's Four Square Gospel and the various utopian schemes of the depression decade — combining elements of Upton Sinclair's EPIC program, Ham and Eggs, and Dr. Francis Townsend's "Old Age Revolving Pension." By casting the leader of the movement as an Aimee Semple McPherson stand-in (the working girl as high priestess, complete with long, flowing robe, gold sandals, and a repertoire of theatrical performances), Hallas suggests the fusion — or confusion — between business and religion, economics and spiritualism, greed and moral uplift in Southern California. Salvation has been, like everything else, commodified for the masses.

To the narrator, who has killed the wrong girl and has been acquitted when the movie director inexplicably commits suicide after confessing to the murder, nothing is real in Southern California, and he prepares to go back home:

> It was like all I had done in California was just a dream. And at first it felt good, and then it felt worse, because Sheila was only a dream like everything else. . . . It was all gone. All of it. The pink stucco houses and the palm trees and stores built

like cats and dogs and ice-cream freezers and the neon lights round everything. (207–8)

Hallas is the pen name of the English writer Eric Knight, author of the children's classic *Lassie Come Home; The Flying Yorkshireman*, a novel set partly in Southern California and featuring another Sister Aimee surrogate; and a World War II novel, *This Above All* (the film version of which starred Tyrone Power). Like his fellow British transplant Cedric Belfrage, who published *Promised Land* the same year, Knight came to Hollywood to work on screenplays and produced a novel that, if not as dense in social reference as Belfrage's work, converges too on a number of local themes. The two novels, though, have little in common in style, scope, or tone. Belfrage's leftist social exposé, with its cast of thousands, is broad in its historical sweep and documentary in style; Hallas's novel is absurdist and parodic. Los Angeles is represented as a place ultimately lacking in reality or substance. As soon as Dempsey crosses the mountains and enters California's coastal plain, he becomes aware that nothing is real. Southern California is a vast amusement park where reality and fantasy blur. There are no boundaries. Although the novel mimics the dark confessionals of Cain and McCoy, it draws, too, on the satiric Hollywood fictions of the Graham brothers (*Queer People*) and Myron Brinig (*The Flutter of an Eyelid*). It anticipates as well the dark, satiric Los Angeles–Hollywood fantasy of another British transplant, Aldous Huxley's *After Many a Summer Dies the Swan*, published just a year later. Edmund Wilson, who placed Hallas in his back room of hard-boiled California writers, dismisses the novel all too briefly as the retrospective account of a man about to leave Southern California, a "vagrant and a rogue" who had fallen under the domination of a "vulgar" woman and "has just crossed the mountains after a great career in love and crime." For Wilson, who never saw Southern California as quite real, Hallas's protagonist is a victim of a delusive environment. He attributes Dempsey's sense of unreality to the climate and landscape, "the empty sun and incessant rains, . . . the dry mountains and the void of the vast Pacific."[7] In the fiction of James M. Cain and Horace McCoy the void of the Pacific becomes the commanding metaphor for dream's end.

IV

Standing at the head of Wilson's gallery of rogue writers was James M. Cain, whose first novel, *The Postman Always Rings Twice* (1934—four years before Hallas's novel), established the formula for the first-person hard-boiled Southern California tale of murder and its consequences. *Double Indemnity* followed in 1936 (published serially that year and in book form in 1943) and *Mildred Pierce* in 1941. Cain, a journalist who wrote for H. L. Mencken's *American Mercury* in his native Baltimore, for Arthur Krock's *New York World*, and briefly for Harold Ross as managing editor of the *New Yorker*, came to Los Angeles in 1931.[8] Like most of the other thirties novelists he wanted to try his hand at screenwriting. Although he remained a screenwriter in Southern California until 1948 and continued writing fiction until his death in 1977, he is best remembered for his three early Los Angeles novels. He wrote, it should be added, two other novels about the region in the 1930s—*The Embezzler* (filmed in 1940 as *Money and the Woman*) and *Serenade* (filmed in 1956). The first of these is an insignificant novella about a wife's attempt to replace money her husband has embezzled from a bank; the second, about a homosexual opera singer, figured prominently in Wilson's essay but is set only in part in Southern California: much of it takes place in Mexico and New York.

In 1969 *Postman, Double Indemnity*, and *Mildred Pierce* were combined in a Knopf hardcover edition titled *Cain x Three* with a roguish introduction by Tom Wolfe and have reappeared since then in separate Vintage paperbacks. Cain's Los Angeles novels, like those of McCoy and Chandler, struck an existential chord almost immediately in Europe (Camus acknowledged *Postman* as a source for *The Stranger*) and since the 1940s have been more highly regarded on the Continent than in this country, where his work has until recently been relegated to the category of pulp fiction or "subliterature." In this country at least, his works are better known by their screen adaptations than their print originals.[9]

Film versions of all three, made in the mid-forties, show up frequently on late-night television, in revival movie houses, and on college campuses where they have attained something of the status of cult classics. *Double Indemnity*, the best of the film adaptations, was directed by Billy Wilder (with a script written in part by Raymond Chandler) in 1944, *Mildred Pierce* by Michael Curtiz in 1945, and *Postman* by Tay Garnett in 1946 (with Lana Turner and John Garfield) and then again by Bob Rafelson in a steamy 1981 version with Jack Nicholson and Jessica Lange. *Postman*, moreover, was the source of two early European adaptations—a French version titled *Le dernier tournant* in 1939 and Luchino Visconti's *Ossessione* in 1942, the film recognized as marking the beginning of Italian neorealist cinema. Lawrence Kasdan's film *Body Heat*, set in Florida but almost a remake of *Double Indemnity*, attests to Cain's continuing presence in, and influence on, American film. Cain keeps his novels so close to the level of concrete, lived experience that they read like screenplays. His work has the feel, Kevin Starr wrote, of a writer "who has left everything but narration on the cutting room floor," and Edmund Wilson called Cain's novels "a Devil's parody of the movies."

"They threw me off the hay truck at noon," *Postman* begins, and the pace never slows after that. In the next paragraph Frank Chambers, a tramp who has hitched up the coast from the Mexican border town of Tijuana, stumbles on the Twin Oaks Tavern, "a roadside sandwich joint" with a filling station and "a half dozen shacks they called an auto court."[10] A few short paragraphs later he discovers the owner's wife, Cora, whose "lips stuck out in a way that wanted me to mash them in for her." Before chapter 1 ends he has taken a job at the Twin Oaks, and before the second chapter ends a few pages later, he already has his wish:

> I took her in my arms and mashed my mouth up against hers. . . . "Bite me! Bite me!"

> I bit her. I sunk my teeth into her lips so deep I could feel the blood spurt into my mouth. It was running down her neck when I carried her upstairs. (15)

By the end of chapter 3 the pair have decided to kill Nick, Cora's husband—to secure each other and the insurance money.

Frank, a highway drifter with a trail of crime stretching across the country, is caught up, like Hallas's drifter-protagonist, in the promise of the highway. Cora, meanwhile, wants to use the insurance money from the murder to refurbish and decorate the Twin Oaks Tavern. The perversity of Cora's domestic desire, grounded in adultery and murder, is blatant. The pair constitute both a travesty of conventional gender roles—the male desire for wandering and adventuring, the female for establishing a permanent home and a sense of respectability—and an expression of the polar extremes of the California dream: mobility and domesticity. The Twin Oaks Tavern, where road and home meet on the landscape, where the pair make love, plot a murder, and then clash, is the perfectly realized backdrop for the lower-middle-class version of the dream gone haywire. Sprawled along the highway, the makeshift diner, filling station, and auto court is the site of the collision between the opposing strands of California desire—highway and home, adventure and settling-in. The meeting ground becomes a battleground for Frank and Cora, a site not of complementary but conflicting versions of the dream.

The highway provides the other setting for disaster, the road that leads not to escape but calamity. On an open stretch of canyon road between Glendale and the coast, the pair murder Cora's husband and make love beside the wreckage of the faked accident. The echo of the dying man's voice reverberates through the canyon, and later Cora, in another grotesque rebound, is killed in a car crash on Pacific Coast Highway not far from the murder site. Events are doubled; every action elicits a counteraction. Acquitted for the murder he did commit, Frank, in the postman's second ringing, is convicted of Cora's murder, an act he did not commit. The road becomes his, Cora's, and Nick's death route.

So fast-paced is the action, so clipped and banal the language, that the novel has offered itself readily to parody—and there have been several over the years. But the novel has its potency. By presenting his male protagonist as the unencumbered drifter on the open road, Cain not only offers a powerful depression image, but introduces a metaphor that will recur in Los Angeles, and California, fiction in the years ahead. As the city became increasingly dominated by the automobile, the central figure in the fiction became the man—or woman—behind the wheel. Five years before the Joads rolled into the Central Valley, Cain offered in his first novel the California highway as the road that goes nowhere, metaphor for the deceptive California promise.

The open road tradition in American literature, stretching back to Cooper, Whitman, and Twain, equated movement west—movement, that is, into the undiscovered country, the territories—with liberation from the strictures of the past. This movement has its final realization at the edge of the continent. After killing Nick, the pair drive west to the ocean to swim and play in the sand. The ocean is a source of cleansing, of regeneration. It promises escape from history, escape from the consequences of their act. They want to wash away their sins in the ocean, to return to a time of innocence before the murder, as if they could retrace their steps back to a mythic California where the dream was still in front of them. But they discover what other California dream seekers discover: that the past has a way of catching up and hanging on. Cora's death at the edge of the ocean signals the inescapability of history, of acts committed in history.

Told in flashback as the death row confession of the condemned male, the story elicits a certain amount of sympathy for its déclassé protagonists, torn between uncontrollable sexual urge and the desire for the California good life, between violent impulses born of lives of frustration and desperation and the impulse to succeed. But while the reader, then and now, may acknowledge their frustration, their stunted lives, and even enjoy vicariously the adventure they share, he or she is repelled by the violence and animalism they exhibit. Cain's formula allows us to go along for the ride, even root for the pair for a while, yet feel relief when they suffer the consequences of their acts. Today's reader, too, is repelled by the blatant racism these marginalized, uneducated people exhibit, their pretensions to Anglo-Saxon superiority. When Frank meets the dark-haired Cora, he takes her for a "Mex," and then when she tells him her maiden name is Smith, he admits his mistake in confusing her with Mexican women who "all got big hips and bum legs and breasts up under their chin and yellow skin and hair that looks like it had bacon fat on it." (7–8) Nick Papadakis is simply called "the Greek" or "the foreigner," a threat to the American respectability they covet. "He's greasy and he stinks," Cora says of him. (23)

In Cain's other novels the drive to succeed, to attain respectability and social position in Anglo California, motivates the violent action. Again the house and the highway—emblems of domesticity and mobility—provide the chief metaphors. The setting in *Double In-*

*demnity* is several steps up from the seedy roadside tavern and auto camp of *Postman*. The fatal encounter between Walter Huff and Phyllis Nirdlinger occurs in a middle-class Spanish-styled house on Beechwood Avenue in the Hollywoodland tract, just beneath the famous sign. Huff, an insurance salesman, drives from Glendale to Hollywood to pick up a policy renewal and is almost immediately (in a pace that rivals that of *Postman*) involved in a murder-for-love-and-money scheme like that of the earlier novel.

An important component of Southern California's lure in the boom of the twenties was the promise of the detached house, the plot of private living space. Houses in every conceivable design found a place on the landscape, giving novelists an inexhaustible supply of images of disarray and dislocation in the eclectic building styles. But while Nathanael West and Aldous Huxley (among others) rendered the absurd pretenses of the Hollywood masqueraders by placing them in exotic fantasy structures that aped almost every style in architectural history and Raymond Chandler appropriated pretentious, barricaded hilltop mansions as metaphors for the deception and corruption of those who rose to wealth and power in the city, Cain avoided the exotic and eccentric. He sets the characters of *Double Indemnity* and *Mildred Pierce* in the conventional Spanish-style houses of white stucco and red-tiled roofs, the style favored by many of the period's subdividers as authentic evocations of the city's past and emblems of the regional "good life." These "ordinary" houses provide ironic contrasts to the "extraordinary" behavior of their inhabitants—commonplace domestic facades behind which adultery, murder, and extortion are played out. In their banality houses express as well the frustrations, failures, and betrayed dreams of their inhabitants. Houses externalize the mental states of their occupants.

In all three novels Cain underscores the monotony of architecture. The Twin Oaks is "like millions of others in California." The Hollywoodland "House of Death" in *Double Indemnity* combines a Spanish revival style ordinariness with grotesque and incongruous details. It was built "cock-eyed," Huff says on first entering it, each room chaotically spilling up the hill. The most conspicuous feature in its living room is a wall of "blood red drapes" run on iron spears, a detail that appears in *Mildred Pierce* as well, foreshadowing in both novels the violent crimes to follow. Mildred Pierce's house in Glendale is described as being "like others of its kind": outside, a Spanish bungalow, with white walls and red-tiled roof; inside, a "standard living room" like those "sent out" by department stores. Such ordinariness underscores the frustration, hidden rage, sublimated sexuality, and resentment of Cain's housewives.

The Glendale house, built by Mildred Pierce's estranged husband, Bert, and "mortgaged and re-mortgaged," is a profile of withered 1920s middle-class elegance, the good life shattered by the depression. Bert Pierce is a prototype of the California real estate developer, his Pierce Homes a reflection of the California domestic promise of the pre-depression years. Mildred's frantic scramble for material success after Bert moves out is portrayed in the spatial metaphor of a journey from middle-class Glendale to Pasadena's exclusive Orange Grove Avenue, where her lover, Monty Beragon, lives. The social distance between her present and the future she so aggressively seeks is rendered geographically as the distance along Foothill Boulevard between the two valley cities. The one symbolizes the constraints of the age, the other the freedom of the dream. Mildred bridges the distance and for a time seems to have gotten a solid hold on Pasadena, only to be dumped back into Glendale at the end.

Both novels take place so much on the roads and streets of Los Angeles that they read almost like grand auto tours of the city, a fact not lost in Wilder's 1944 screen version of *Double Indemnity*. Phyllis's husband (in the novel but not the film) is killed in his own car, and Huff is shot by his lover-accomplice while sitting in his car in Griffith Park waiting for her—in order to kill her first. Murder has implicated the pair, as it did in *Postman*, in a cycle of suspicion, distrust, and fear. When each has guilty knowledge of the other, neither is safe.

Fast driving is a compulsion for both Mildred Pierce and Frank Chambers. Like Frank, who equates freedom with the road, Mildred finds stepping on the gas pedal of her car a source of exhilaration, pleasure, even sexual excitement. She craves highway speed, confusing it with freedom, autonomy, power, and social mobility. Behind the wheel of her car she transcends her environment.

She gave the car the gun, exactly watching the needle swing past 30, 40, and 50. . . . The car was pumping something into her veins, something of pride, of arrogance, of restrained self-respect that no talk, no liquor, no love could possibly give.[11]

In a key scene near the end of the novel Mildred is trapped in her car between Glendale and Pasadena in a flash flood and is forced to abandon it and stagger home on foot in the middle of the night—Cain's way of revealing that the freedom and power promised by the highway are illusory.

The three restaurant/pie shops Mildred commands—stretching over a vast triangle from Glendale to Beverly Hills to Laguna Beach—connect and contain, like the Twin Oaks, the opposing versions of the dream, mobility and domesticity. Her highway restaurants are in fact precursors of the "drive in" restaurants, which in the thirties began to appear along the miles of highway strips, the "linear cities," of Southern California. They are the characteristic commercial structures (like the new supermarkets and department stores fronted by large parking lots) in a place dedicated to the marriage of business and the automobile.

*Mildred Pierce* reflects a major shift in Cain's fiction away from the hard-boiled first-person stance of his earlier novels to a more traditional, slower-paced third-person narrative. In place of the lean, spare prose and rapid-paced action sequences that defined his hard-boiled earlier work, the novel is a detailed portrait of middle-class life in the thirties. The reader is dazzled, if not overwhelmed or even bored, by the massing of details and presumably factual information he doles out. Even *Double Indemnity*, with all its talk about the insurance business, doesn't prepare one for the lore he offers, particularly about the restaurant business. The "inside dope" strain in the novel reflects Cain's earlier careers as journalist, food writer, teacher, insurance salesman, even singer (a career that figures in his novel *Serenade*). In *Mildred Pierce* he gives us countless details about running a restaurant—serving a table, baking pies, cooking chicken croquettes, balancing three plates on one arm, operating a cocktail bar, even dealing with sexual harassment from customers.

Still, the novel obeys the formula Cain established at the beginning of his career: the dream-come-true that turns into nightmare. In each of the three novels the principals, driven by sexual passion or a passion for wealth or for respectability, or all three, commit desperate acts, experience a taste of victory, and then lose everything. The hunger for sex, money, and goods leads to reckless acts and these acts to terrible consequences. Frank and Cora beat a murder rap and collect the insurance money but can't escape each other. Walter Huff nearly gets away with the perfect crime, but his lover-accomplice turns out to be a psychopathic killer with no qualms about killing him. *Mildred Pierce* contains no murder (a fact remedied in the 1945 Michael Curtiz noir screen version) but follows a similar pattern: here, though, the heroine is brought to her knees not by a complicitous guilty act but by her pathological need to control her daughter Veda and the vengeful counterplot of Veda, a person capable of even greater duplicity than her mother.

However duplicitous, Veda Pierce is no match for the elemental villainy of Phyllis Nirdlinger in *Double Indemnity*. Phyllis is perhaps the most brutal and cold-blooded female in the period's fiction, although the Billy Wilder film, working with a Raymond Chandler script, plays down her murderous, psychopathic history. In the novel she has murdered more than one victim before she meets Huff and entices him into murdering her husband. Even Dashiell Hammett's Brigid O'Shaughnessy, whom Sam Spade unmasks in the famous ending to *The Maltese Falcon*, and Raymond Chandler's duplicitous females such as Carmen Sternwood, Helen Grayle, and Eileen Wade are the softer sisters of Phyllis Nirdlinger.

## V

If Phyllis Nirdlinger is the deadliest of the femmes fatales in the period's hard-boiled fiction, Gloria Beatty in Horace McCoy's *They Shoot Horses, Don't They?* is the most nihilistic, the most death obsessed. When Robert Syverton, her partner in the dance marathon that constitutes the setting of the narrative, puts a bullet in her head, it is in response to her urging to be put out of her unending misery. She tells Robert, as they stagger on the dance floor: "The whole thing is a merry-go-round. When we get out of here, we're right back where we started."[12] But as the lame horse on that merry-go-round, Gloria will not end where she started but in death. Like Cora in *Postman*, Gloria has come to California to chase the dream, but unlike Cora her past has molded her into a cynicism that Hollywood can only harden.

In Texas she had been the victim of an uncle's sexual advances, lived miserably with a string of men, and attempted suicide. In a hospital she began reading fan magazines—another source of infection—and migrated to Hollywood in a desperate last gesture.

Although the novel is told from Robert's perspective, Gloria's nihilistic vision dominates the novel and determines its outcome. Nothing matters, nothing is immoral, nothing is meaningful. (Not until Joan Didion's 1970 novel, *Play It as It Lays*, do we encounter another Los Angeles woman so filled with despair.) Lee Richmond, an astute critic of the novel, has remarked that with the exception of West's *Miss Lonelyhearts* and *The Day of the Locust*, McCoy's novel is "indisputably the best example of absurdist existentialism in American fiction," anticipating Sartre's *La nausée* (1938) and Camus's *L'Etranger* (1942) in France.[13] Indeed McCoy's novel was widely discussed in France, and McCoy's name was linked with Cain's, Hemingway's, and Faulkner's in the late thirties and early forties.

Surprisingly, the novel was not translated into film until the 1969 adaptation by Sydney Pollack, thirty-four years after its publication and fourteen after McCoy's death. McCoy came to Hollywood from Dallas in 1931, the same year as Cain, and like Cain remained on the coast for most of the rest of his life. Over the next twenty years he worked on about one hundred (virtually all "B") scripts. He had been, like Cain, a journalist (a sports reporter), but also an actor who worked for the Dallas Little Theater, and had hopes of becoming a screen actor as well as a writer in Hollywood. With the almost back-to-back publication of *Postman* and *They Shoot Horses*, the two writers were quickly linked. Wilson, who gave only a few sentences to McCoy in "The Boys in the Back Room"—an equivocal judgment buried in a paragraph on Cain—described him as a follower of Cain, a judgment that rankled McCoy, who in fact completed a draft of the novel in 1933, before *Postman* appeared. His real kinship is with the *Black Mask* school, its editor Joseph Shaw identifying him as one of the writers who helped to establish it.

The two novels bear some strong similarities. Cain's is narrated as a death row confession, McCoy's as the courtroom flashback of a man standing trial for murder. Both men have been condemned to death for the "murder" of a female partner. In both cases, though, the act— like the "wrong woman" murder in Hallas's *You Play the Black and the Red Turns Up* — carries considerable irony and ambiguity: Cora's death in Cain's novel is an accident, and Gloria's death in McCoy's is rendered as a mercy killing. Frank is rushing the pregnant Cora to the hospital after a threatened miscarriage when the car hits a culvert; Robert accedes to Gloria's urging that he "pinch hit for God" and put her out of her misery. This kind of ambiguity — a rupture of the boundary between cold-blooded murder and other kinds of violent death — runs through the hard-boiled genre. The confessional, flashback narrative stance in both novels (and in *Double Indemnity*, which is the confessional narrative of a man who has committed murder and is about to commit suicide), moreover, has the effect of implicating the reader as confidant and arousing some sympathy for the doomed men. As narrators, though, the two men are very different. Frank remains tough, detached, and dispassionate, while Robert, a movie hopeful, is romantic and naively optimistic. The tough quality of McCoy's narrative derives not from the language and tone of its narrator but from the relentless brutality of its subject matter.

There is a another difference in narrative stance. Cain's novel is a straight, unframed, chronological flashback. Only in the last chapter is the death row perspective revealed. McCoy's is framed from the start by the murder trial, which is the present tense of the novel. It opens with the judge's words, printed alone on the page: THE PRISONER WILL STAND. Each of the thirteen sparse chapters is preceded by another fragment of the judge's sentence in increasingly larger typeface until the final words of the book, MAY GOD HAVE MERCY ON YOUR SOUL, covers the full page. Each of the intervening chapters is a silent recounting, an act of memory of the condemned man as he stands before the judge. The events of thirty-seven days of the dance marathon leading up to the killing are compressed, thus, into the moment of actual sentencing. The effect is that of hearing, or overhearing, the thoughts and memories of a condemned man, not of being told a story whose ending is held back from the reader; we read McCoy's novel with the fatalistic knowledge that everything has already happened, that the ending has already been determined. Sydney Pollack, who directed the film, remarked that the structure of the novel is that of the "flashforward," an effect he tried to achieve by making the marathon the present and flashing forward to the trial and sentencing.

Whatever the differences, the two novels converge in their use of highway's end as metaphor for the end of California possibilities. At the edge of the ocean, one runs out of space. McCoy's dance floor and Cain's highway represent not zones of movement and freedom but of entrapment and claustrophobia. That McCoy's novel is set not only *against* the ocean but *over* it as well, on the pier in Santa Monica, intensifies this sense of being at the very end of the road, the place from which there is no return. The back-and-forth movement of the dancers across the floor—movement without progress—is accompanied by the monotonous, relentless ebb and flow of the ocean beneath their feet. In *Postman* the highway, always doubling back on itself, betrays its promise of mobility and freedom, leading to death and not the fresh start. Every action in Cain's novel is followed by a counteraction, an echo or recapitulation; events are rhymed. There are two attempts to murder Nick; the second, botched but successful, is accompanied by the echo of Nick's final sounds bouncing across the canyon. In McCoy's novel the dance marathon, with its endless circularity, repetition, and essential meaninglessness, serves as symbolic setting of the betrayal of the promise of California as a site of freedom and new beginnings. Pairing Robert's hopefulness with Gloria's despair, McCoy underscores the tension between Hollywood-engendered dreams and an existential awareness of futility. Like Cain's Frank Chambers and Nick Papadakis, the pair in McCoy's novel represent opposing visions of California migrants' expectations. Like the other participants, Robert Syverton and Gloria Beatty join the marathon for the meals and lodging, the possibility of prize money, and the hope (which Gloria sees as a ruse) of being discovered by a movie talent scout. The cumulative exhaustion has the effect, though, for Robert of subverting a too easily held hopefulness and for Gloria of intensifying her death wish. When Robert, "out there in the black night on the edge of the Pacific," obliges Gloria by putting a bullet in her head, he is indicating that if he has not quite come around to her nihilistic vision, he has come a long way toward it.

The marathon itself is both pure theater—an elaborate, staged spectacle cynically manipulated by its criminal promoters to draw crowds of thrill seekers—and a parody of the Hollywood dream factory. Dance, traditionally a celebration of life, becomes a rite of death, a *danse macabre.* There are no celebrants and no winners, only an abrupt and crashing halt after 897 hours of futile movement, underscored by the insistent presence of the ocean pounding against the pilings. The pier, "groaning and creaking," is almost an extension of the bodies of the dancers. After the marathon has been shut down following a shooting in the hall, Robert and Gloria stand at the edge of the pier, looking out to the movie star houses on the shore and back to the dance hall where they have spent the last thirty-seven days: "So that's where we've been all the time. . . . Now I know how Jonah felt when he looked at the whale," Robert says. (123) The dance hall is the demon that has swallowed them, then spit them out. The image is claustrophobic, reflecting their constant sense of entrapment, the entrapment of the dream itself.

McCoy followed *They Shoot Horses* in 1938 with a second Hollywood-linked novel whose title says it all: *I Should Have Stayed Home.* Less hard-boiled in tone, less clipped in its telling, and more discursive and conventional in structure, it is nonetheless a blunt indictment of the betrayal of the dream. Again the leads are a young pair of Hollywood seekers with opposing expectations—the male hopeful and romantic, the female tough and pessimistic. Mona Matthew, though, while possessing some of Gloria Beatty's cynicism, has none of her paralyzing despair. A third character, Dorothy Trotter, takes on Gloria's role, committing suicide while in jail for stealing a car. A reporter, taking pictures at the morgue, asks for a shot of the death instrument, and Mona places some fan magazines in the dead girl's hand: the Hollywood publicity network with its small-town-girl-makes-good message is the weapon.

Set in Hollywood (near a sign that reads "All Roads Lead to Hollywood—And the Pause that Refreshes") the novel is filled with conventional movieland types: the lady who lays wreaths at Valentino's grave, the rich nymphomaniacal widow and collector of young actors, the homosexual star, the lesbian screen goddess, the cynical and hard-drinking writer, the tyrannical producer. These are the cameo players who have inhabited Hollywood fiction since the twenties. The constant display of theatrics and role-playing and the exploitive use of sex point to the sense of the West Coast as the place not of new beginnings but of disastrous endings—an anarchic, moral wilderness where high hopes lead to desperate acts and those acts to destruction.

*I Should Have Stayed Home* is a weaker novel than *They Shoot Horses* chiefly because it lacks the tautness, the symbolic compression provided by the controlling metaphor of the dance marathon. Neither Cain nor McCoy was able to do again what they did in their tougher, leaner first novels: concentrate their fables in powerful images drawn from the built and natural landscape of the region, images that would carry the weight of their themes. The haphazard Twin Oaks Tavern sprawled along the highway in Cain and the dance hall perched over the edge of the Pacific in McCoy provided them with symbolic, representative, California landscapes they were not to find again. Makeshift architecture, highways that go nowhere, a claustrophobic dance hall hanging on to a pier, glaring sunlight, and the constant presence of an ocean that could be both inviting and menacing gave *Postman* and *They Shoot Horses* the symbolic compression needed to transform individual tales of murder, greed, and adultery into cultural fables about the failure of the dream.

# 5

## DOWN THESE MEAN STREETS
### *The Tough-Guy Detective Story*

Down these mean streets a man must go who is not himself mean, who is neither tarnished nor afraid. The detective . . . must be such a man. He is the hero, he is everything. He must be a complete man and a common man and yet an unusual man. He must be, to use a weathered phrase, a man of honor, by instinct, by inevitability, without thought of it, and certainly without saying it. He must be the best man in his world and a good enough man for any world. . . . He is a lonely man and his pride is that you will treat him as a proud man or be very sorry you ever saw him.
RAYMOND CHANDLER, *"THE SIMPLE ART OF MURDER"*

The wish-fulfillment fantasy that fuels the mystery-detective genre is the wish to penetrate façades, to know secrets forbidden to ordinary mortals, and the "private eye" takes us to such places and describes what he/we see in such ways that the "seeing" is both information and sensation.
JOYCE CAROL OATES, *LOS ANGELES TIMES BOOK REVIEW* (OCCASIONED BY THE PUBLICATION OF THE WORKS OF RAYMOND CHANDLER IN THE LIBRARY OF AMERICA SERIES)

I

The tough-guy detective came to California in the 1920s. He came as the violent private eye who worked both sides of the street in *Black Mask* stories of writers like Raoul Whitfield and Carroll John Daly, as the Continental Op in Dashiell Hammett's early fiction, and as Sam Spade in *The Maltese Falcon*. He has real-life local antecedents in detectives like William Burns, who worked the 1910 *Los Angeles Times* bombing, and Harry Raymond, whose investigation of municipal corruption led to his near-assassination by a car bomb in 1938. It was Raymond Chandler, though—himself a *Black Mask* story writer— who established Los Angeles as the permanent home of the tough-guy detective in seven Philip Marlowe novels from *The Big Sleep* in 1939 to *Playback* in 1958.[1] Ross Macdonald followed, midway in Chandler's career, with his first Southern California detective novel in 1947. Two years later in *The Moving Target* Macdonald established Lew Archer as the Marlowe-derived California private eye who would be the hero of nineteen novels written over the next three decades. And in the most recent two decades the genre has spun off a number of new, and new age, versions of the Southern California private eye. Among them are Roger Simon's Jewish ex-hippie, Moses Wine; Joseph Hansen's gay detective, Dave Brandstetter; women sleuths like Sue Grafton's Kinsey Millhone, Wendy Hornsby's Maggie Macgowen, and Jan Burke's Irene Kelly; and African-American detectives like Gar Anthony Haywood's Aaron Gunner, Gary Phillips's Ivan Monk, and Walter Mosley's Easy Rawlins. With Joseph Wambaugh as a literary model, James Ellroy and Michael Connelly have brought back the Los Angeles police detective story, with its good cop/bad cop dichotomy, grisly murders, and high-tech forensics.

Although there is no inherent reason that the tough-guy detective story should have retained such vigor and staying power in Los Angeles, there are compelling causes. Detective fiction, for one thing, is essentially an urban form, dependent, as Edgar Allen Poe and Arthur Conan Doyle have shown, on a dense social matrix—on crowds, strangers, and anonymity. There are exceptions, of course—the village and country estate settings of Agatha Christie and in contemporary America the small-town Montana of James Crumley and the Navajo reservation of Tony Hillerman among them—but most practitioners of modern detective fiction have appropriated the large city: London, Amsterdam, New York, and Chicago. Most conspicuously in twentieth-century America, that city has been Los Angeles, the sprawling up-for-grabs city lying at the end of the frontier.

Los Angeles was, in the 1930s, a big city layered on a Wild West frontier town. Its booster legacy encouraged a get-rich-quick mentality that even the depression didn't shake. And supporting its ambitions was a corrupt municipal government. Under Mayor Frank Shaw and his henchmen, notably Police Chief James Davis and Lieutenant Earl Kynette, the city supported, and colluded with, a vast network of underground activities. Everything was for sale, from phony petroleum stocks (the Julian oil stock fiasco was recent memory in the thirties) to police protection of rackets. Scandals rocked the biggest local industries—oil and movies—and gangsters who migrated west controlled gambling, drugs, and prostitution. Headlined warfare between reformers like Clifford Clinton and the mob and between state attorney general Earl Warren and Tony Cornero Stralla's offshore gambling ships turned a national spotlight on local crime, graft, and racketeering. Since the 1920s pulp magazines like *Black Mask* and *True Detective* had been creating an urban mythology of gangsters and detectives. Increasingly, these magazine stories found their way to the West Coast city—San Francisco and then Los Angeles. When Chandler made Los Angeles the locale of his fiction, he was stepping into a city that had already established itself in myth and literature as America's new Babylon.

Moreover, as a decentralized built landscape stretched across a vast basin and inhabited by a largely migrant population, Los Angeles could offer the detective novelist a seemingly unlimited range of physical and human geography. Frank McShane, who has written the most authoritative biography of Chandler, explains the concomitance of Los Angeles and detective fiction.

> There is something appropriate in Chandler's choosing the detective story as his vehicle for presenting Los Angeles. . . . The detective story, so peculiar to the modern city, can involve an extraordinary range of humanity, from the very rich to the very poor, and can encompass a great many different places. Most of Chandler's contemporaries who

wrote "straight" fiction—Fitzgerald, Hemingway, and Faulkner, for example—confined themselves to a special setting and a limited cast of characters. The detective story, however, allowed Chandler to create the whole of Los Angeles in much the same way that such nineteenth-century novelists as Dickens and Balzac created London and Paris for future generations.[2]

One line of descent to Los Angeles detective fiction leads from the traditional, or "classical," detective story invented by an American a century earlier, Edgar Allan Poe, and carried into the twentieth century by British practitioners like Arthur Conan Doyle, Agatha Christie, and Dorothy Sayers. The classic detective story posits an essentially rational and orderly society; crime is an aberration, usually the act of a single deranged person. The detective, using powers of logic and observation beyond the reader's scope, solves the crime the way an intricate puzzle is solved. (And then, conventionally, he gathers all the suspects in a room, reconstructing the crime, establishing the motive, and pointing the finger at the guilty one.)

By contrast, in the brand of detective fiction pioneered by Hammett and the *Black Mask* writers, and anchored in Los Angeles by Chandler, crime is not just an aberrant act—a murder in the vicarage or country estate—but a pervasive feature on the urban landscape, a network that crosses neighborhood, class, and racial divisions. The city itself is corrupt, and the private detective is not there as meliorist assuring readers that society (thanks to him or her) is correctable and essentially sound but as a social critic, a proletarian hero (to Chandler, a knight) battling forces of urban corruption rooted in the rich and powerful. No longer the rational problem-solver, the detective is the street-wise, hard-hitting tough guy who digs for answers in the urban muck, mixes it up with people of all classes from the criminal rich to the exploited poor, gets beaten, drugged, and shot at for his trouble, and often comes away without really "solving" anything. For Chandler, who likened the solution to the crime to the olive in the martini and noted that a good detective story is one that can be read for pleasure even if the last chapter has been torn out, the city itself was always more interesting and book-worthy than the solution to the puzzle or the apprehension of the perpetrator of the crime.

Seen from the historical perspective of American fiction, folklore, and film, the tough-guy detective is not so much a new hero type as an urban recasting of the traditional Western American hero as outsider and individualist. With the end of the frontier and the growth of cities, particularly after World War I, the frontier hero migrated to the city, entering it not as society's representative, the man inside, but as the man standing outside. He lives in the city but maintains his independence from its sources of power, relying instead for his validation on his own instinctive sense of justice and morality. He belongs neither to the police nor to the criminals, neither wholly to his clients nor to those who prey on them. (The "he," it should be added, could be a "she" in some recent detective fiction.) With Chandler, the solitary western hero found a permanent home in America's fastest-growing city.

Frederic Jameson has written suggestively about the linkage between Los Angeles and the kind of detective fiction Chandler wrote. Los Angeles in the years between the wars, he noted, "is already a microcosm and forecast of the country as a whole, a new centerless city in which the various classes have lost touch with each other because each is isolated in his own geographic compartment." Since there can be no "privileged experience" to take in the entire city, he goes on, a "figure must be created who can be superimposed on the society as a whole . . . to tie its separate and isolated parts together."³ That figure, Marlowe, the first motorized private eye in the most thoroughly motorized city in America, is analogous to the picaresque hero who moves from one place to another, linking neighborhoods, characters, and episodes together. In a mobile city Marlowe moves with the kind of fluidity encouraged by the city's network of roads and highways into every enclave. (By way of coincidence, the first, and only, prewar freeway, the Arroyo Seco, was laid out in 1939, the year Chandler's first novel, *The Big Sleep*, appeared.)

## II

Chandler, who arrived in Los Angeles in 1912, knew the vast reaches of the city as it extended itself across the basin. Marlowe's beat stretches from the affluent coastal cities like "Bay City" (Santa Monica), the most thoroughly corrupt enclave in Chandler's geography, to the hills and canyons of the Santa Monica Mountains laced with the temples of sham spiritualists and the fortresslike houses of the criminal rich, and to the inland regions—the derelict inner-city neighborhoods harboring the city's large underclass. His beat extends north to Pasadena, home to old money, and to the gated, suburban San Fernando Valley communities of the new rich like "Idle Valley." Beyond the basin Marlowe races as far as Big Bear Lake in the San Bernardino Mountains to find the "Lady in the Lake" (in the novel that bears that title). Characteristically, though, his territory is closer to the city's commercial center—to the shabby office buildings in Hollywood, along Wilshire Boulevard, or downtown, places where medical quacks hang their shingles, "mail order mechanics with a license to cut corns or jump up and down on your spine . . . [where] a well-heeled patient with incipient DTs could be money from home to plenty of old geezers who have fallen behind in the vitamin and antibiotic trade."[4]

Chandler, like almost everyone else in early-twentieth-century Los Angeles, was a migrant. He was born in Chicago in 1888. When his father, an alcoholic and womanizer, deserted the family in 1897, his mother took him to England where they lived as poor relations with his mother's sister. With some financial backing from his uncle, he attended public school in Upper Norwood and then Dulwich College from which he graduated at seventeen. He traveled for a time in Europe, then worked for a time as a newspaper reporter and wrote poetry. He returned to America in 1912 and with the encouragement of a couple he met on the ship went to Los Angeles where he got work with an independent oil company, first as an auditor and later as a vice president in charge of acquisitions. He lived with his mother in Los Angeles and shortly after her death in 1924 married Cissy Pascal, a woman eighteen years older than he. Lively and attractive when they married, Cissy became a semi-invalid late in her life. She died in 1954, five years before Chandler's death. Chandler, then living in La Jolla (north of San Diego), fell into a deep depression, attempting suicide at least once.

Biographical and psychoanalytical critics have had a field day with his marriage to Cissy, commenting on the Oedipal bond, his mother complex, and a need both to take care of and be taken care of by older women. Conversely, they cite the misogynistic portraiture of women in the fiction as evil, threatening, wholly deceptive figures.

The negative depiction of women, though, would seem to derive more from traditional American literary stereotyping than from biographical sources: women, conventionally, were offered up by male writers as either sexual temptresses or domesticating agents (or both); either way they spelled trouble for the male. Whatever the source of Chandler's representation of women, McShane stresses the strong, caring bond between the Chandlers and the fact that Cissy was a vivacious woman before her illness.

In 1932, in what now has to be seen as a break for Los Angeles, and American, literature, Chandler was fired from the Dabney Oil Company, owing to his heavy drinking and frequent absences. Almost immediately he began publishing stories in *Black Mask*, learning his craft by imitating the plots of the stories in the magazine. His first story, "Blackmailers Don't Shoot," came out in 1933, and in the next five years he published sixteen stories, apprentice work for the novel he was to begin in 1938, *The Big Sleep*. The stories not only served as warm-up exercises for the novels, but provided their plot lines. In a practice he called "cannibalizing," he recycled plots from his stories into the novels. Often several different stories found their way into a single novel. The attempt to integrate multiple plot strands led to some byzantine and almost incomprehensible story lines. Howard Hawks, the now-familiar story goes, when working on the 1946 screen adaptation of *The Big Sleep* (assisted by a William Faulkner script), wired Chandler to ask who killed Owen Taylor (the chauffeur whose car was run off the Santa Monica pier); Chandler replied that he didn't know. Careful plotting, the kind one finds in Ross Macdonald, was not Chandler's strong suit, a point Chandler himself acknowledged many times.

Readers disagree (as they do about most good writers) about what is his best work. The strongest contenders are *The Big Sleep*, *Farewell, My Lovely* (1940), and *The Long Goodbye* (1953)—his first two novels and one published near the end of his career. As confusing as it is in its details, *The Big Sleep* offers an accessible path to an understanding of the version of the California story Chandler was to tell in all his novels. At the opening of the novel Marlowe is summoned to the hilltop mansion of General Guy Sternwood, to protect the family from blackmail threats engendered by the reckless acts of his younger daughter, Carmen. What Marlowe finds out, though, in the novel's final revelation, is that Carmen's real crime, the secret and "primal" crime—and the real reason for the blackmail—is neither gambling debts nor the nude photos she had posed for but her murder of Rusty Regan, an Irish roughneck and young friend of the general, who had spurned her sexual advances. Carmen has killed Regan, long before the novel begins, in the oil field that lies below the Sternwood mansion. The corpse in the oil field is the family secret (secret even to Guy Sternwood) that must be discovered, the crime lying hidden in history and buried deep in the landscape. As in all of Chandler's fiction, the plot moves in two directions at once: forward in time to the discovery of clues and backward in time to the discovery of the original crime, hidden in past time (a narrative structure Macdonald employs with more psychological complexity). Marlowe discovers the buried truth by having Carmen reenact, with him as intended victim, the original crime on the same landscape, the oil field, and for the same motive—this time, though, with blanks in Carmen's gun.

Marlowe's role, as the man who uncovers secrets, is analogous to that of the blackmailer, who knows secrets and turns that knowledge into power to extort money. The role of blackmailer is played in the novel by Eddy Mars, a racketeer who runs a gambling den that serves as a front for his other enterprises, extortion among them. Unlike the blackmailer, though, Marlowe doesn't use his knowledge for power over others; his power derives from his independence from others, his refusal to be bought or to sell anything, a refusal that extends to sleeping with women involved in the case (he evicts a naked Carmen from his bed, angrily ripping out the sheets, and remains chaste until *The Long Goodbye*) or to taking more than his fee of $25 a day and expenses (raised to $40 in the later novels).

Tough and independent, Marlowe is also a contemplative man who likes to work out chess puzzles in his apartment and who has a penchant for reflecting on the world around him. He has a nostalgic side, too, a hankering for the older, simpler city of the booster era. "I used to like this town," he reflects in *The Little Sister* (1949):

A long time ago. There were trees along Wilshire Boulevard. Beverly Hills was a country town. Westwood was bare hills and lots offering at eleven hundred dollars and no takers. Hollywood was a bunch of frame houses on the interurban line. Los Angeles was just a big dry sunny place with ugly homes and no style, but goodhearted and peaceful. It had the climate they just yap about now. People used to sleep out on porches. Little groups who thought they were intellectual used to call it the Athens of America. It wasn't that, but it wasn't a neon-lighted slum either.[5]

With an eye to the growth and changes the city underwent from the time of his arrival in 1912, Chandler invests its physical and architectural landscape with symbolic and moral meaning. In Chandler's geography the corrupt and criminal rich have moved high up into the hills, into large, pretentious houses (done up in a variety of historical, most often Mediterranean, styles) surrounded by high walls that isolate and insulate them from the consequences of crimes they have committed on the flatland below. General Sternwood, not a criminal himself, has nonetheless made millions exploiting the city's oil reserves and then moved up to the high ground, above the site and source of his wealth. In Chandler's next novel, *Farewell, My Lovely*, this kind of geographic relocation recurs. Velma Valenti, torch singer and gangsters' moll, has committed a crime, framed a man for it, married a rich man, moved up into the hills, and taken a new name (Helen Grayle) and identity (wife of a respectable judge), barricading herself in "one of those great silent estates with twelve-foot walls and wrought iron gates and ornamental hedges."[6]

Such movement is consistent with the demographics of the city. In the sprawling landscape of Los Angeles, as commentators from Carey McWilliams to Frederic Jameson have pointed out, status and respectability are achieved not by movement to a higher floor in the same apartment building, as, say, in Paris, or even by movement to a better house or better street in the same neighborhood, but by movement to a different neighborhood. In Los Angeles this usually means one on higher ground. McWilliams put it this way in 1946:

The heights of the town are occupied by the extremely wealthy, between the heights and the lowlands live the well-to-do townspeople, below the middle-class townspeople are the lower middle-class residents, and still farther down the slope, and across the tracks, are the Negro domestics and the Mexican field workers.[7]

Just as James M. Cain's Mildred Pierce sought to erase her past and attain a new identity by moving from middle-class Glendale to the higher ground of Pasadena, Chandler's upwardly mobile migrant families seek the abrogation of past time, and past acts, by movement to the high ground.

To move up the hill in Chandler's fiction is to move away from the scene of the crime. Living in the hills is living with a "prospect," which taken literally means living with a *view*, and metaphorically with a *future*. In Chandler's world both the view and the future are purchased by the gains of brutal acts committed in the past. The job of Marlowe, as detective, is to drag the criminal rich *down* to the flatland, carry them *back* to their histories, their crimes. He destroys their view, their prospects, and anonymity. He makes them remember past acts, sometimes, as in *The Big Sleep*, by forcing them to reenact those events. Marlowe's task is to cure them of their amnesia. This is what makes Chandler's novels so distinctly Californian: in the land dedicated to the proposition of the fresh start, the detective is there as a reminder that history is inescapable. One carries one's past into the present, and however successful one is in burying that past for a time, it resurfaces. There are always blackmailers and detectives.

The case is clearest in *The Big Sleep*. Near the beginning of the novel Marlowe, having just penetrated, room by room, the pseudomedieval trappings of the Sternwood mansion, and having interviewed the general and encountered his two daughters, looks out and down from the patio to the oil fields below that have made Sternwood his millions:

> On this lower level faint and far off I could just barely see some of the old wooden derricks of the oilfield from which the Sternwoods had made their money. Most of the field was public park now, cleaned up and donated to the city by General Sternwood. But a little of it was still producing in groups of wells pumping five or six barrels a day. The Sternwoods, having moved up the hill, could no longer smell the sump water or the oil, but they could still look out of their front windows and see what made them rich. If they wanted to. I don't suppose they would want to.[8]

To look out is to enjoy a prospect, a rustic mountain view; to look back down the hill is to see the past, to see where one has come from. Beneath the house are the covered-over wounds of the oil derricks and the site of the murder. Although ignorant of that murder, Stern-wood has made deep gouges in the city's bedrock and fathered, late in his life, two reckless daughters—"the moral consequences," Richard Lehan has written, "of a state of mind founded on commercial exploitation, the movement from the desire to control the land to the desire to control other people."[9]

When Marlowe interviews Sternwood in the first chapter, the old man is sitting in a wheelchair wrapped in a faded robe and blanket in his greenhouse, existing like "a new-born spider." The air is "thick, wet, steamy, and larded with the cloying smell of orchids in bloom." The flowers that surround him have "nasty meaty leaves and stalks like the newly washed fingers of dead men." (5) The image is an example of one of Chandler's trademarks, the ironic simile in which things are like other things in revealing and surprising ways. Such similes, often tossed off as wisecracks, are always suggestive, carrying hints of truths that lie beneath the surface. The hothouse flowers, personified this way, evoke not life and growth but death and decay: the "newly washed fingers of dead men" suggest the living death of Sternwood himself and the corpse beneath the house as well.

Throughout Chandler's fiction surfaces are simultaneously deceptive and revealing. Marlowe discovers truth by both observing and penetrating exteriors, looking at and beneath surfaces. Nothing is what it looks like at first, and people are not who they appear to be. The pervasive performative behavior found in Hollywood fiction runs through the crime fiction of Chandler, as well as his followers, providing the strongest link between the two dominant genres in Los Angeles fiction. In *The Big Sleep* the blackmail attempt is not about gambling debts or nude photos but murder; the rare book dealer Arthur Geiger runs a pornographic lending library; and the flirtatious ingenue is a dope addict and killer. In the other novels as well roleplaying preempts reality: the wife of the judge in *Farewell, My Lovely* is a killer, the little sister from Kansas in *The Little Sister* (1949) is a swindler, the corpse rising from the water in *Lady of the Lake* (1943) is not who she is supposed to be, and the respectable widow in *The High Window* (1942) has eased her husband out of that window. Doctors, more often than not, are "barred window boys" operating dope-dispensing hideaways fronting as "clinics" (one would have to go back to Hawthorne to find a more cynical appraisal of doctors). The police, more often than not, are on the take. Lawyers are usually crooked and incompetent, the kind, Marlowe says, you hope the other guy has. And spiritualists (who label themselves "psychic consultants") are in business to bilk rich, bored, frustrated housewives.

Chandler consistently underscores the rampant deception and masquerade by using architectural details emblematically. "Dope doctors" like Sonderberg in *Farewell, My Lovely*, Almore in *The Lady in the Lake*, Lagardie in *The Little Sister*, and Verringer in *The Long Goodbye* cater to alcoholics, drug addicts, and criminals on the lam in establishments disguised as ranches and country estates. Their job is to make sure that those who want to get lost stay lost. The sham spiritualist Jules Amthor in *Farewell, My Lovely* consults his rich clients in a mountaintop aerie with rooms designed, like the Gothic out-of-time-and-space rooms of Edgar Allan Poe, to obliterate any sense of ordered space. The elaborate houses of the rich, though, are Chandler's most compelling images of deception and disguise, architectural façades behind which criminals live as if past acts were of no consequence. The Grayle house in *Farewell, My Lovely* is Chandler's consummate image of the monumental, impenetrable, and wholly counterfeit fortress. Inside the high walls is a garden with stone benches, crouching griffins, a pool with water lilies and a stone bullfrog, a sun dial against a wall designed to look like a ruin, and "a special brand of sunshine, put up in noise-proof containers just for the upper classes." (101) Here, and throughout Chandler's fiction, description fuses objective detail with subjective reaction; through Marlowe's eyes we know both *what*, in a literal sense, a place looks like and *how*, usually in the form of a wisecrack, Marlowe responds to it. The response to place is a response to the people who inhabit that place.

Inside the pretentious, counterfeit Grayle house, down a long corridor, Marlowe finds himself in front of a French window that reveals a patch of blue and remembers with a sense of shock that he is at the border of the Pacific. The vast emptiness of the ocean stands in violent opposition to the man-made dream castles perched at its edge. The proximity of the ocean beyond and beneath the house is the reminder that one has reached the end of the line: there is nowhere else to go, nowhere else to hide. As in the fiction of James M. Cain and Horace McCoy, the ocean is the place where the dream runs out and history catches up. In dragging criminals from their mountain-top or beachfront sanctuaries, Marlowe forces them to confront their pasts and acknowledge what all California migrants must acknowledge: that history may be side-stepped for a while but never escaped.

## III

"It makes me wonder if certain things aren't fated. Do you think they are?"

"Of course. By the place and the time and the family you're born into. Those are the things that fate most people."

ROSS MACDONALD, *THE BLUE HAMMER*

Ross Macdonald, Chandler's heir to the Southern California detective story, acknowledged that while he derived his detective hero's name, Lew Archer, from Sam Spade's partner (murdered in *The Maltese Falcon*), his detective's character is modeled on Marlowe. The resemblance is more apparent in the earlier novels when Macdonald was most clearly under Chandler's influence. By 1959, beginning with *The Galton Case*, Archer becomes less angry, less bitter, less tough. He emerges as a man more sympathetic with those he works for and with, more emotionally involved with them, more painfully implicated in their lives. The mature Archer seeks reconciliation and restoration more than the punishment of guilt.

Archer's own past difficulties have conditioned his responses, prompting pity more often than demands for punishment. Scattered through the Archer novels are bits and pieces of the detective's personal history. We know more about him than we do about Marlowe. We know he was born in Long Beach in 1914, attended high school in Oakland, belonged to youth gangs and got in trouble with the law, served in Army Intelligence in World War II, joined and then quit (or was fired from) the Long Beach Police, and went through a painful divorce. He is thirty-five in the first Archer novel, *The Moving Target* (1949), and approaching sixty in the late works. He lives and works in Santa Teresa (Santa Barbara, one hundred miles up the coast from Los Angeles) and, unlike Marlowe, has a good working relationship with local police detectives, who can be both honest and smart. He cooperates with the police and takes advantage of modern law enforcement methods and technology.

Crime in Macdonald's enactment of the California story is not ordinarily rooted in gangland activity and racketeering but in family histories. Characteristically, the detective is hired (sometimes by someone he knows) to find a missing person or recover a stolen object. The search carries Archer into the past. Present problems are the consequence of acts committed in the past—acts motivated by greed, egoism, jealousy, love, or hate that may have occurred a generation or more earlier. The past acts are hauntings, ghosts in the family attic. Archer discovers the original crime, brings past acts into the present, links one generation to another. To some degree Macdonald is reworking the Chandler story told in *The Big Sleep*, but he invests his tales with deeper psychological insight. The children, the sons and daughters in the present generation, bear the sins of their forebears, suffer the trauma of historical violence. Archer sees his role as analogous to that of a psychotherapist; though haunted by his own past, he seeks truth by discovering the secrets of others. He reflects on his task in *The Blue Hammer* (1976):

Take a look at your own life, Archer. . . . My chosen study was other men, hunted men in hunted rooms, aging boys clutching at manhood before night fell and they grew suddenly old. If you were a therapist, how could you need therapy? If you were the hunter, you couldn't be hunted, or could you?[10]

As in Chandler's fiction, the California myth of new beginnings, with its corollary of the irrelevance of history, is undercut by the detective's revelation that past acts give rise to contemporary disturbances. Moving through a labyrinth of mistaken and assumed identities, he finds historical truth by distinguishing the real from the counterfeit. The assumption of a new name, a new home, or a new neighborhood fails to insulate people from history. Macdonald in the Archer novels doesn't invent a new story or a new genre but extends beyond Chandler the bitemporal California story, realizing its full potential in the family crime narrative.

Macdonald's work reflects not only the influence of Chandler but also his own academic training in literature and psychology—graduate work at the University of Michigan culminating in a doctoral dissertation on the psychological criticism of Coleridge's work. His interest in Freudian psychology, voguish in the post–World War II years, derives from personal sources, too: his own sense of doubleness and exile. Like Chandler, he was American-born but raised in another country, the consequence of a father's abandonment. He was born Kenneth Millar in Los Gatos, California (near San Jose), in 1915 but was brought up, after his parents' divorce, in Canada (first in Alberta, then Ontario). The parallels with Chandler's early life are striking: the boy, suffering the father's abandonment, grows up in poverty in another country, dependent on the support of the mother's family. Moved from place to place, raised essentially by women, he grows up feeling the loss of both father and home. Macdonald, aware of the parallels with Chandler's childhood, identified with the sense of exile in the older author, noting in *The Writer as Detective Hero* that "[it] is Marlowe's doubleness that makes him interesting: the hard-boiled mask half concealing Chandler's poetic and satiric mind. Part of our pleasure derives from the interplay between the mind of Chandler and the voice of Marlowe."[11] He saw this doubleness, a migrant quality, as informing his own work. In a foreword to a three-novel compilation of his novels, *Archer in Hollywood*, he writes that his hero, like Chandler's, has "the fresh suspicious eye of a semi-outsider, who is fascinated but not completely taken in by the customs of the natives."[12]

The "natives" on whom Macdonald casts his suspicious eye are themselves wealthy California migrants, men and women who have made their fortunes in other places—sometimes in the flatland below their hilltop houses, sometimes in other states. They have moved up into the hills above Santa Teresa in stratified communities, insulated by walls and mountain terrain, close to but segregated from the Mexican field hands and working-class whites below, who have made the hill dwellers' affluence possible. In the first Archer novel, *The Moving Target*, the drifting haze in the mountains and canyons is like "thin smoke from slowly burning money."[13] Archer in this novel is hired to find a missing alcoholic oil man named Sampson who has disappeared after getting off his private plane in Los Angeles. The source of family troubles, though, goes back in time before the kidnapping. The trauma lies in family history: the wartime death of a son. It lies, directly or indirectly, behind the whole chain of events in the novel: alcoholism and adultery, the hatred between husband and wife, the alienation of children, the drifting into occultism, then the kidnapping itself, and ultimately the killing of Sampson by the family lawyer. Everything leads back in time, has antecedents.

The search for the missing father, for paternity, is in some of the novels fused with, or transformed into, the search for the missing son — or grandson. In *The Galton Case*, Macdonald's favorite of his books, the search touches three generations: an old, wealthy Santa Teresa widow hires Archer to find her missing grandson, her only heir. Her son, the boy's father, ran off with a woman twenty-three years earlier and is presumed dead. In the present his decapitated skeleton is uncovered and identified; he was murdered by a man who then took on, as protective mask, the role of the boy's father, marrying the mother. The young John Galton, victim of the false father, becomes avenger of the real father and in the end returns to reestablish his place in the original family. Disappearance and reappearance, exile and return, are themes that recur in Macdonald's novels, themes that may well have their sources in the author's own childhood exile. Seeking historical truth, Archer moves though a web of true and false fathers, true and false sons. In the novel's strangest twist on the missing son theme, the young man is set up by gangsters to impersonate the man he really is—but isn't sure he is—to claim an inheritance. Similarly, in *The Underground Man* (1971) domestic conflict reaches back three generations. A son, witness to the pickax murder and burial of his father in a Santa Teresa forest clearing, attempts years later to dig up the body and is killed and buried in the same spot. The original crime, as in Chandler's *The Big Sleep*, has been committed in history and the victim buried on the landscape; the attempt to uncover that original crime leads to its reenactment. Archer's task is the same one he performed in *The Galton Case*: to restore order by linking past and present and returning the grandson, the child-victim, to the family.

The vulnerability of the mountain and forest landscape of Santa Teresa is linked in Macdonald's fiction with human vulnerability. Through much of *The Underground Man* a forest fire rages in the hills close to the site of two murders and burials. Fire, a natural and recurring event in the chaparral-filled hills ringing Southern California (now, however, more and more the result of arson), functions as metonymy for, and ecological counterpart to, human transgression. The fire in Macdonald's novel was started by a carelessly tossed cigarette, but in larger terms it signals man's violation both of the landscape and of his fellow man: the heedless real estate plunder of the vulnerable hills, the greedy attempt to dominate nature and other people. The drive for power over others is reflected in the drive to transform the landscape, to commodify and exploit it for what it will bear. There is in Macdonald, as Jerry Spier has written, "a developing tension between nature and man, between the eternal landscape and its temporal inhabitants."[14] The fire in *The Underground Man* is followed by heavy rains, pouring mud down the denuded hills onto the houses of the violators. The house of Kilpatrick, a real estate agent, is buried in mud, and Lennox, who has made his fortune in oil, has stains of ooze on his windows. Nature and human nature bear a correspondence; the harm done to the fragile ecology of the coast, mountain, and forest through greed and carelessness is the consequence of, and counterpart to, violations inflicted on other people.

Fire—what Joan Didion has called the city's deepest image of itself and what Nathanael West's painter-protagonist Tod Hackett envisions in his painting, "The Burning of Los Angeles," as the force that will accompany the city's destruction—is in Macdonald a reminder that the houses built by the rich in the hills have no power to immunize them against either the destructive force of nature or their own greed. In *The Underground Man* fire is equated with war. "Under and through the smoke," Archer comments, "I caught glimpses of fire like the flashes of heavy guns too far away to be heard." The fire, he says later, "hung around the city like the bivouacs of a besieging army."[15]

War signals disruption in Macdonald, the end of one time and the beginning of another. In *The Moving Target* war lies at the root of modern history. World War II is the real source of family troubles that are unearthed years later. A painter, a returning veteran, has murdered his brother in 1943. The killer camouflages that murder by assuming the dead man's identity. Seven years later the murderer has to kill again when his act is discovered by another. He buries the second corpse in a greenhouse and once again assumes a second dead man's identity. In a perverse version of the California myth of the fresh start (reminiscent of Cain's *Double Indemnity*), the murderer must kill and kill again to secure his fresh start, which is dependent on his anonymity. He takes on a series of disguises. Identity is never fixed but fluid, contingent, assumable; one becomes who he or she wants or needs to become in order to escape the consequences of past acts. Archer, like Marlowe, is the agent of history, forcing people to remember and acknowledge the past. Hired to recover a stolen painting, he moves back in time to the identity of the missing painter, the model for that painting, the corpse in the greenhouse, and finally the identity of the man killed during the war, in 1943. In the inward-turning plot, the history and fate of two families, one upper and one working class, intersect. The families mirror each other, the rich and poor families linked by spousal hatred, alcoholism, adultery, and the Oedipal love/jealousy of alienated children. In the final revelation the families are shown to be even more intimately connected: they are the same family.

As the place at the end of the West, California is the final destination of five hundred years of European westward movement, movement first across one ocean and then west across a continent to another ocean. At the Pacific the European American makes his last stand, builds, in Macdonald's appropriation of the myth, his dream house in a stratified community in the hills and canyons fronting the ocean. Even the sea, though, is no barrier to man's advance. The ocean itself is vulnerable. In *The Sleeping Beauty* (1973) an oil spill, the product of the heedless exploitation of offshore oil deposits, turns the beach at Santa Teresa into a black, thick, slick liquid. Surfers, bathers, and sun worshipers stand at the edge of the ocean, staring in disbelief at the dark sea, an image of the violent apocalyptic end of the dream that harks back to the finale of West's *The Day of the Locust* but set here—appropriate to Los Angeles disaster fiction—at the very edge of the continent.

In an interview for *Esquire* in 1972 Macdonald elaborated on the notion of the California coast as nexus of nature and man, the place where the natural world confronts human desire and the ability to transform it: "Here in California what you've got is an instant megalopolis superimposed on a background which could almost be described as raw nature. What we've got here is the twentieth century right up against the primitive."[16] Psychological and ecological vulnerability merge in Macdonald's fiction; the fate of characters is reflected, doubled on the landscape. The land heals in time, just as the detective, in time, uncovers the truth that leads to the healing of selves and families.

## IV

One of the themes that I have been stressing in this book is the migrant theme: Los Angeles as the place to which people have come in search of new lives. Characters come to the new land with histories in, and memories from, other places. Like the characters in all immigrant and migrant literature, those in Los Angeles fiction are poised between imagined futures and remembered pasts. What they learn is that history has a way of remaining in the present tense; the quest for the new beginning comes up against a past that surfaces in the present. In the tough-guy detective fiction that is the subject of this chapter, criminals have committed brutal acts in the past, individually or in collusion with others, that have permanently defined and disfigured them. The move into Southern California in the fiction of Chandler and Macdonald is a deliberate move away from a past life and the consequences of past acts. The Los Angeles detective story is in this sense part of, and in response to, the larger story of American literature and mythology: freedom in the national myth has always been identified with mobility, with the open road—the road that points west, away from the history-bound East and into the open, future-oriented West. The West is the geographic site, the destination, of the invented self, the new, free, self-made American. For Twain's Huckleberry Finn traveling west was "lighting out for the territory"; for Fitzgerald's Jay Gatsby, in the imaginative reconstruction of his narrator, Nick Carraway, the West was linked with the journey of the earliest European explorers of the New World who came astonished upon "the fresh green breast" of America. The West has been rendered in European and American literature and mythology as the fresh, green garden, ready for occupation by adventurous travelers. But in twentieth-century versions of the story, the past is always present to challenge the notion of a fresh start, unencumbered by history. *The Great Gatsby* reminds us that history has already happened; the past is paradoxically both irrecoverable and inescapable.

In the Southern California detective novel the past is as determinative, as fatal, as it is in *The Great Gatsby*. Chandler's Marlowe and Macdonald's Archer, hired to investigate present troubles in the arcadian setting of Southern California, find the source of the troubles lying deep in history, in long-buried corpses that surface in the present. As urban heroes who have arrived by way of the frontier adventurer, the western hero, and the tough, unreflective *Black Mask* gumshoe, Marlowe and Archer reveal little of their own pasts, but unlike the reticent western hero who rides into town, rids it of its villains, and then rides off, they have histories in the city. In a city of newcomers they are old-timers. The migrants in the Chandler/Macdonald tradition are the detectives' guilty clients and antagonists, men and women who have moved from somewhere else into exclusive estates and neighborhoods in an attempt to erase their histories. The luxurious, gated houses they inhabit are sanctuaries they believe will isolate them from soiled pasts.

Houses stand between the self and the world. They are man-made interventions on nature, impositions of human will exerted on the landscape. In the Los Angeles brand of the detective novel—as in the Hollywood novels I discuss in the following chapter—the architectural landscape is represented not only as the preemption of nature, as takeover and makeover of the land, but also as metonymy for pervasive masquerade and performative behavior. Unlike the Thoreauvian notion of the house representing, organically, the authentic self of the builder/dweller, houses in Los Angeles crime fiction (and Hollywood fiction) represent the desire to construct a new self-image, to erase former identities and to be what one wants others to believe one to be. Chandler's ironic similes, as tropes, are analogous to the architectural façades, suggestive of the erasure of boundaries between organic and made worlds; they mediate the space between the natural and the constructed, the landscape and its representation in language.

Traditionally in American writing the open, unbuilt landscape has been linked with the timeless, with what endures and is outside history (as in much conventional western fiction). But space is always altered by history, by natural forces or by human need or greed; landscapes change in time. The houses of Chandler's and Macdonald's rich, butting up against raw nature, are built as stays against the ravages of time, but time and history intrude either because the blackmailer knows past truths or because the detective finds hidden truths. The inescapability of history is the lesson of the Chandler/Macdonald California crime story, one that would be carried into the present by dozens of followers.

## V

To be sure, there have been significant changes in the form since the time of Chandler and Macdonald. For one, the contemporary Los Angeles detective may no longer look like a Marlowe or an Archer. The white Anglo male no longer occupies the dominant position he did in earlier decades. The detective today can be a woman, a Jewish ex-hippie, an African American, or a homosexual. For another, the detective's tastes have sometimes been elevated: he or she may be educated and bookish, wear fashionable clothes, be a gourmet cook, a connoisseur of fine wines, or owner of a large, well-furnished house. He or she may be an environmentalist, yoga practitioner, opera fan, or outdoor adventurer. The genre, as one observer put it, has moved from "mean streets to Easy Street."[17] The detective as proletarian hero persists in inner-city detective stories of writers like Walter Mosley, Gary Phillips, John Shannon, and Gar Anthony Haywood, but the characteristic new detective has definitely been mainstreamed. And in contrast to the loner like Marlowe, the new detective has personal and sexual relationships that sometimes constitute a significant part of the narratives.

The new detective story has come, in other words, to reflect contemporary, postmodern America's, and Los Angeles's, diversity. Issues of race, gender, and class have been foregrounded and highlighted. Racial and ethnic minorities, relegated to the margins in Chandler and Macdonald, have become major characters. Women are less often stereotyped as threatening figures, bearers of dangerous sexual allure, deception, or (worse yet) domestication. In the fiction of Sue Grafton, Jan Burke, Wendy Hornsby, Faye Kellerman, and others, the female—and sometimes feminist—detective has found a place in the genre.[18] And in the novels of Haywood, Phillips, and Mosley, the African-

American detective, operating out of South Central Los Angeles, has found a place in the fiction.

Closest in tone and setting to Ross Macdonald among the newer detective writers is Joseph Hansen, whose Dave Brandstetter appears in a two-decade series of novels beginning with *Fadeout* in 1970. Brandstetter is a gay and more refined Archer—rich, sophisticated, and famous (having appeared, as a successful insurance investigator, on talk shows and magazine features). He is about sixty in the later novels, drives a Jaguar, drinks Glenlivet, and lives comfortably in a rambling three-building ranchlike compound, converted from stables, in Horseshoe Canyon (probably Laurel Canyon). Independently wealthy (having inherited money from his father, who owned an insurance company), he lives a very different life from the spartan, financially strapped Marlowe, and as a homosexual detective, he represents the antithesis of the characteristic homophobic detective in the tough-guy detective tradition from *Black Mask* through Hammett to Chandler. In Brandstetter the detective has become a liberal. He has none of the racism or misogyny that runs rampant in the tradition either; he is not threatened by women and has female companions as well as male friends and lovers, including, in the later fiction, Cecil Harris, a black television technician who becomes Brandsetter's lover in the novel *Gravedigger* (1982) and remains so in subsequent novels.

In another transformation of the Chandler/Macdonald tradition, Brandstetter's investigations carry him into a world seedier and poorer than his own. In *Gravedigger*, for instance, he confronts Arazel, a totalitarian, homophobic leader of a cannibalistic religious commune in the desert. Deserts and mountains are, as in Chandler, refuges for an assortment of cultist and occultist practices, but the city itself, in Hansen's representation, is not pervaded by crime, not a microcosm of a "world gone wrong," as it was for Chandler. Los Angeles, except for its lunatic fringe, is generally a tolerant, cosmopolitan, and civilized place. Crimes are linked, most often, to the city's poor nonurban margins. Hansen's vision is an "anti-pastoral" one, as Ernest Fontana has written: threats to urban stability come from "rural and primitive settings and atavistic belief systems that are totalitarian, religious, and violent."[19]

The urban and urbane Brandstetter, though, finds much that is wrong with the city. Living in a designer house in the hills, he finds

much of the architecture of the flatlands appalling. He responds dis-
paragingly, for instance, to the kind of buildings that the architectural historian Reyner Banham called "dingbats"—the squarish, two-
story, nondescript stucco apartment houses built from the 1950s to
the 1970s in every neighborhood of the city:

> The buildings were beige stucco boxes propped on tall
> steel pipes, living quarters above, parking below. The
> structures turned square blind faces to the street. Stairs
> climbed to galleries along the side, where doors and
> windows showed. . . . the main effect of the street was
> of dreary tidiness.[20]

As with Chandler and Macdonald, description functions both as information and as personal response.

The updated Macdonald-like plots of Hansen center on bizarre
killings committed in the past and unearthed by Brandstetter. In
*Early Graves* (1987), for instance, the graves of the title are inhabited
by six men, all gay, all victims of AIDS, who have, over a period of
time, been slashed to death with a knife. Brandstetter finds the sixth
victim on his own patio. His investigation leads back to a former lover
of five of the men: the killer has killed in revenge for the disease he
contracted. But the sixth victim, the corpse on his patio, has not been
killed by the same man or for the same reason. The victim has deserted a wife and son in Arkansas, broken out of prison, and migrated
to California, where he assumed a new name and identity as a land
developer, his life divided between business affairs and leather bars.
His killer, it turns out, is his demented son from Arkansas, who has
come to California in search of the father, intending to make him
pay for his abandonment and his evil ways. In dealing both with greedy,
exploitive land development and the "sins of the father" theme,
Hansen touches on two of the concerns that were central to Ross
Macdonald's California crime stories.

Roger Simon's Moses Wine is the proletarian flip-side to the bour-
geois Brandstetter. He is a younger man, a tough, independent loner,
and a Jewish, heterosexual, dope-smoking, ex-radical Berkeley dropout.
Recently divorced, he lives alone in Echo Park, struggles to keep up
child support payments for his two sons, and drives an old Buick. His

ex-wife, meanwhile, lives in the more upscale Laurel Canyon, Brand-stetter's territory, and has taken on as lover a new-age guru who drives an XKE (parked, no doubt, near Brandstetter's Jaguar). In mobile, fluid Southern California, the kind of car one drives is the clearest sign of status: by their cars shall ye know them. Wine's closest rela-tionship is with his Trotskyite aunt who lives in an old age home in the Jewish Fairfax district. In a comic allusion to Marlowe's solitary chess puzzles, Wine, alone in his apartment, plays the board game Clue.

Simon's debt is both to Chandler and to Macdonald. His detec-tive is as tough as Marlowe, and in his best-known work, *The Big Fix* (1973), he is enmeshed in a Macdonald-like family plot focusing on the evil parent and victimized son. Hired to investigate and prevent a threatened freeway explosion, allegedly a plot to smear liberal presi-dential candidate Miles Hawthorne by linking his supporters with violent anarchism, Wine finds that the true motive, the real "big fix," is the scheme of a rich man who has bet $10 million against Hawthorne in the primary election. Oscar Procari, the gambler, has murdered those who have stood in his way and bullied his weak-willed son, who has been working for Hawthorne's election, to go along with the plot. As frequently happens in Macdonald's novels, the detective in Roger Simon's novel is brought into the case by someone he has known in the past. Lila Shea, a Hawthorne campaign worker, is a former lover and fellow Berkeley activist. "The first time I met her," he recalls, "we were being firehosed down the steps of San Francisco City Hall at the HUAC protest in May, 1960."[21] Shea's car is subsequently run off a cliff into the Pacific; she is one of two murder victims who meet the same fate—an echo of the coastal highway murders that turn up regularly in Cain and Chandler; cars, in the California crime story, are both status symbols and death instruments.

Wine drives across a vast landscape in his battered Buick from the Mexican-American barrio in East Los Angeles where he gets involved with an agitprop Chicano theater company, to a Hollywood Hills sa-tanic cult run by a faded movie queen, to a Nevada desert gaming/ prostitution resort for members only. He covers more territory by car than either Marlowe or Archer. After driving all day through the hot desert to the Nevada ranch, he gets drugged, beaten, and imprisoned before untangling the truth about the fix. Simon, working in a tradition closer to Macdonald than to Chandler, focuses his tough-guy tale on two interrelated Macdonald themes: the victimization of a son by a ruthless parent (Wine himself feels like a failed parent to his two boys) and the representation of California as destroyed Arcadia. The idealism represented by 1960s Berkeley (Wine's past) is set off against political corruption and patriarchal greed in 1970s Los Angeles (Wine's present). Even the name of the liberal candidate, Miles Hawthorne, may be Simon's allusion to failed idealism, evoking the name Miles Coverdale, the disillusioned idealist and failed utopian dreamer in Nathaniel Hawthorne's *The Blithedale Romance*. Wine, who was an English major, imagines Miles Hawthorne as looking like "a New England transcendentalist who got lost trying to find the twentieth century."(46)[22] There may be something ludicrous, even parodic, about the erstwhile radical Moses Wine, a man whose life is in such chaos, going against the real lines of urban wealth, power, and privilege with nothing more than a pistol and his old Buick, but Simon makes it convincing. *The Big Fix*, whatever the excesses and twisted convolutions of its plot, holds up well as a gritty exploration of the nexus of politics and greed, idealistic 1960s California dreams and 1970s corruption.

Kem Nunn's *Tapping the Source* (1984) and T. Jefferson Parker's *Laguna Heat* (1985) are not private eye novels as such but like Simon's and Hansen's novels involve searches deep into Southern California's demonic underworlds. The site of both novels is the beach community, where glittering surfaces betray, as they did in Brinig's *The Flutter of an Eyelid* and Hallas's *You Play the Black and the Red Turns Up*, dark and satanic realities. Nunn's book is about eighteen-year-old Ike Tucker's search for his missing sister in the surfer and biker world of Huntington Beach, a search that leads to drugs and to a satanic cult on a Santa Barbara ranch that links sex with human sacrifice. The novel culminates in a bloody, apocalyptic massacre as a biker attacks the ranch, rifle blazing. Grisly and melodramatic, Nunn's novel, his first, carries some real power in its exploration of the dark side of beach culture. Parker's *Laguna Heat* also explores the violent and sadistic netherworld of the Southern California beach town in a Macdonald-like story of the crimes in one generation coming back to haunt the next: here, in a highly implausible plot, a man named Azul Mercante, framed for a murder he did not commit (the killing of the Laguna Beach detective Tom Shepard's mother), comes out of prison seeking revenge against the men who colluded in the frame, including Shepard's father, an ex-cop who accidentally shot his wife when he caught her with Mercante.

The California beach town is also the turf of the best-known local female private eye, Sue Grafton's Kinsey Millhone, who, like Maconald's Lew Archer, is stationed in Santa Barbara (and like Macdonald calls it Santa Teresa). Grafton has been naming her Kinsey Millhone series alphabetically since *A Is for Alibi* appeared in 1982, followed by *B Is for Burglar* in 1985. She has reached, at this writing, the letter "O" with *O Is for Outlaw* (1999). Her detective is a twice-divorced former insurance investigator who lives alone in a "bachelorette"— no kids, no pets, no plants. She combines a tough-talking exterior with a compassionate, caring interior, particularly in dealing with female victims, in front of whom she is likely to get quite emotional. Millhone works by gaining the confidence of women, by getting them to talk, and by intuitive hunches, verified by tedious computer checking and cross-checking. One of her strengths is technology; another is her contacts. Although a loner in her private life, she knows and works with police detectives, Department of Motor Vehicles workers, newspaper reporters, and forensic experts. She makes mistakes sometimes, trusting the wrong people. In *A Is for Alibi*, for instance, she gets sexually and emotionally involved with a murderer and barely gets away with her life.

Grafton is one of several women who are writing novels featuring a female detective. Her best-known contemporaries are Sara Paretsky (creator of Chicago-based detective, V. I. Warshowski) and Marcia Muller (whose Sharon McCone mysteries are set in San Francisco). Recently there have been a good number of women writers writing about women detectives in Southern California. *Detecting Women 2*, edited by Willetta L. Heising, lists more than two dozen Southern California women detective series.[23]

One of the hottest writers in new Los Angeles detective fiction is Robert Crais, a Louisiana-born writer who lives in Encino in the Santa Monica Mountains. More than a half dozen Elvis Cole novels have appeared since *The Monkey's Raincoat*, published in 1987. Cole is a tough, wisecracking, and smart but sometimes hapless detective who lives in Laurel Canyon (the neighborhood of choice, it would seem, for the new detective), does yoga and Tai Chi on the deck of his "A-Frame" house, and has a decided preference for salade niçoise, Evian water, and Falstaff beer. He shares an office with his enigmatic, taciturn partner Joe Pike—who appears as deus ex machina to rescue Cole when he fumbles, which is often. Cole is a blend of Chandler's Marlowe and Robert Parker's Spencer—the knight who can't resist trying to save a woman in trouble and the detective who loves the good life. His 1966 Corvette is part of that good life, and when the garrulous detective isn't tracking down leads, karate-chopping evildoers, or rescuing damsels in distress, he drives the city. He truly loves Los Angeles and describes it lovingly from the windshield of his car, measuring distance traveled, as Angeleno commuters tend to do, in minutes, not miles. In *Free Fall* (1993) we get this description, with only the slightest irony:

> Driving along Santa Monica Boulevard through West
> Hollywood and Beverly Hills is a fine thing to be doing in
> late March, just at the end of the rainy season. It was warmer
> than it should have been, with highs in the mid-eighties and
> mare's-tail cirrus streaking in the sky with feathery bands,
> and there were plenty of men in jogging shorts and women
> in biking pants and Day-Glow headbands. Most of the men
> weren't jogging and most of the women weren't biking, but
> everyone looked the part.[24]

*Free Fall* takes its story from the Rodney King case—the videotaped beating of an unarmed black man, the acquittal of the police of criminal charges, and the subsequent urban uprising of 1992. One of the policemen in the novel, part of an elite squad with the acronym REACT, is named Mark Thurman (Mark Fuhrman was the policeman whose racist remarks heard in the courtroom during O. J. Simpson's trial enraged listeners). The novel's Thurman, though, is not a seasoned racist cop but a young, inexperienced member of the squad who clearly is in over his head; he stands by and does nothing while several other members of the squad beat to death a young black pawnshop operator in a sting operation. Drawing on recent history, Crais depicts in this novel racism and violence in the Los Angeles Police Department. Several African-American crime novelists have been representing the African American in the empowering role of private detective, investigating crimes inside and outside the ghetto — without the cooperation of the Police Department.

## VI

In the 1990s fiction of Gar Anthony Haywood, Gary Phillips, and Walter Mosley the African-American detective operating in Watts and South Central Los Angeles has come to represent a significant component of the local tough-guy novel. Haywood writes about detective Aaron Gunner, who works out of the back of a barbershop in South Central, his office separated from the barber by only a bead curtain. Gunner is tough, violent, and smart. In *When Last Seen Alive* (1998), the fourth in the series, the detective's search for a missing man takes him into an inner-city milieu of lost people, hidden and mistaken identities, a murderous black liberation group called Defenders of the Bloodline, and a lethal hit man named "Razor" Jack Frerotte, who is locked throughout the novel in a death struggle with Gunner. While the center of Haywood's activities is the inner city, he deals with the larger contemporary Los Angeles in which black and white worlds intersect. Phillips's Ivan Monk is also enmeshed in contemporary multiethnic Los Angeles. In *Violent Spring* (1994), for example, he investigates the murder of a Korean liquor store owner (followed by other murders) near the corner of Florence and Normandie, the site of the Rodney King beating. In *Perdition USA* (1996) he offers a nightmarish postmodern inner city of gangs, serial killers, and skinheads. Mosley, by contrast, looks back to an earlier Los Angeles in a series of novels set between the late 1940s and the 1960s, when Watts, the heart of the black community, was a more isolated, segregated zone.

Mosley thus is something of a cultural historian, a chronicler of the buried history of African Americans in Los Angeles, many of whom migrated from the South in the 1940s to work in the defense industry. His territory is one he knew from childhood. Born in 1952, he grew up in South Central Los Angeles at the very boundaries of the black and white city. His mother was a white Jewish schoolteacher, his father a black laborer. The world he puts in his novels, he has said in interviews, is one he knew firsthand as a child and from the stories his father would tell friends late into the night. Drawing on the memories and oral history of a place and time, Mosley, now living and writing in New York, has evoked a complex cultural landscape.

Easy Rawlins is a reluctant investigator, not a PI with a license but a man simply trying to survive in Watts. He has served in the war (part of the force that liberated the Nazi death camps) and has been fired from his job at an aircraft plant. Like his Watts neighbors, he is a migrant, a transplant from Houston. He shares his neighbors' migrant history, speaks their language, eats their food, drinks with their men, and sleeps with their women. He struggles to stay afloat, pay a mortgage, and raise two adopted kids in a place where the law has broken down and where the racist police cannot be counted on to help. As a man who knows the turf and has an "easy" relationship with his Watts neighbors, Easy is seduced, sometimes coerced, into solving problems, usually the problems of white men who need information or want to find missing people who have disappeared in the ghetto. What he discovers, though, and what he discloses are often two different things, as he negotiates the ground between loyalty to his community and the job he is paid to perform. He acts, reluctantly, as a cultural mediator, as link between black and white worlds. To the whites who represent the city's power elite—politicians, corporate heads, government agents—Watts is terra incognita, a city apart, a black city within a white city, unknown and incomprehensible to them. He is their link, their hired access.

Like so much Los Angeles fiction, the novels of Mosley are about two places and two times: history is a different place, a prewar era in the South that exists in memory and that the migrants try to replicate in postwar Los Angeles. Watts is geographically close to the city's center but culturally a place apart, rendered by Mosley almost as a southern country town. Easy finds information by dropping in on neighbors, sitting with them and chatting. He calls it a "country way" of doing business. "At that time," Easy says in A Red Death, "everybody in my neighborhood had come from the country around southern Texas and Louisiana."[25]

Easy moves through history in the novels, each a kind of time capsule of black Los Angeles, a recovery of a lost time—the postwar forties, the cold war McCarthyite fifties, the social cataclysms of the sixties. Living through changing times, he gets older, acquires rental property, gets divorced, raises his children, tends the fruit trees and flowers around his house. In the first novel, *Devil in a Blue Dress* (1990) (each novel is color-coded), he is a twenty-eight-year-old veteran hired by a white man to find a missing woman. In *A Red Death*, where he confronts postwar anti-Communist hysteria, he has become a businessman, a property owner who is being harassed by the IRS and the FBI. In *White Butterfly* (1992), which focuses on the serial killing of four prostitutes, one white, Easy's marriage has come to an end and he is struggling to support two children. *Black Betty* (1994) engages him again in a search instigated by a white man for a mysterious woman who has disappeared. And in *A Little Yellow Dog* (1996) Easy, now living on Genesee Street in the Fairfax district and working as a school custodian in Watts, is drawn into the disappearance of a woman teacher and the subsequent uncovering of two corpses in a garden on the school grounds. At the end of the book his sidekick, Raymond "Mouse" Alexander, a ruthless assassin but loyal friend, has been killed; it is the same day President Kennedy is shot.

In the sequence of novels Easy is revealed as both a local fixture and a bridge to the surrounding white world. He is an intermediary standing both inside and outside his community. His work takes him into every corner of Watts and also into the affluent Westside white world. His positioning in the ambiguous zone between racial and cultural worlds is brought home in the opening of *Devil in a Blue Dress*. In an ironic reworking of the opening of Chandler's *Farewell, My Lovely*, in which Marlowe finds himself in a black bar on Central Avenue, Easy is sitting in a bar in Watts when a white man walks in. The perspective is Easy's, the black patron, the insider, not, as in Chandler's novel, the white intruder:

> I was surprised to see a white man walk into Joppy's bar.
> It's not just that he was white but he wore an off-white linen
> suit and shirt with a Panama straw hat and bone shoes over
> white silk socks. His skin was smooth and pale with just a few
> freckles. One lick of strawberry-blond hair escaped the brim
> of his hat. He stopped in the doorway filling it with his large
> frame, and surveyed the room with pale eyes; not a color I'd
> seen in a man's eyes.[26]

The white man in Mosley's mirroring of Chandler is a fat blond man in a white suit who represents, caricatures, the power of the white world. His name is DeWitt ("de white") Allbright ("all bright"), and he is a study in white on white. He is, in this representation, the white devil (one thinks of Hammett again, who called Sam Spade a "blond satan"), tempting Easy Rawlins with money he desperately needs to pay his mortgage in exchange for finding the missing Daphne Monet. Easy becomes the detective, the black Marlowe hired by the white stranger to find a woman in Watts who, it turns out, is herself a marginal figure, literally both black and white.

The sense of Watts as a black community where the appearance of a white stranger would raise eyebrows is strong in the early novels but becomes weaker as the novels follow. Freeways in the 1950s and 1960s diminished the isolation of Watts from the larger city. Migration and urbanization pushed the borders of communities out, partially dissolving old cultural boundaries (black, white, Latino). What were farmland and fields between Watts and the rest of Los Angeles became housing developments. The black community, which, Mosley posits, drew some of its strength and regional identity from its isolation, begins in the more recent novels to erode. In the meeting of black and white worlds racism becomes more blatant and visible. Easy becomes more cynical, more bitter. In *Black Betty* the landscape reflects his mood. Feeling the pain of discrimination after being arrested and jailed by racist cops, and plagued by the traffic and smog in the city, the now-middle-aged Easy responds to a city "dense with smog, gray all around with a deepening amber color hanging low at the horizon." "If I took a deep breath," he says, "I felt a sharp pain in the pit of my lungs."[27] He still has affection for his home territory and its people, though. He is repelled by discrimination, consoled by acts of black heroism. We get this in *A Little Yellow Dog*:

> Southeast L.A. was palm trees and poverty; little neat
> lawns tended by the descendants of ex-slaves and massacred
> Indians. It was beautiful and wild; a place that was a nation,
> populated by lost people but that were never talked about
> in the newspapers or seen on the T.V. You might have read
> about freedom marchers; you might have heard about a
> botched liquor store robbery (if a white man was injured) —
> but you never heard about Tommy Jones growing the biggest
> roses in the world or how Fiona Roberts saved her neighbor

by facing off three armed men with only the spirit of God to guide her.[28]

With Walter Mosley the boundaries of the tough-guy private eye novel have been immeasurably stretched. However much he is working in the tradition begun by Chandler, he has realized new possibilities in the form. The detective is no longer the lone wolf whose personal life remains outside, and distant from, the criminal world he investigates. The mean streets he travels are his own. Although as cultural intermediary he ventures outside the black community when he has to, he is personally and intimately connected to that community, complicit with and loyal to it. He is implicated by everything he shares with his neighbors—race, language, poverty, a migrant history that began in the South, and the neighborhood itself. He knows who the people are, where they live, where they work. What he doesn't know, he finds out. He learns his neighbors' secrets, solacing and protecting them when he can. The care he gives to his orphaned children and his fruit trees and the pain he feels at the loss of his marriage, the death of friends, and the breakdown of community are qualities of mind that place him at a considerable distance from Philip Marlowe, the loner who stalked streets that were not his own, possessing so little in the way of friends and intimate connections.

Beyond the neighborhood, though, Easy Rawlins finds, as Marlowe does, that the city is impenetrable and ultimately unknowable. This unknowability is what, Mosley claimed, makes Los Angeles such fertile ground for detective fiction. In a 1995 interview he remarked, "It's impossible to know L.A. It's an extremely diffuse and diverse city. . . . a place of hiding. To be able to know a place, it has to at least in some ways want to be known. And L.A. just doesn't want to be known. L.A. is a big secret, which is why it is so good for the genre."[29] The uncovering of secrets is the task of the detective story, but Los Angeles remains at bottom impenetrable.

The tough-guy detective story from Chandler to Mosley has always posited an underground city, a hidden, invisible city beneath the revealed city, one that can be only incompletely known. Perhaps one can say this about the crime fiction of any large city, but Los Angeles presents a special case. There are, it seems, at least four reasons. In part it is a consequence of the city's vast geographic spread and its diverse, diffuse multicultural neighborhoods, in part a response to the city's long history of under-the-table corruption and law enforcement/criminal alliances, in part the fact that its writers have been until very recent times migrants or outsiders, and in part the fact that detective writers, like the Hollywood novelists, have been engaged, collectively, in the act of subverting the Los Angeles as Paradise myth propagated by the boosters.

Boston-based crime writer Robert Parker, who created the Spencer series of detective stories (and completed Chandler's unfinished novel, *Poodle Springs*, in 1989 and subsequently wrote a sequel to *The Big Sleep* called *Perchance to Dream*), offers a sense of the impossibility of comprehending Los Angeles when he takes Spencer to Los Angeles in *A Savage Case*:

> I didn't know any place like it for sprawl, for the apparent idiosyncratic mix of homes and businesses and shopping malls. There was no center, no fixed point for taking bearings. It ambled and sprawled and disarrayed all over the peculiar landscape—garish and fascinating and imprecise and silly, smelling richly of bougainvillea and engine emissions, full of trees and grass and flowers and neon and pretense. And off to the northeast, beyond the Hollywood Hills, above the smog, and far from Disneyland were the mountains with snow on their peaks. I wondered if there were a leopard frozen up there anywhere.[30]

Frozen leopards in the hills or not, the detective's conviction that he or she can know the city, discover its secret lines of power—get a fix on it and then fix it—becomes delusional in much of the fiction. The unknowability of Los Angeles is the theme of the most popular local detective film, Robert Towne's 1974 *Chinatown*. Noah Cross tells the detective Jake Gittes, "You may think you know what it's all about, but you don't." In the end Gittes's not-knowing leads to the death of the woman he has been trying to protect. Restrained by the police who are there to protect the rich and powerful, Gittes, in handcuffs, can only watch as his lover-client Evelyn Mulwray has her face shot away. "Forget it, Jake, it's Chinatown," his partner tells him— Chinatown meaning here, as trope, the unknown and unknowable dimension of the city.

This sense of an invisible city, an urban hell beneath the visible city, is the central, obsessive concern of James Ellroy's Los Angeles detective fiction. Like Mosley, Ellroy in the past decade has been reconstructing the city of the fifties and sixties, a postwar and cold war city in which the detective, no saint with gun, is complicit with the criminal underworld he investigates. But while Easy Rawlins, in the business of doing favors, gets caught up in the violence and killings in the ghetto, he is no match for the corrupt cops of Ellroy's "L.A. Quartet"—*The Black Dahlia* (1987), *The Big Nowhere* (1988), *L.A. Confidential* (1990), and *White Jazz* (1992). In an allusion to Raymond Chandler's remark that he wanted to take crime out of the drawing room and give it back to those on the streets who were really good at it, Ellroy said in an interview:

> I wanted to give crime fiction back to the leg-breakers of history, to soldiers of fortune, to bad white men, to racist shit-birds and the corrupt cops. I think the chief rule I've taken is to ignore the old warning of crime fiction editors worldwide: Namely that you've got to create sympathetic characters your readers identify with.[31]

No one would accuse Ellroy of giving his audience—a substantial audience now, since Curt Hansen's successful film adaptation of *L.A. Confidential*—sympathetic characters. The four novels of the Quartet offer a rogue's gallery of psychopathic cops, crooked politicians, corporate thugs, serial killers, violent strikebreakers, paid hit men, and organized crime kingpins. There are no good guys. Los Angeles is a demonic underground city controlled by alliances of the rich and powerful who want to be more rich and powerful and have the police on their payrolls. The legions of his satanic city, his shadow city, are fallen men who, like Milton's fallen angels, would rather rule in hell than serve in heaven.[32] Real-life figures (in name at least) like Howard Hughes, Mickey Cohen, and Sam Giancana mix it up with corrupt cops, some of whom—like Ed Exley, Danny Upshaw, Bud White, Jack Vicennes, Junior Stemmons, and Dudley Smith— reappear in different novels. For Ellroy's ruthless cops crime work is an obsession and a route to power, promotion, and wealth.

In the work of this self-proclaimed "demon dog of literature," we are given the darkest, most relentlessly brutal crime writing about

Los Angeles. No one is innocent, no one untainted. In Chandler's fiction the police were often on the take and could not be trusted. But there were honest cops, too. In Ellroy's fiction virtually every detective is eye-deep in slime. *L.A. Confidential* begins with a re-creation of the Christmas Day massacre of 1950 in which Los Angeles policemen drunkenly celebrating the holiday at police headquarters brutally attack a group of Mexicans who had been brought in after the breakup of a tavern brawl. *White Jazz*, arguably the most violent of the novels, is set in 1958. The multiple plot strands range over the personal and political crimes of an entire city, hinging on the red-baiting attempt (powered by Howard Hughes) to break up a studio union, a series of grisly killings by a psychopath, sexual perversion (incest and bestiality), an Iranian drug dealer who operates in the black ghetto, the eviction of Mexicans from Chavez Ravine to build a stadium for the relocated Brooklyn Dodgers, and the internecine warfare between Mickey Cohen and Howard Hughes when Cohen cuts in on Hughes's territory to make a movie called *Attack of the Atomic Vampires*, a production clearly reflecting cold war paranoia with its cast of atomic mutants.

Beginning with *L.A. Confidential* and reaching manic dimension in *White Jazz*, Ellroy evolved a style to match the ruthless subject matter and frenzied pace of his narratives. He described it in the interview cited above as "a paranoid tone, a stream of consciousness style that made the book[s] read like a fever dream." (242) It is what Dave Klein, the racist, homophobic, murderous detective in *White Jazz*, called "mind-jumping," a disconnected, discontinuous leaping from image to image, a semitelegraphic, free association projection of the mind of his characters. Here is the mind-jumping of Dave Klein, the most ruthless cop in Ellroy's lineup—slumlord with a law degree, communist hater and anti-Semite, murderer who has killed eight men and thrown a witness from a high window at the beginning of the novel, and a man harboring incestuous fantasies of his sister Meg as he twirls the dial on his car radio:

> Easy: My "crush" stretched me too thin—catch her stealing
> and snitch her—TODAY. Kicks: Get her a Commie lawyer
> enraged at big money—Morton Diskant, just the ticket.
> Arraignment, trial—Glenda plays cunthound. Morty off

in trade. "Guilty," State time, Dave Klein there with flowers
when they boot her.

Play the radio, drift.

Bop — maybe queer cops prowling Darktown — too jangly,
too frantic. Skim the dial, ballads — "Tennessee Waltz" —
Meg '51, that song, the Two Tonys — Jack Woods probably
knew the whole story. Him and Meg back on; I dumped a
witness and she got suspicious — and Jack wouldn't shit her.
She'd know, she'd be scared, she'd forgive me. Her and
Jack — I wasn't jealous — call him dangerous and safe —
and safer than me.

Back to bop — jangly good now — think.[33]

Ellroy's police detective fiction has roots in his own tortured personal history. In 1958 the ten-year-old Ellroy, who had been living
with his mother in El Monte, returned home to the San Gabriel Valley
city after visiting his father in Los Angeles to learn that his mother
had been murdered. Her body had been found near a high school
athletic field. Years later — after a troubled childhood with his father,
the death of the father, and a series of voyeuristic house break-ins,
burglaries, and drug and alcohol addiction — he was seized to the
point of obsession by the connection between his mother's unsolved
killing and that of Elizabeth Short, the "Black Dahlia," whose mutilated body had been found in an empty lot in Los Angeles in 1947.
Jean Ellroy and Elizabeth Short fused in his mind.

Ellroy's autobiographical memoir, *My Dark Places*, acknowledges
his childhood sexual attraction to and incestuous fantasies about his
mother.[34] Returning to the memory of these fantasies as an adult, he
hired a retired police detective, Bill Stoner, to reopen his mother's
case and traveled with Stoner down a long trail of leads that failed to
produce a killer. He wrote about the investigation in *Gentleman's
Quarterly*, and it became the occasion that propelled him into writing crime fiction. His compulsive quest for knowledge of the past and
resolution of the case after all the years that had passed was, he wrote,
his journey into self-knowledge, his exploration of the dark side of

his psyche. By attempting to exorcise his ghosts, he would come to understand himself. His 1987 novelistic revisiting of the Elizabeth Short murder, *The Black Dahlia* — discussed in detail in chapter 8 — is his most thoroughgoing probe of the obsessions that haunted him.

Ellroy has also stated in various places that his decision to write about police detectives stemmed in part from the model of Joseph Wambaugh, himself an ex-cop, who in the sixties and seventies wrote several tough LAPD detective novels, the best-known of which was *The Onion Field*, about an actual cop killing. It is, after all, Ellroy has reminded us, police detectives and not private eyes who solve murders in real life. Ellroy went far beyond Wambaugh, though, in his exploration of the underbelly of Los Angeles, beyond his contemporary in the police detective genre Michael Connelly, who has created in Detective Hieronymous "Harry" Bosch a "good cop," though violent and capable of irrational behavior,[35] and farther yet from Chandler, pushing the boundaries of the form almost beyond recognition, almost to the point of parody. In tracing the evolution of the genre from *Black Mask* stories of the twenties through Hammett, Chandler, and Macdonald up through the nineties, one has to ask where we go from here.

# 6

# SARGASSO OF THE IMAGINATION
## *The Hollywood Novel*

He thought of Janvier's "Sargasso Sea." Just as that imaginary
body of water was a history of civilization in the form of a marine
junkyard, the studio lot was one in the form of a dream dump.
A Sargasso of the Imagination! And the dump grew continually,
for there wasn't a dream afloat somewhere which wouldn't sooner
or later turn up on it, having first been made photographic by
plaster, canvas, lath and paint. Many boats sink and never reach
the Sargasso, but no dream ever entirely disappears.
NATHANAEL WEST, THE DAY OF THE LOCUST

People here
have become
the people
they're pretending to be.
SAM SHEPARD, THE MOTEL CHRONICLES

Writers we don't need. Indians we can always use.
—LINE FROM THE COEN BROTHERS' FILM, BARTON FINK

I

Toward the end of Nathanael West's *The Day of the Locust* Tod Hackett, artist turned set designer, stands on a sound stage where the film *Waterloo* is being shot. He watches in horror as the extras playing Napoleon's troops storm the unfinished wood and canvas set of Mt. Saint Jean. The hill collapses under their collective weight, dropping the soldiers to the floor beneath, sending dozens to the hospital. The scene not only foreshadows the novel's apocalyptic ending—a movie premiere riot in front of "Khan's Persian Palace" (Grauman's Chinese Theater)—but in a bizarre way recapitulates Napoleon's own miscalculation at Waterloo. History and fiction converge in a way wholly unintended by the filmmakers, and the consequences of taking the facade for the reality, the prop for what it represents, is graphically realized. It is this kind of confusion that lies at the center not only of West's novel but also of the greater number of novels that have taken Hollywood—place and industry—as their subject.

From its beginnings in the 1920s, the Hollywood novel has taken for its essential theme the confusion of reality and illusion, of lives lived and lives performed, of real and reel life. The results of such confusion can be disastrous. In West's dark Hollywood fable this conflation reaches a hallucinogenic level in the inability of his characters to distinguish living and acting. Identity is an utterly performative act, a matter of adopting screen poses. Characters walk the streets of Hollywood as if they are playing to the cameras, and the exotic houses they inhabit, aping and parodying every style in architectural history, look like they have been constructed on the movie lot by studio carpenters. Hollywood the town is represented as an extension of the movie lot—what West called the "dream dump" and the "Sargasso of the Imagination"—a pastiche of fantasy structures and costumed locals who appear to have just walked off a movie shoot. Although West's take on Hollywood has its antecedents in earlier fiction—like the novels by Harry Leon Wilson, Carl Van Vechten, Carroll Graham and Garrett Graham, and Myron Brinig discussed earlier—*The Day of the Locust* in its pervasive theatricality, its relentless tracing of the consequences of confusing real life and screen life, stands as *the* Hollywood novel, the essential source for almost every Hollywood novel written since.

Like the hard-boiled crime story and tough-guy detective story, the Hollywood novel had its real beginnings in the 1920s, reached its apex in the late 1930s and early 1940s, and then over the next half century persisted in acts of imitation, transformation, or parody. A single figure in each case—James M. Cain in the hard-boiled tradition, Raymond Chandler in the detective story, and Nathanael West in the Hollywood novel—gave the genre its definitive expression in the 1930s. In the immediate wake of West's novel came F. Scott Fitzgerald's *The Last Tycoon* (incomplete but published in 1941) and Budd Schulberg's *What Makes Sammy Run?* (1941). Thereafter fiction about Hollywood and filmmaking underwent a number of shifts, as filmmaking itself changed. The vertically organized, hierarchical studio system, with its despotic studio heads, contract stars, and disaffected writers that form the spine of the early novels, is long gone, but Hollywood fiction continues to be written, largely as romans à clef by people who grew up as Hollywood sons or daughters or have been, as adults, connected with the industry. Further, with the rise of independent filmmakers working all over the world, Hollywood becomes less identifiable as a geographic place; Hollywood is wherever movies are made.

## II

The starting point for any discussion of the Hollywood novel—as it is for the discussion of any Los Angeles novel until the most recent decades—is the fact that with the exception of the Hollywood-raised Schulberg, son of a producer, the creators of the genre were outsiders, writers drawn to the movie capital to write film scripts. With the invention of sound movies at the end of the twenties, the trickle of writers drawn to Hollywood turned into a tidal wave. The Vitaphone created a demand for dialogue—writers who could write it as well as actors who could speak it—and hundreds of writers, seduced by Hollywood dreams of steady work and high salaries, poured into the film capital—relatively unknown young writers like Cain, McCoy, and West, major literary figures like Fitzgerald, O'Hara, and Faulkner, and expatriate writers from England like Hallas, Belfrage, Huxley, Waugh, and Isherwood.

West, one of the early recruits, made the first of two sojourns to

Hollywood in July 1933. A shy, lonely New Yorker ironically nick-named "Pep," West had at the time two books behind him, both com-mercial failures. He had been working as a night manager in a Man-hattan hotel owned by his father when *Miss Lonelyhearts*, his second novel, was bought by the producer Darryl F. Zanuck. Hired to do the screenplay, he boarded a train for the West Coast, hoping to earn enough money to enable him to continue as a novelist. His brother-in-law, the humorist S. J. Perelman (married to West's sister, Laura), was already in Hollywood, having scripted the brilliant dialogue for the Marx Brothers films *Monkey Business* and *Horse Feathers*. West's first Hollywood encounter ended before the year was up; the novel was assigned to a team of hacks who managed, alchemically, to trans-mute a brilliant gem into a piece of innocuous fluff about a news-paperman and a murder. When the picture, renamed *Advice to the Lovelorn*, was released, the disheartened Pep was on a train heading back to New York.

In 1935 West was back in Hollywood working as a low-paid writer for Republic Studios ("Repulsive Studios" to the writers), scripting B movies, living in the tawdry Pa-Va-Sed apartment house on North Ivar Street (near Hollywood and Vine), and storing up material for the Hollywood novel he had been contemplating. His experience on the margins of Hollywood, unlike the experiences of his higher-paid "insider" contemporaries like Fitzgerald, Schulberg, and Huxley, situ-ated him to write the kind of book he did. His Ivar Street neighbors were an assortment of Hollywood discards—has-been comics, bit play-ers, stunt men, drugstore cowboys, and prostitutes. West came home one night and saw a prostitute kick what appeared to be a bundle of laundry in the corridor. The bundle moved and a dwarf emerged from it. The incident found its way into the opening of *The Day of the Locust*.

The surreal ambiance of West's Hollywood, the grotesque "half world" of outcasts and hangers-on, misfits and freaks, exotic cultists and disillusioned midwesterners he constructed, was grounded in ob-served reality—heightened and distorted, but real fixtures on the landscape. He observed it all: the exotic and eclectic architectural mix, the cultists and prophets preaching the way to regeneration through such means as chest weights and Aztec "brain-breathing," the throngs of extras who hounded Central Casting and paraded

Hollywood Boulevard decked out in full costume, and the masses of desperate migrants who simply stared at the masqueraders. These are the people, West wrote, who hung out at Glendale Airport anticipating plane crashes and at funerals hoping for the excitement of being witness to uncontrollable outbursts of grief. "Their boredom becomes more and more terrible," Hackett thinks. "They realize they've been tricked and burn with resentment. . . . The sun is a joke. Oranges can't titillate their jaded palates. Nothing can ever be violent enough to make taut their slack minds and bodies. They have been cheated and betrayed. They have slaved and saved for nothing."[1]

West's real subject in this novel he originally titled *The Cheated* is the pernicious effect of mass culture on individual and collective identity. The effect was more than local. With the coming of the movies, Hollywood became the epicenter of an entire culture cheated by the puerile fantasies of the industry. Fed on dreams of glamour and celebrity (which in the Hollywood myth is just around the corner), the migrant crowd in West's novel wanders the streets of Hollywood, in costume, striking movie poses, impersonating screen types. Along Vine Street, Hackett, in the novel's first chapter, sees people who "wore sports clothes which are not really sports clothes."

> Their sweaters, knickers, slacks, blue flannel jackets with brass buttons were fancy dress. The fat lady in the yachting cap was going shopping, not boating; the man in the Norfolk jacket and Tyrolean hat was returning, not from a mountain, but an insurance office; and the girl in slacks and sneaks with a bandanna around her head had just left a switchboard, not a tennis court. (60)

Here clothing, as signifier, is detached from conventional referents; outfits tell us nothing about class, wealth, status, occupation, social relations, or occasion. Consumer society has erased the old meaning of dress. What clothing does signify, self-referentially, is costuming itself, the *act* of dressing up. Dress is a way of constructing and performing an identity. With the Vine Street masqueraders, the walkons in the novel, and the major characters as well, the deliberately, self-consciously constructed self is the only self.

Alongside the Vine Street masqueraders are a different breed, those who wear "mail-order" clothing, "somber and badly-cut." These are the people who stare at the masqueraders, and when their stare is returned, "their eyes filled with hatred." They are the real cheated, the ones who have been fed on the dream and find that oranges and sunshine are not enough to satisfy their palates. Illusion feeds disillusion, and disillusion breeds envy, resentment, and anger, the kind that erupts in the orgiastic mob violence and sexual assault that brings the novel to a screaming halt in front of Khan's Persian Palace. "It was a mistake to think them harmless curiosity seekers," Tod thinks as he watches the premiere crowd gather. "They were savage and bitter, especially the middle-aged and old, and they had been made so by boredom and resentment." (177)

The thousands of bit players, those without speaking parts, the locusts of the title, become in the final reel the leading performers, tearing the Hollywood props down in a palace revolt that becomes one of the most devastating finales in American fiction. They enact, or actualize, the painting Tod has been working on throughout the novel, "The Burning of Los Angeles." The unfinished canvas pictures a mob of defeated Angelenos carrying baseball bats and torches, "a great united front of screwballs and screwboxes" fleeing the burning city, which is depicted along the top of the canvas as "a great bonfire of architectural styles, ranging from Egyptian to Cape Cod colonial" (184). Both apocalyptic and satiric, the painting frames the written narrative, gives it containment and form, embedding the chaotic events of the novel in the structure of art.

The critique of the culture of capitalism and consumerism that the left-leaning West offered was not directed, like the leftist novels of the thirties (by Dahlberg, Gold, Steinbeck, and others), at the industrial exploitation of the proletariat or the battle between organized workers and ruthless captains of industry, but at the manipulation of mass society, the kindling and betrayal of consumer dreams. Hollywood is both place and metaphor for this manipulation. If the novel is the severest indictment we have of the Hollywood dream, it is also the most far-reaching in its implications for American culture. More relentlessly than the Hollywood novelists who came before him, West traced the connection between the fantasies produced by the studios and the fantasies so desperately pursued by the American public. And coming as it did just as Hitler's storm troopers were marching through

Eastern Europe, "liberating" Poland and Czechoslovakia, the novel is also a cautionary tale about the manipulation of power—the power to control and harness the masses, narcotizing them with daydreams of regeneration and redemption.

The fantasy architecture West appropriates as a principal metaphor in the novel is one expression of the daydream: an expression of the West Coast migrant desire to step outside history. Houses, as simulacra, as ersatz replicas of historic designs, are spatial representations of the desire to abrogate history, to deny past time by domesticating it—as the movies themselves did by reconstituting history as escapist drama. Each of the main players in West's book lives in a fantasy house: Hackett and the Greeners in an apartment house fronted by a mustard yellow "Moorish" facade, Homer Simpson in an "Irish cottage" with fake thatched roof, Claude Estee in a masquerade of an antebellum plantation house. Hackett, a Yale-trained artist who has brought his eastern sensibilities with him, dwells on this movie-lot architecture with a blend of amusement, derision, and sadness. "It is hard to laugh at the need for romance and beauty, no matter how tasteless, even horrible the results are," he thinks as he walks along the slope of a canyon above Hollywood Boulevard. "But it is easy to sigh. Few things are sadder than the truly monstrous." (61) "Only dynamite," he muses, would be of any use against the ubiquitous architectural masquerades.

For West, who drew exclusively on the fantasy designs of Hollywood for his architectural imagery, the built landscape functions as projection, externalization, of the compulsive daydreaming and role-playing of an assortment of characters who have lost the ability to separate living and acting. Faye Greener lives each day as if she were in a costumed movie; her father, an ex-slapstick fall guy, suffers, or feigns, a heart attack, plays the role to its dramatic hilt, then dies; Claude Estee, a screenwriter, saunters back and forth on the veranda of his plantation house ("an exact reproduction of the old Dupuy mansion near Biloxi, Mississippi"), calls to his "black varmint" for a mint julep, and gets the Scotch and soda he really wants from his Chinese servant. Living and performing are one and the same.

In such a place even the natural world is rendered metaphorically in terms of the unnatural—the man-made, the movie-made, the painterly. Houses appear in "the soft wash of dusk." The edges of trees

against the sunset form "a violet piping, like a Neon tube." The sky
is rendered as a "blue serge sky" in which the moon pokes through
"like an enormous bone button." Food in supermarkets, bathed in
artificial light, takes on unnatural colors (oranges are red, fish pale
green). Looking out through a window, Tod sees "a square of enam-
eled sky and a spray of eucalyptus." What such images suggest, beyond the painterly eye of the narrator, is the sense that the organic
world has been replaced by the inorganic, by a man-made and commodified world from which we stand twice removed. It is the landscape of the movies, produced by technical skill, well-placed props,
and effective lighting.

Here a recurring theme in this and other Hollywood novels suggests itself: the disjunction between, on the one hand, sophisticated
technology and a high degree of competence and skill, and, on the
other, the meretricious ends to which this know-how has been put.
This is one representation of the familiar opposition in American literature between art and commerce, the creative mind and philis-
tine, marketplace values. In Hollywood it has elicited the myth of
the "sellout," the story of the writer as artist adrift in, and at odds with,
an industry concerned only with profit. The writer willingly sells himself to the industry for what he thinks will be a short time, finds himself by chance or accident in Hollywood (like the Graham brothers'
"Whitey" White), or is literally a captive, unable to escape (like Van
Vechten's Ambrose Deacon or Joe Gilles in Wilder's film *Sunset
Boulevard*).

The sellout myth—like every other myth about Los Angeles—was
an import. It was invented in the East by writers and critics who believed nothing good could come out of Hollywood—or anywhere
west of the Rockies, or, for that matter perhaps, the Hudson River.
Hollywood was the burial ground of talent, the place where fat salaries
ensnared writers and kept them from doing serious work. The very
financial success of the industry offered further proof of its egregious-
ness: anything that successful couldn't be good; anything that ap-
pealed so strongly to the masses was suspect. The industry, after all,
was run by immigrant rag merchants and glove dealers (references
to Goldwyn, Zukor, Laemmle, et al.) who knew nothing, and cared
nothing, about art. The writers were wage slaves (never mind that
some of these slaves earned big salaries) in a factory system that mass-

produced lowest-common-denominator entertainment. Edmund Wilson, who had high praise for Nathanael West's and F. Scott Fitzgerald's Hollywood fiction, nonetheless castigated the system that held them in captivity and had the power to vitiate their talents. Hollywood, to him, was the great destroyer.

The writers perpetuated the myth, particularly those like West who worked for the Poverty Row studios like Republic and Monogram. West wrote Josephine Herbst that "this stuff about easy work is all wrong. . . . All the writers sit in cells in a row and the minute the typewriter stops someone poked his head in to see if you are still thinking."[2] The myth has been dispelled by critics like Tom Dardis (in *Some Time in the Sun,* for instance) and more recently by others who have offered the counterargument that the Hollywood years were often the most creative and productive years for novelists, furnishing them with the material for a number of remarkable novels.

West, who worked by day at the studio and at night on his novel, wrote the most remarkable of them. It sold exactly 1,464 copies when it appeared in 1939. A year later West was killed along with his wife, Eileen McKenny (the sister Eileen in Ruth McKenny's play *My Sister Eileen*), when he ran a stop sign returning from a hunting trip in Mexico. He was thirty-seven. West's achievement, essentially four short novels, has been recognized most recently in its Library of America publication, edited by Sacvan Bercovich, a compilation of the four novels and almost four hundred pages of previously unpublished material including stories and screen work.

III

1939, the annus mirabilis in West Coast fiction and film, marked, in addition to the publication of West's novel, the appearance of John Steinbeck's Central California classic, *The Grapes of Wrath*; Raymond Chandler's first Philip Marlowe detective novel, *The Big Sleep*; Aldous Huxley's Hollywood fantasy/satire, *After Many a Summer Dies the Swan,* and John Fante's down-and-out Bunker Hill novel, *Ask the Dust.* Hollywood, seemingly undeterred by international events (Hitler's advances and Franco's crushing of the Spanish loyalists) and bolstered by the arrival of directors, actors, and film technicians who were fleeing war-torn Europe, continued to do what it did best: make films and make money. That year it invested some $170 million in more than five hundred features, among them some that are indelibly imprinted on our collective movie consciousness. It was the year of Victor Fleming's *Gone with the Wind* (which took most of the awards), Fleming's *The Wizard of Oz*, John Ford's *Stage Coach*, Ernst Lubitsch's *Ninotchka*, and Frank Capra's *Mr. Smith Goes to Washington*. It was also a year that demonstrated decisively Hollywood's ongoing infatuation with British and European material, releasing *Gunga Din*, *Wuthering Heights*, *Goodbye Mr. Chips*, *The Hunchback of Notre Dame*, and *The Private Lives of Elizabeth and Essex*.

Hollywood was clearly internationalizing in the thirties, both in terms of its story material and in terms of its employment of émigré auteurs. If it was ignoring the war clouds at the end of the decade (it was to change its tune in the next few years with a host of anti-Nazi stand-up-and-be-counted films like *Manhunt*, *Watch on the Rhine*, *To Have and Have Not*, and *Casablanca*), it was making good use of its talented refugees and expatriates. From its beginnings, though, Hollywood moviemaking was enmeshed in Europe. The industry's founders were by and large Jewish immigrants who were part of the mass emigration from central and Eastern Europe before and after the turn of the century, a generation before the exiles from Nazi Germany arrived: Carl Laemmle was born in Germany, William Fox and Adolph Zukor in Hungary, Samuel Goldwyn in Poland, Louis B. Mayer and David O. Selznick in Russia. That they gave America a steady diet of "American," that is, Christian and patriotic, movie fare both attests to their assimilationist values and reflects their defensive, don't-make-waves response to rampant anti-Semitism.[3]

Paradoxically the Jewish movie moguls who were excluded from the reactionary old-wealth downtown Protestant establishment were businessmen essentially as solidly Republican and anti–New Deal as the Christian oligarchs who had rejected them. To the movie tycoons, Upton Sinclair's EPIC campaign of 1934, the struggle to establish a writers' guild, and Roosevelt's labor policies each carried the specter of socialism or the fear of higher costs or taxes. Los Angeles, the town that Otis built, was an open shop, antiunion, laissez-faire place, and the studio heads wanted to keep it that way. That the majority of the writers they hired in the 1930s were the sons and daughters of eastern European ghetto Jews (estimates of the percentage of Jewish writers in the film capital vary from 60 to 80 percent) raised, often enough, on socialism and trade unionism and drawn, in some cases, to communism, put fear in the hearts of the Jewish studio heads. They wanted the writers' brains but not their politics.

During the 1920s and 1930s a second wave of European filmmakers arrived in Hollywood. When Billy Wilder and Fritz Lang came in 1934, refugees from Hitler's Europe (both born in Vienna), they joined a contingent of German, Austrian, and Eastern European filmmakers who had come in the previous decade: Ernst Lubitsch, Erich von Stroheim, Lewis Milestone, and Michael Curtiz among them. As the war approached, a host of actors, actresses, composers, conductors, architects, and novelists emigrated to Los Angeles. Among the novelists were Thomas Mann and his brother, Heinrich, Bertolt Brecht, Berthold Viertel and his screenwriter wife, Salka, Franz Werfel, and Lion Feuchtwanger. Exiles from Nazi Germany, they settled on the western fringes of the city (Pacific Palisades and Santa Monica), where, along with expatriate composers Arnold Schoenberg and Hanns Eisler, they constituted the artistic and intellectual elite of the Westside German-speaking community. But although their years in Southern California were productive, the German exiles wrote little fiction about the region. Jack Warner and other studio heads kept some of them on the payroll, more as acts of charity than anything else, but the expatriate writers produced little significant screen work. Mann spent his days completing the final volume of his Joseph tetralogy, *Joseph the Provider,* and writing his major work, *Doctor Faustus.* Werfel wrote his novel *The Song of Bernadette* in Los Angeles (almost immediately a best-seller, it was bought and filmed by MGM). Brecht's contribution to local writing was a series of poems, his "Hollywood Elegies," which excoriated Hollywood's money worship, its commercialism and disregard for art, and its commodification of sex. In 1942 and 1943 he collaborated with (and fought with) Fritz Lang on the film *Hangmen Also Die* (about the assassination of the Nazi commander in Czechoslovakia). In 1947, collaborating with his British-born friend Charles Laughton, he translated and adapted his play *Galileo* for an American audience. The play, which was directed by Joseph Losey and featured Laughton as the tortured astronomer, premiered at the Coronet Theater in West Hollywood in 1947.

Laughton was one of a good many British émigrés who arrived in Hollywood over the years, an impressive list that included Charles

Aubrey Smith, Charlie Chaplin, Stan Laurel, Cary Grant, Ronald Coleman, David Niven, Basil Rathbone, Alfred Hitchcock, Merle Oberon, P. G. Wodehouse, Deborah Kerr, and Laurence Olivier. Aldous Huxley came in 1937, planning to stay only a short time—just long enough to work on a screen version of the story of Madame Curie for MGM—but the impending war turned the journey into permanent resettlement. Isherwood arrived two years later, and he, too, became a permanent settler. In 1947 Waugh arrived on assignment to adapt *Brideshead Revisited*, returning to England after six weeks, the film adaptation never getting beyond the conference stage.

Unlike the German refugees, Huxley and Waugh plunged almost immediately into writing Hollywood novels, novels not focused specifically on the making of movies but on the pervasive fantasy and pretense they found in and around Hollywood: the moviemaking that takes place off-camera. In contrast to Isherwood's Los Angeles novel, *A Single Man* (1964), which took as its subject a single day in the life of a British-born college professor, Huxley's *After Many a Summer Dies the Swan* (1939) and Waugh's *The Loved One* (1948) are broad, extravagant comic and satiric fantasies encompassing Hollywood studios, cemeteries, and architecture. Central to both is the death industry, epitomized by the fantasy burial ground Forest Lawn.

Huxley's novel takes as its theme the California quest for eternal youth, reified in the novel by Jo Stoyte, an old millionaire dedicated to the proposition of living forever. He lives in an ersatz medieval castle on top of the Santa Monica Mountains with his "bit of yum yum," Virginia Maunciple, the daughter/mistress figure—both innocent child and sexy woman, madonna and whore. Virginia is, to Huxley, what Hollywood is about: the worship of youth, glamour, beauty, and innocence (in her case a façade masking prurience). She is the sister of West's Fay Greener and would reappear as Lulu Meyers, "queen of Supreme Pictures," in Norman Mailer's *The Deer Park* in 1955. Also on hand are Stoyte's retainers, one a quasi-scientist/spiritualist who advises him on the secret of eternal life (a diet of carp guts). And underlying the novel as a mythic presence is the story of Tithonus (Tennyson's version of which provides the novel's title), the Trojan prince who was granted eternal life by the gods but not eternal youth.

The perspective is that of a transplanted English scholar, Jeremy Pordage, who has been brought over to edit some rare manuscripts owned by Stoyte. Bookish and intellectual, he is totally out of place in Los Angeles. He is a Jamesian ambassador in reverse, encountering not an Old World of sophistication but a New World of seeming innocence and guilelessness, a Los Angeles of cheap and gaudy illusion. Met at the rail station on his arrival, he is driven through a landscape dominated by commercial buildings shaped like animals ("zoomorphs," Pordage calls them) and billboards and neons that shout at him: EATS, COCKTAILS, MILE HIGH CONES, JESUS SAVES, DRIVE-IN NUTBURGERS, BEVERLY PANTHEON, PSYCHIC READINGS, ABIDING WITH YOUTH IN THRILL-FORM BRAS.[4]

Stoyte's holdings include the "personality cemetery," Beverly Pantheon, and Huxley, anticipating his countryman Evelyn Waugh's fixation on Forest Lawn and the California death industry, renders the place as giant theme park, a tourist-trap repository of replicas of Old World churches and Greek statuary. The statues, all nude, all female, all "exuberantly nubile," are, Pordage reflects, "the kind one would expect to see in the reception room of a high class brothel in Rio de Janeiro." (7) They represent to him not the victory of spirit over matter, heaven over earth, but precisely the opposite: the victory of body, "the well-fed body, forever youthful, immortally athletic, indefatigably sexy." They offer the viewer "the promise of everlasting tennis, eternal golf, and swimming." (12) This is one promise of Hollywood: the denial of old age and mortality, the suspension of time and history, and a decidedly un-Tithonusian celebration of an ever-present now of sensuous pleasure.

Stoyte's castle, like the cemetery, signals the erasure of time, tradition, and moral authority. It is represented as "more medieval than any building of the thirteenth century . . . medieval not out of vulgar historical necessity, but out of pure wantonness . . . medieval as only a witty and irresponsible modern architect would wish to be medieval, as only the most competent modern engineers are technically equipped to be." (13) Inspired by William Randolph Hearst's castle in San Simeon, where the Huxleys had spent a weekend (just as Virginia Maunciple may have been inspired by Hearst's mistress, Marion Davies), the castle stands as symbol not only for the denial, or domestication, of history but also for the Hollywood yoking of technical skill and artistic irresponsibility, a theme West dealt with the same year. The extravagant architectural masquerade as well as the voluptuous cemetery statuary are Huxley's metaphors for Hollywood's trivializing of history, aesthetics, and significant ritual.

Evelyn Waugh, though in Los Angeles only a short time in 1947, visited Forest Lawn too—even dining with its visionary founder Hubert Eaton—and wrote a comic piece for *Life Magazine* titled "Death in Hollywood," which focused on that fantasy burial ground. *The Loved One* is broader in scope than Huxley's Hollywood novel, more international in implication. Walter Wells has written that it "makes Hollywood a metaphor for the fate of western civilization in the mid-twentieth century." Waugh's postwar Los Angeles, Wells adds, "has become the place to which the torch of European barbarism has been passed from a defeated Germany to an ascendant America, over the moribund body of English culture."[5]

The novel focuses on three displaced Englishmen. One commits suicide, another tries to get by with his British stiff upper lip, and a third, the poet Dennis Barlowe, works for a time as a studio writer, then takes a job at a pet cemetery adjoining Whispering Glades (the Forest Lawn cemetery) where he pursues the elusive cosmetologist, Aimee Thanatogenos. Whispering Glades, like Huxley's Beverly Pantheon, epitomizes the fantasy cemetery. The grounds have electronic sound effects imitating birds chirping and bees buzzing. The "loved ones" are cosmetically made up and outfitted by the chief mortician Mr. Joyboy and his assistant Aimee (allusion to Sister Aimee?) in a send-up of Hollywood movie costuming; as directors of production, they create roles for the corpses. Whispering Glades, resting place of "loved ones," museum of ersatz European art treasures (suggesting the overcoming of death through the permanence of art), and site of the pet cemetery, Happier Hunting Grounds, run by a German named Schultz (this only three years after the war), is Waugh's consummate image of the collapse of world culture; Hollywood is the ultimate dumping ground, the cemetery of civilization.[6]

Fantasy architecture recurs as metaphor in the novel, as it does in West's and Huxley's Hollywood novels. Barlowe, who has come to Hollywood to do a screenplay on the life of Shelley, is struck by the studio architecture.

When as a newcomer to the Megalopolitan Studios he first toured the lots, it had taxed his imagination to realize that

those solid-seeming streets and squares of every period
and climate were in fact plaster facades whose backs revealed
the structure of bill-boarding. Here the illusion was quite
otherwise. Only with an effort could Dennis believe that the
building before him was three-dimensional and permanent;
but here, as everywhere in Whispering Glades, failing
credulity was fortified by the painted word.[7]

Hollywood architectural illusion plays a less central role in Fitzgerald's *The Last Tycoon* and Schulberg's *What Makes Sammy Run?*
(Fitzgerald's was issued with the author's notes for its completion in
an edition edited by Edmund Wilson.)[8] Near the beginning of *The
Last Tycoon*, though, Fitzgerald does offer a scene of built landscape
illusion that launches the plot: producer Monroe Stahr (Fitzgerald's
rendering of MGM's "boy wonder" Irving Thalberg, the man who
commandeered the anti-EPIC faked newsreels of 1934) surveys the
flooded studio lot after the 1933 Long Beach-centered earthquake and
encounters the illusion of his dead wife floating on the severed head
of the Hindu goddess Siva. A case of mistaken identity, it evokes the
Gatsby-esque daydream that time, history, and mortality can be sus-
pended and that one can recapture the past, become again what one
once was. This bit of illusion aside, Fitzgerald makes little use of the
architectural landscape in the novel, surprisingly since he was so preoccupied with masquerade houses in *The Great Gatsby* and since
fantasy architecture plays so central a role generally in Hollywood
fiction. In this novel, however, his narrator, Cecelia Brady, unlike
Nick Carroway, West's Tod Hackett, or Huxley's Jeremy Pordage, is
not an outsider, a newcomer, but an insider, daughter of a studio
head. Valentino, she tells us, came to her fifth birthday party. Perhaps, too, the scant reference to local architecture reflects the fact
that the novel is not about Hollywood the place but Hollywood the
industry, the making of movies at a particular time in their history.
"My father," Cecelia writes, "was in the picture business the way another man might be in cotton and steel, and I took it tranquilly."[9]

Colored by her school-girl adoration of Stahr, Celia's patched-
together story (much of it composed of imagined scenes and events —
like the what-it-must-have-been-like narrative perspective of Nick
Carroway in *The Great Gatsby*), is a romantic idealization of the man

"who led pictures way up past the range of theatre, reaching a sort of golden age, before the censorship." (28) The tale she tells of Stahr's fall becomes a fable about the end of the line for the powerful, individualistic Hollywood moviemaker. (Thalberg died in 1936, before Fitzgerald's final trip to Hollywood.) Stahr is a Jew who rose from the immigrant ghetto of New York's Lower East Side, achieved success in the film world, and tried to use his power to serve both art and commerce. A benevolent despot, he is dragged down by forces that are both personal and industrial. Worn out by his futile love affair with the woman he mistook for his wife and trapped between capitalistic studio power wielded by eastern money interests and the rise of a collectivized workforce (the founding of the writers' guild, abetted by a visiting communist organizer named Brimmer), Stahr sinks downward toward total exhaustion.

The fall of a Monroe Stahr portends the rise of a Sammy Glick, the Hollywood tycoon as ruthless wheeler-dealer. In *What Makes Sammy Run?* Schulberg takes over in his first novel where Fitzgerald ends in his last.[10] The benevolent despot of the studio, the man willing to make a good movie even if it doesn't promise to repay its budget, surrenders to the slick operator, the Hollywood hustler, whose rise to studio head is achieved through a combination of plagiarism, deception, and sheer chutzpah. Schulberg, who grew up mainly in Hollywood, the son of former Paramount head B. P. Schulberg, tells the story with a mixture of fascination and contempt from the point of view of Al Manheim, a New York newspaper columnist who comes to Hollywood as a screenwriter. Whereas Fitzgerald, the outsider, tells his story from the perspective of an insider, Cecelia Brady, Schulberg, the insider, tells his from the perspective of a cynical outsider.

The perspective allows Schulberg to expose Hollywood—and Glick, as its success model—as corrupt parody of the American Dream, an industry that celebrates and rewards image over substance: the self-constructed image of a Glick over real talent and ability. The barbarians have taken over the palace and there is little place left for the honest craftsman. Sammy Glick is what Hollywood has become. Manheim, a German Jew, son of a reform rabbi, is, as narrator, the liberal conscience of the novel, given unfortunately to sometimes overbearing moralizing and pontificating about what Sammy means in terms of the death of art in the industry—as if indeed art had ever been alive in Hollywood. He spends much of his narrative trying to answer the title's question. Sammy Glick, who has risen from the same ghetto as Monroe Stahr, is running, Manheim discovers, from the poverty of his immigrant Jewish childhood; history, personal and cultural, is simply a hurdle to jump. The past counts for nothing in this twisted Horatio Alger reading of the American Dream. History is erased, debased, and trivialized—as it is in Fitzgerald's novel where, to cite two instances, the Jewish writer Manny Schwartz commits suicide in front of the Andrew Jackson shrine in Tennessee (icon of heartland America) and Abraham Lincoln (in full costume) stuffs a piece of pie in his mouth in the studio commissary between takes.

Glick is the archetypal performer who finagles his way to the top. After a few weeks in Hollywood, he rises from errand boy to scriptwriter (largely by stealing story ideas) and soon after bluffs his way into real studio power. When Kit Sargeant, the liberal screenwriter friend of Al Manheim (and one of those savvy, sophisticated, uncorrupted studio women who have always been fixtures in Hollywood fiction), meets Glick, he is soliciting payroll contributions to defeat Upton Sinclair's EPIC campaign: a day's pay for Frank Merriam. When the writers try to organize a guild, Glick double-crosses the writers by attempting to form a rival guild, a company union.

Schulberg's novel was attacked (as, a couple of decades later, Philip Roth's early novels would be) for its self-hating portrait of the unsavory Jew, which would allegedly fuel anti-Semitism. The attack came from both directions—left and right. The screenwriters in the Communist party criticized the book as offensive to Jewish party members and as failing to follow the party line in demonstrating the class basis for the struggle in Hollywood and the role the party played in the formation of the writers' guild. Reactionary Jewish studio heads were just as furious with the novel: Sammy Glick would contribute to stereotypes both about the movie industry and about Jews in the industry; the novel would contribute to anti-Semitism at home just at a time when Jews were being persecuted in Europe. Louis B. Mayer was incensed, shouting at B. P. Schulberg, "I blame you for this. God Damn it, B. P., why didn't you stop him?"[11] Schulberg, perhaps anticipating the criticism from the party of his father, may have attempted to deflect some of it by putting three other Jews in significant roles in the novel, all sympathetic figures. There are Manheim, the novel's moral register; Julian Blumberg, the nebbish writer but man of integrity whose stories Glick plagiarizes; and the producer Sidney Fineman, whom Sammy replaces as head of World Wide Pictures. Fineman, a foil to Glick, is an echo of Monroe Stahr, a man who wants to make good pictures but is ground down by the system. Sammy's rise is made possible by, and measured against, the fall of Fineman and the victimization of Blumberg. Still another character who represents the defeat of energy and ability in Hollywood is Henry Powell Turner, a Pulitzer Prize-winning writer, reduced to an alcoholic hack. Schulberg's portrayal of the grasping, finagling Jew as lead character, though, led to his being roundly criticized from all sides in Hollywood.

In his appearance before the House Un-American Activities Committee (HUAC) as a friendly witness, Schulberg told the committee how the Communist party, which he joined in 1937, criticized the stories he began publishing in the late thirties for being too "individualistic," including the one he was to expand into his novel. He left the party in 1939, he claimed, and went to Vermont to write the novel. At his hearing on May 23, 1951, he named fifteen Hollywood Communists, defending himself, disingenuously, by declaring that the writers had already been named, and so he was doing no further damage to them. He accused the party of "thought control" and blamed the party loyalty of his fellow writers, oddly enough, on guilt: the writers, he argued, were paid high salaries for doing little or nothing, and so paying 10 percent of their salaries for dues made them feel better about being hacks.

Writing many years later (1987) in the *Los Angeles Times*, Schulberg complained that Glick had become by the 1970s not the greedy, ruthless capitalist antihero he intended him to be but a positive role model for yuppies. Referring to comments made by college students and young adults at talks he had given, he concluded that Glick had been transformed into "a character reference: How to succeed in America when really trying" and the novel had become a tract on "looking out for No. 1." But as Terry Curtis Fox had pointed out in his 1985 article, "The Hollywood Novel," in *Film Quarterly*, it was perhaps Schulberg himself who might have become Sammy Glick, citing his HUAC testimony—the kind of testimony he says that Julian Blumberg, defending the guild against Sammy in the novel, would refuse to give. "In the thirteen years between *Sammy* and *On the Waterfront*," Fox wrote, "Schulberg turned into Glick."[12]

## IV

Both *The Last Tycoon* and *What Makes Sammy Run?* offer the fable of Hollywood in decline from a golden age. A fall, though, assumes a previous height, and one has to question whether, in Hollywood's history, there was ever such a time. Moviemaking in America has always been a commercial venture, a business enterprise, and if real geniuses, real artists, did come along—a Griffith, a Chaplin, a Keaton, even a Thalberg—they were never part of the original thinking. Writing at the end of the depression decade and in the eye of the international storm, Fitzgerald and Schulberg, like West and Huxley immediately before them, imposed their own, and the culture's, anxieties on Hollywood. The representation of the decline of Hollywood was, implicitly, a representation of the decline of American civilization, and by extension, particularly in West and Huxley, Western civilization itself. Hollywood was both metaphoric site and cultural symbol of the declivity of Western values.

In the years after the war, after West's, Huxley's, Fitzgerald's, and Schulberg's Hollywood novels, the studio system began its long unraveling. Antitrust legislation stripped the studios of their monopolies on production, distribution, and exhibition. Television, meanwhile, rose to challenge movie hegemony, and the HUAC hearings led to the blacklisting of hundreds of writers, actors, and directors, forcing the Hollywood left underground and depleting the industry of some of its best talent. Independent production companies were in the process of preempting the big studios, which in time would become pieces of huge media conglomerates. No longer would the major studios be averaging a picture a week.

In fiction, as in fact, Hollywood became less and less a place on the map. Hollywood was everywhere, everywhere that movies were made and moviemakers congregated. Peter Viertel's *White Hunter, Black Heart* (1953), about John Huston and the making of *The African Queen*, was set on that continent. Norman Mailer's portrait of the movie colony, *The Deer Park*, was set closer to home in a Southern California resort called Desert D'Or, a thinly disguised Palm Springs, as was much of *West of the Rockies* (1971) by Daniel Fuchs. Rudolph Wurlitzer's *Slow Fade* (1984) takes place all over North America — Mexico and New Mexico, New York and Newfoundland — with a subplot in India. And Josh Greenfeld's *The Return of Mr. Hollywood* (1984) is set largely in New York.

Displaced, the Hollywood novel continued to exploit the same themes: the confusion between reality and illusion, the conflict between commerce and art, the commodification of sex, and the erasure of both identity boundaries and an ordered sense of time and place. Mailer's *The Deer Park*, though set in the desert, features a commercial and domestic built landscape that, like West's Hollywood, is a purely deceptive construct. Even the name of the place, Desert D'Or, is a glamorous dressing up of the name of an old miner's town, Desert Door. Everything in town is disguised to look like something else. Stores look like living rooms, their goods hidden in drawers. A jewelry store is shaped like a cabin cruiser, moored strangely in the desert. Bars, where most of the activities and talk of the movie colony take place, look like jungles, grottoes, or theater lobbies. With their false ceilings, irregular shapes, and garish colors, they distort both a sense of time and a sense of place. Sergius O'Shaughnessy, the narrator, says of one watering hole, "Drinking in that atmosphere I never knew whether it was night or day, and I think that kind of uncertainty got into everyone's conversation."[13]

The movie people in the novel live with this sense of uncertainty. The performance of identity so pervasive in West's novel is a constant in Mailer's, too. Lulu Meyers, "queen of Supreme Pictures," is another version of the madonna/whore, love goddess blend, a Faye Greener or Virginia Maunciple who has made it big. Lulu, who has a penchant for making love while she speaks on the telephone or in the backseats of cars, is engaged to leading man Teddy Pope, a closeted homosexual — a match urged by Herman Teppis, tyrannical studio head, for its star-publicity value. Teppis is Glick, grown to middle age. Paternalistic, sentimental, and despotic, he is the consummate stereotype of the Jewish studio head, harking back to Jacob Schmalz in *Queer People*. He is a version of Pat Brady as well, the Irish Louis B. Mayer in *The Last Tycoon*. In a scene in Fitzgerald's novel Cecelia Brady, having just had a conversation with her father in his office, opens a closet door and a naked secretary pops out. In Mailer's novel

Teppis lectures Lulu on moral purity and the importance of marriage, and then when she leaves his office, a prostitute walks in, sits on his lap, then drops to her knees under his desk. Mailer, like the other writers of Hollywood fiction, constructs a movie colony of moral hypocrisy and sexual confusion. Sexual alliances are nothing more than stays against boredom and fatigue, signs of the failure of love, commitment, and loyalty. The lead male characters all suffer from some sort of emotional or sexual ambivalence: Teddy Pope, the leading man engaged to a starlet, is a secret homosexual; Sergius O'Shaughnessy, the guilt-ridden Korean War veteran, struggles with sexual impotence; Marion Faye, Mailer's familiar hipster/psychopath/ existential saint figure, rants about the coming apocalypse; and Charles Francis Eitel, blacklisted screenwriter, torn between leftist integrity and desire to remain in the industry, cooperates with HUAC.

Peter Viertel's *White Hunter, Black Heart* stands at the head of a line of contemporary Hollywood romans à clef, novels that would take their material from real-life movie encounters and real-life moviemakers, dissolving in some cases the boundaries between fact rendered as fiction and fiction rendered as fact. Viertel, son of émigré writers Biertold and Salka Viertel, wrote an earlier novel, *The Canyon* (1940), about growing up in Santa Monica Canyon in the twenties and thirties, a coming-of-age story focusing on his friendships with poor Mexicans living in a collection of shacks built helter-skelter up the canyon. When a raging brush fire, followed by torrential rains, destroys the shacks, real estate developers have their way and turn the canyon into a clean, new white suburb. Viertel's early novel (written when he was only nineteen or twenty) anticipates both the multicultural and environmental concerns of later Los Angeles writers. *White Hunter, Black Heart*, published thirteen years later, is his rendition of the shabby treatment he experienced working as a screenwriter on John Huston's *The African Queen*. It is not a memorable novel, though Huston casts a long shadow as a bigger-than-life dictatorial director who, though often either drunk or out hunting game, still manages to get the picture done.

Leo Wurlitzer's *Slow Fade* also deals with a screenwriter's experience with a contentious, bigger-than-life director—here not a single figure but a composite, it would seem, of Huston, Howard Hawks, and perhaps John Ford. The novel begins on one of those reality/

illusion confusion scenes: a rock band promoter named A. J. Ballou wanders on horseback onto a movie set and is shot by an Apache arrow. Wesley Hardin, a crusty, hard-drinking old director, while making what is to be his final western, has been trying to pull his son Walker out of a semicatatonic state by prodding him to write a screenplay about his sister's disappearance in India—the reason for the son's mental collapse. To compensate Ballou for the arrow wound, he hires him to hang out with Walker and co-write the script—a project the old man is less interested in than he is in finding out what happened to his daughter and what has paralyzed his son. The novel intercuts sections of the emerging India script with the story of Wesley Hardin's failed but heroic attempt to make one last film in Durango. The clear, precise imagery of the script is set off against the confused narrative of the fall of a once-powerful director, a narrative that itself becomes a movie when Ballou, an opportunist of the Glick variety, rolls the camera on Hardin's real-life collapse.

Erica Jong's *How to Save Your Own Life* (1977), Jill Robinson's *Perdido* (1978), Josh Greenfeld's *The Return of Mr. Hollywood*, and John Rechy's *Marilyn's Daughter* (1988) are still other recent Hollywood romans à clef, set wholly or in part in places other than Hollywood. Jong's Isadora Wing is the author's unflattering self-portrait, an expression of her anxieties over an unhappy marriage and the fame that followed the publication of *Fear of Flying*. A satirical novel set mostly in New York, *How to Save Your Own Life* focuses on the attempts of a tough, brittle agent named Britt Goldstein, a kind of female Sammy Glick, to get Isadora to sign a movie contract for her novel *Candida Confesses*. Robinson's *Perdido* is a coming-of-age story of a Hollywood daughter (Robinson is the daughter of MGM's Dore Schary) set in Pacific Palisades, Hollywood, and the East Coast. Robinson draws on her own childhood to tell the story of a girl searching for her identity by seeking the absent father. Hollywood actors like Ethel Barrymore, Cesar Romero, and Danny Kaye make appearances in this novel, set against the backdrop of the studio system's decline in the age of television. Rechy, the author of other local novels including *City of Night* (1963), about Los Angeles's homosexual underworld, and *The Amazing Day of Amalia Gomez* (1991), which I discuss in chapter 9, takes as his premise in *Marilyn's Daughter* a child born to Marilyn Monroe (fathered probably by Bobby Kennedy, perhaps Jack). In 1980 the daughter, Normalyn, at eighteen, leaves her Texas foster home for Hollywood in search of her identity, giving Rechy a chance to play off her present-day experiences with past scenes from Monroe's life. Greenfeld's *The Return of Mr. Hollywood* focuses, like Viertel's and Wurlitzer's novels, on a director—not a seasoned old-timer from the golden age, but one of the new breed of film-makers, a man who resembles Paul Mazursky. As Larry Lazar, the director is portrayed as a man who considers himself an auteur and in no need of collaborators. Returning to New York for his mother's funeral, he reestablishes contact with old friends (including figures who very much resemble the artist Larry Rivers, the film critic Pauline Kael, and the novelist Philip Roth) and on returning to Hollywood discovers in a final epiphany that he needs both friends and collaborators. Greenfeld, who received an Academy Award nomination for the screenplay for *Harry and Tonto* (directed by Mazursky), turns the title of Lazar's movie into *Herbie and Milty*, and the ongoing gag in the novel is that everyone Lazar meets has heard of the film but hasn't actually seen it—a reference to the film's fate as artistic success but commercial failure.

In telling tales about real movie people in their novels, writers like Viertel, Jong, Wurlitzer, Robinson, Rechy, and Greenfeld were doing in serious fiction what Hollywood "nonfiction" exposés (of the Christina Crawford *Mommy Dearest* type) or memoirs (of the Brooke Hayward *Haywire* type) or popular novels (of the Jacqueline Susann *Valley of the Dolls* type) had been doing for years: milking the public's fascination with the "inside stories" of the lives and personalities of movie stars.

Hollywood, recognizing the box office potential of sanitized confession, has been telling screen stories about itself since the thirties, since, for example, George Cukor's 1934 film, *What Price Hollywood?* (about Hollywood's use and abuse of stars) and William Wellman's 1937 spin-off of Cukor's film, *A Star Is Born* (about the rise of one star and the fall of another). In telling the tale of a powerful man's obsessive drive to make a opera star of his no-talent mistress (the Marion Davies figure), Orson Welles's *Citizen Kane* (1941) offers still another critique of the celebrity star system. Hollywood self-reflexiveness has also given us stars playing themselves: Billy Wilder's *Sunset Boulevard* (1950), for instance, which features Gloria Swanson portraying a version of herself as aging, delusional former silent screen star with a supporting cast of Eric von Stroheim and Cecil B. DeMille, each playing a version of himself. There have also been films in which stars play other stars: Faye Dunaway as Joan Crawford, the "dear mommy," and as Sister Aimee Semple McPherson, another Hollywood performer. In a recent twist Kim Basinger plays a prostitute who impersonates Veronica Lake in *L.A. Confidential*, based on the James Ellroy novel.

That a number of recent Hollywood novels, like those of Wurlitzer and Greenfeld, focus not on stars or powerful studio heads of the old type, but on hardworking if sometimes demonic directors reveals the change in the power lines of Hollywood. The old production-chief-on-top studio system that the Graham brothers, West, Fitzgerald, and Schulberg wrote about is gone—and with it the old power struggles and antagonism between writer and producer, craftsman and mogul, leftie and rightie, that framed many of the narratives of the thirties and forties. Hollywood, too, is gone, that neon and nutburger zone that externalized a state of mind. Hollywood has become the world and the world Hollywood. The place gone, what remains is the metaphor, which has been, in the end, the most real, most substantial thing about Hollywood since the beginning.

# 7

## DOWN AND OUT IN LOS ANGELES

### *From Bunker Hill to the Barrio*

You'll eat hamburgers year after year and live in dusty, vermin-infested apartments and hotels, but every morning you'll see the mighty sun, the eternal blue of the sky, and the streets will be full of sleek women you will never possess, and the hot semi-tropical nights will reek of romance you'll never have, but you'll be in paradise, boys, in the land of sunshine.
JOHN FANTE, ASK THE DUST

The shortest route between Heaven and Hell in contemporary America is probably Fifth Street in downtown L.A.
MIKE DAVIS, IN NEW LEFT REVIEW

I

Because most of Los Angeles's novelists until the most recent decades were men and women who came to the city as screenwriters, Hollywood and the affluent Westside — its beach communities, hills, and coastal canyons — have been the chief settings of the city's fiction. They are the sites the migrant writers knew best, the territories they could appropriate in fictions ranging in tone from the satiric to the hard-boiled to the apocalyptic. The instability of the land at, or near, the ocean's edge has repeatedly been invoked in the fiction and equated with the instability of the migrant population itself. The site of the meeting of land and sea, what Robinson Jeffers called "the drop off place," has provided the recurring locale and metaphor for dream's end: at the edge of the west coast the land turns back on itself, offers no farther place to go. But however seductive coastal and hillside Los Angeles has been to novelists, there is the fact that the vast majority of greater Los Angeles's residents do not live anywhere near the Hollywood Hills, the Westside, or the coast but inland, in the vast, flat zone that Reyner Banham called, "the Plains of Id," stretching in every direction from a downtown core: east across the Los Angeles River to the large Mexican-American barrio, south to Watts and South Central, south again all the way to San Pedro and Wilmington. This is the Los Angeles one sees from a plane coming in to land at LAX or from the freeway. This is undeniably and historically the heartland of Los Angeles, although a side of the city that Westside or San Fernando Valley residents seldom see — except from the window of a jet or the windshield of a car — or when they catch television images of it in flames.

Thomas Pynchon, writing just after the 1965 riot, reflected on the invisibility of vast reaches of the city to the white population. His direct reference is to Watts and to black-white relations in Los Angeles leading up to and just following the riot, but his remarks can be taken more generally to indicate the city's geographic and cultural segregation:

The two cultures do not understand each other, though
white values are displayed without let-up on black people's
TV screens, and though the panoramic sense of black

impoverishment is hard to miss from atop the Harbor
Freeway, which so many whites must drive at least twice
every working day. Somehow it occurs to very few of them
to leave at the Imperial Highway exit for a change, go east
instead of west only a few blocks, and take a look at Watts.
A quick look. The simplest kind of beginning. But Watts is
country which lies, psychologically, uncounted miles further
than most whites seem at present willing to travel.[1]

Although Don Ryan, in *Angel's Flight*, and Raymond Chandler,
particularly in *Farewell, My Lovely* and *The High Window*, explored
this vast inland territory in their fiction, they did so as outsiders, observers. But works like John Fante's *The Road to Los Angeles* and *Ask
the Dust*, Chester Himes's *If He Hollers Let Him Go*, Danny Santiago's *Famous All over Town*, Ron Arias's *The Road to Tamazunchale*,
Oscar Zeta Acosta's *The Revolt of the Cockroach People*, and the novels of Walter Mosley and Charles Bukowski offer a solid, if smaller,
body of fiction, largely ethnic, converging on inner-city Los Angeles.
For such writers the flat inland neighborhoods were home, not regions glimpsed in transit. They are urban places that exist almost as
different worlds from the Hollywood/Westside territory only a few
miles to the west, places inhabited today substantially by nonwhites,
zones marked and scarred by issues of race and racial conflict, poverty
and subsistence. In inner-city fiction, "making it" is not about rising
to the top but just surviving, hanging on.

## II

At the head of the list of down-and-out Los Angeles writers who have
represented the inner city is John Fante, an Italian American who
migrated to Los Angeles from Colorado in 1930, determined to be a
writer. In 1980, fifty years later and three years before his death, Black
Sparrow Press of Santa Rosa, California, reissued the author's long
out of print 1939 Bunker Hill novel, *Ask the Dust*, initiating an eleven-
year, twelve-volume publishing project that would make available in
paperback editions all the work of one of Los Angeles's most original
and engaging writers.[2] As the volumes appeared, one by one, the circle
of Fante readers widened. A writer who had made Los Angeles his

home and literary territory for more than fifty years was thus rescued from near-oblivion by this ambitious publishing project.

Fante's arrival on the Los Angeles literary scene in the early 1930s has its comic and bizarre side, an occasion appropriate to the comic nature of his writing. He was born in Denver in 1909, the son of an Abruzzi-born father and a Chicago-born Italian-American mother, and raised in nearby Boulder, where he attended a Jesuit school and for a short time the University of Colorado. In 1930 he hitchhiked to Los Angeles. When his first story, "Altar Boy," was accepted by H. L. Mencken for his *American Mercury* publication, Fante was living in a tiny apartment hotel on downtown's Bunker Hill and working as a busboy. News of the story's publication reached the *Los Angeles Examiner* and a reporter and a photographer were dispatched to Marcus Barbecue at the foot of the hill. The August 7, 1933, issue of the *Examiner* contained an article on the twenty-two-year-old "literary dish juggler" under the headline, "Bus Boy by Day, At Night He's Author." An accompanying photograph showed him serving a woman who, the caption read, was "casting admiring glances" at him. The article reported that he had a contract from Alfred Knopf for a novel. Although that novel, *The Road to Los Angeles*, the first to feature his autobiographical hero Arturo Bandini, was rejected by Knopf and remained unpublished until Black Sparrow issued it in 1985, the career of John Fante, literary "dish juggler," had its flamboyant launching.

Fante may be one of the few migrant writers who didn't go west to write for the movies, but a few years after his short stories began appearing in magazines ("Altar Boy" was followed by several other stories in *American Mercury* and other magazines), he landed a scriptwriting contract with MGM. He was to earn his living as a screenwriter for the rest of his life, although, like West, Faulkner, and others, he complained constantly that screen work kept him from fiction writing, his real love. In fact, while he did continue to write fiction until the end of his life, his best work was done in the 1930s, during and soon after his down-and-out years on Bunker Hill. His best and most characteristic work, *Ask the Dust*, which looks back to his time in the early thirties on Bunker Hill, was published in 1939—the Los Angeles/Hollywood annus mirabilis that also saw the publication of Chandler's *The Big Sleep*, West's *The Day of the Locust*, and Huxley's *After Many a Summer Dies the Swan*.

Forty-five years after his café launching in the *Examiner*, nearing the end of his life, his books out of print, Fante was again rescued by a strange and comic fate when novelist-poet Charles Bukowski cited Fante's 1938 novel, *Wait Until Spring, Bandini*, in his own 1978 novel, *Women*. Bukowski's publisher, Black Sparrow Press's John Martin, thought the title was some sort of joke (a reference to a popular brand of fertilizer). When things got straightened out, Martin, who like almost everyone else had never heard of Fante, enthusiastically began reissuing Fante titles. Thus, nearly a half century after Fante's newspaper "arrival"—a case of early, instant, and short-lived celebrity— he was rescued by a writer and a publisher with strong affinities to his work.

In the introduction to the first of the Black Sparrow reprints, *Ask the Dust* in 1980, Bukowski recalled his discovery of that novel on the shelves of the downtown public library in 1940:

> Then one day I pulled a book down and opened it, and
> there it was. I stood for a moment reading. Then like a man
> who had found gold in the city dump, I carried the book to
> a table. The lines rolled easily across the page, there was a
> flow. Each line had its energy and it was followed by another
> like it. . . . And here at last was a man who was not afraid of
> emotion. The humor and the pain were intermixed with a
> superb simplicity. The beginning of that book was a wild
> and enormous miracle to me.[3]

Now, thanks to Bukowski, and Black Sparrow Press, all of Fante's books are in circulation, some for the first time. In translation his works, like Bukowski's, have also been selling widely in France, Germany, Norway, and Italy. There is considerable film interest in his work too, both here and abroad. *Wait Until Spring, Bandini* was filmed in 1989 in a U.S.-Italian-Belgian coproduction directed by Dominique Deruddere (with Faye Dunaway and Joe Mantegna), and several other Fante titles have been optioned to the movies. The film interest in Fante's work has, moreover, spawned a number of magazine articles bearing such titles as "Fante Fever," "Fante's Inferno," "The Fante Phenomenon," and, most bizarrely, "The Hottest Dead Man in Hollywood."[4]

Fante lived to experience only the beginnings of this recognition. He died on May 8, 1983, at the Motion Picture and Television Country House, at the age of seventy-four. Although blind as a result of complications from diabetes, he worked right up to the end. Buoyed up by the new publishing interest in his work, he dictated a final novel, *Dreams from Bunker Hill*, to his wife, Joyce, from his hospital bed and their home in Malibu. The novel completes the "Bandini cycle" of four novels, begun in 1933 with *The Road to Los Angeles* and followed by *Wait Until Spring, Bandini* and *Ask the Dust*. From the 1940s movie writing and the need to support a growing family took up most of his energy, although he managed over the years a few good non-Bandini works like the exuberant *Full of Life* (1952, filmed with a Fante script in 1955) and the novellas *My Dog Stupid* and *1933 Was a Bad Year* (published for the first time by Black Sparrow in 1986 under the title *West of Rome*).

These works grow out of Fante's middle age and represent the writer in his more affluent screenwriting years. His early Bunker Hill and Wilmington period, though, offered him the materials for his best fiction. Bunker Hill in particular is Fante's real literary territory. Once an elegant neighborhood of 1890s Victorian houses standing between Temple and Fourth streets and Figueroa and Broadway, west of the commercial zone, Bunker Hill had become by the time Fante settled there a zone of rundown rooming houses and transient hotels inhabited by a multiethnic population of pensioners, laborers, and hangers-on.

Other writers knew the neighborhood in its decline from Queen Anne refinement. In *Angel's Flight* (1927) Don Ryan uses the vantage point from the top of the hill, terminus of the Angel's Flight funicular car, to satirize the boosterism and small-town religiosity of the downtown crowd at the foot of the hill. "Along with the religious farrago," he wrote, "marches the cult of the Booster. . . . And at the weekly luncheon [of the chamber of commerce] the reverend pastor of the Temple Baptist Church [is] proclaiming in solemn accents that if Jesus Christ were on earth today he would be a Rotarian."[5] Raymond Chandler, whose territory was all of Los Angeles, also knew the neighborhood. In *The High Window* (1943) Bunker Hill is the zone that marks the city's deterioration. Philip Marlowe calls it "lost town, shabby town, crook town," a neighborhood "inhabited by women with faces like stale beer . . . men with pulled down hats."[6] Some of the old Bunker Hill houses, he observes, are still standing, "the jigsaw Gothic mansions with wide circle porches and walls covered with round-end shingles and full corner bay windows with spindle turrets." Now, though, they have become cheap rooming houses with staircases "dark with time and with cheap varnish laid on generations of dirt." (167)

For Fante, newly arrived in the early thirties, the neighborhood was not an index of the city's physical or moral decay but the site of both a vital community and the frustrated dreams of a migrant population that crowded into the city in the twenties and thirties. Fante's fiction, like that of his thirties contemporaries, peels away the city's booster varnish, but as Stephen Cooper has written, "while he skewers the polished surface of pretense and illusion endemic to the city, it also celebrates, even exalts the rough substance of life as he finds it in the rented rooms and sooty streets of old L.A."[7] His Bunker Hill, as he offers it in *Ask the Dust*, is a region of both hope and despair, the California promise and its betrayal. It is where Bandini lives, dreams, hopes, where he completes his first novel and has his first sexual experience, but also the place where, for the dream seekers from the Midwest, last acts are played out:

> Dust and old buildings and old people sitting at windows,
> old people tottering out of doors, old people moving
> painfully along the dark street. The old folk from Indiana
> and Iowa and Illinois, from Boston and Kansas City and
> Des Moines, they sold their homes and their stores, and
> they came here by train and by automobile to the land of
> sunshine, to die in the sun, with just enough money to live
> until the sun killed them. . . . Smith and Jones and Parker,
> druggist, banker, baker, dust of Chicago and Cincinnati and
> Cleveland on their shoes, doomed to die in the sun, a few
> dollars in the bank, enough to subscribe to the *Los Angeles
> Times*, enough to keep alive the illusion that this was paradise,
> that their little papier-mâché homes were castles. (45)

The passage recalls West's description of the deracinated masses who roam the streets of Hollywood, gawking, zombie-like, at the

Hollywood masqueraders. But while West's voice is detached and derisive, Fante's reveals a genuine sympathy for the inhabitants of the city, tinged more with sorrow than irony; he is one of them: "The uprooted ones, the empty sad folks, the old and the young folks, the folks from back home. They were my countrymen, these were the new Californians. With their bright polo shirts and sunglasses, they were in paradise, they belonged."(45) Fante's Bunker Hill may not be "paradise," but neither is it the locus of dream's end, as it is to West. It is the place Bandini encounters the world, confronts his desires to be both writer and lover. His voice is not that of the prophet of doom, commenting sardonically, contemptuously, on the fallen land.

The irony in *Ask the Dust* is not directed so much outward at the city as failed paradise as it is inward toward its narrator Bandini's own self-deception, the ridiculous figure he cuts, and knows he cuts, as he negotiates his world. Early in the novel, for instance, he sees an attractive Mexican-American waitress, Camilla Lopez, working in a greasy spoon café and he chuckles, convincing himself for the moment that the gesture "had a powerful effect on her." We know, of course, and Bandini knows too, that it has no such effect. Posturing and ego-preserving affectation are exposed for what they are. Sexual bravura masks sexual fear. Bandini, nursing his own insecurity, may hurl insults, sometimes racial, at Camilla and at his neighbors, but he is also drawn irresistibly toward them. His sympathy extends to the even less fortunate ones, those who can't afford the sunglasses and cheap polo shirts and who live to the east of Broadway—on the streets and flophouses of Skid Row, along Fifth Street, Main Street, and Los Angeles Street. This neighborhood hasn't changed the way Bunker Hill (the locus of the city's downtown redevelopment) has since Fante's day. The streets east of Pershing Square have yet to undergo major renovation, though in districts like Little Tokyo one can see the eastward reach of international capitalism. Bandini forays east from Bunker Hill in *Ask the Dust*: to the burlesque houses on Main Street, to cheap bars and cafés, and once on a drug-buying trip to the black ghetto with Camilla, but Bunker Hill is home territory.

Fante's Bunker Hill is peopled not only by déclassé migrants from the Midwest but also by an assortment of immigrants and ethnics— blacks, Filipinos, Portuguese, Mexicans—crowded together with poor whites in a few square blocks in the center of the city. He is one of the first local novelists to give us this ethnic mix. His downtown is an enclave of dance halls and taxi dancers (catering to lonely Filipino cannery workers), saloons and Mexican cafés, vagrants and pensioners who roam the streets. There are some wonderful comic characters among the down-and-outers in *Ask the Dust*: Mrs. Hargraves, Bandini's landlady with her middle-class pretensions and Anglo-Saxon pieties; Hellfrick, his rooming house neighbor, who guzzles gin and fries cheap steaks in his room, dressed only and always in a bathrobe; and Vera Rivkin, the lonely, crazed, scarred, middle-aged Jewish woman who recites Edna St. Vincent Millay and provides Bandini with his sexual initiation, possessing him like a demon.

The seduction, enacted in Vera's Long Beach apartment and narrated as pure black comedy like something out of Nathanael West's *Miss Lonelyhearts*, is followed by Bandini's postcoital Catholic guilt. He contemplates walking out into the ocean when, like a cosmic response to his personal sin and that of the city, the 1933 earthquake strikes: "It was an earthquake. Now there were screams. Then dust. Then crumbling and roaring. I turned round and round in a circle. I had done this. I had done this." (98)

"Los Angeles was doomed," he concludes. "It was a city with a curse on it. This particular quake had not destroyed it, but any other day another would raze it to the ground." (102) Granted, this is the fluster of a guilt-ridden Catholic boy, but the symbolic appropriation of Los Angeles as the site of the apocalypse has been a pervasive feature in the city's fiction. Fitzgerald uses the same 1933 quake to bring on the studio flood that precipitates producer Monroe Stahr's descent from his Heaven, and Myron Brinig—prophetically, since his novel was published in the earthquake year 1933—has the entire coast slide into the sea in *The Flutter of an Eyelid*.

The destructive encounter with the natural landscape is often matched, or counterpointed, in Los Angeles fiction with an absurd, comic encounter with the built landscape. Here was another disaster zone that writers could use as an emblem for human and cultural failing. Exotic fantasy architecture in and around Hollywood, as I have indicated in an earlier chapter, provided the newly arrived writers with a principal metaphor for the pervasive role-playing and masquerading of the city's inhabitants. Fante, whose chief territory was the inner city and not the dreamscape of Hollywood, was less preoccupied than his screenwriter contemporaries with fantasy architecture, but he nonetheless plays on the odd, improvisational character of the built landscape in his description of Bandini's rooming house. The Alta Loma Hotel is seemingly built upside down, against the side of the hill. The entrance is on top of the hill and the floors go down as their numbers go up. Bandini lives on the tenth floor—level with the ground beneath the hill. He enters and exits his room through the window. Outside the window stands a single palm tree, grotesquely black at its branches, stained by carbon monoxide from cars coming out of the Third Street Tunnel that cuts through the hill.

Fante was neither a Hollywood novelist (though as screenwriter he touched on his movie career in his later work, particularly *Dreams from Bunker Hill*) nor one of the hard-boiled boys in the back room. The city he offered in his 1930s work is less the graveyard of California dreams—as it appeared to most of his contemporaries—than a place alive with hope and possibility, desire and allure. His unglamorous, un-Hollywood central-city neighborhood is a diverse, multiethnic enclave represented without sentimentality, derision, or a sense of impending doom. The young Bandini may envision the earthquake as apocalypse, but Fante makes it clear that the envisioning is that of an impressionistic, guilt-haunted Bandini, not the author's own apocalyptic haunting.

## III

Soon after Fante's arrival in Los Angeles in 1930, he began a long correspondence with his literary idol H. L. Mencken that was released in a Black Sparrow volume in 1989. The letters were largely one-sided. Fante, from rented rooms in Bunker Hill, Wilmington, and other places, wrote long, sometime obsequious epistles to his master, alternatively boastful and self-reproachful. He bragged about his talent and berated his failures. In response to his passionate, urgent letters, Mencken, thirty years his senior, sent back cool, clipped, commonsensical notes, supportive if not encouraging of his young worshiper in California. The letters are of interest not for what they say about the life lived but for what they reveal about the inner life of the writer-in-the-making. They display a personality compounded of comic bravura and apprehension about his talent, passionate desire and angry frustration, self-aggrandizement and self-contempt. It was a life Fante was spinning out of his own emotions and re-creating as the life of Bandini. In the end Mencken, who urged him to write from his own Italian Catholic life, became Fante's chief short story publisher.

Mencken, the self-styled "village atheist," had friends in town and was generous in making introductions. Through Mencken Fante came to know Carey McWilliams, journalist and author of some acute social and political histories of California before leaving for New York in 1951 to take on the editorship of *Nation*—books like *Factories in the Fields, North from Mexico, California: the Great Exception,* and *Southern California: An Island on the Land.* The last remains, more than a half century after its 1946 publication, the liveliest social history of Los Angeles, *the* certified antibooster, debunking treatise. McWilliams, in that book, cites Fante as one of the best novelists he came across in his Los Angeles years.

Like Fante, McWilliams was a migrant from Colorado. He arrived in Los Angeles in 1922, went to work for the *Times*, completed law school at the University of Southern California, wrote an early book on Ambrose Bierce, and became in the thirties and forties the vital center of several overlapping literary, intellectual, and political circles in Los Angeles. Fante and McWilliams became fast friends in the thirties. McWilliams's diary contains dozens of references to Fante: their dining and drinking (frequently and copiously) together at Hollywood restaurants like Lucy's and Musso and Frank's, car trips to Santa Barbara, and water taxi voyages to the gambling ship *Rex*. McWilliams introduced Fante to Louis Adamic, the radical Yugoslav-born author of *Laughing in the Jungle* and *My America,* and William Saroyan, an Armenian American from Fresno who spent a considerable amount of time in Los Angeles. Through McWilliams Fante also met the screenwriters Jim Tully, Ross Wills, Frank Fenton (who wrote an unimpressive Los Angeles novel, *A Place in the Sun*), A. I. Bezzerides (author of a California trucking novel, *The Long Haul*), and Humphrey Cobb (author of *Paths of Glory* and later a target of the HUAC Hollywood witch-hunts).

McWilliams's vital role in the city's intellectual and literary life extended to his involvement in the founding of two famous local bookshops. He helped organize the first bookstore of Jake Zeitlin, At the Sign of the Grasshopper, near the downtown library. Zeitlin then moved his shop west to a location on Sixth Street (a Lloyd Wright-designed building), west again to Westlake Park in the Wilshire district, and then again to his Red Barn on La Cienega Boulevard in West Hollywood. His shops with their rare books and vintage editions became a meeting ground of local literati like Phil Townsend Hanna (editor of *Westways*, the auto club magazine), Paul Jordan Smith (the *Times* literary editor), Lawrence Clark Powell (essayist and novelist who became head librarian at the University of California, Los Angeles), the poet Hildegarde Flanner, and the journalist-activist Herbert Klein.[8] McWilliams also helped to set up the bookshop of another Texan, Stanley Rose, first on Vine Street and then on Hollywood Boulevard, next to Musso and Frank's. Rose was a noted raconteur and entertainer who was rumored to have a business on the side peddling pornography to the studios and had a reputation as well for being a con man, though McWilliams, not one to suffer fools, sees him more as an innocent dupe of his business partners than as a villain. His store, like Zeitlin's, became a hangout in the 1930s, but for a far different crowd: it was the proletarian—and Hollywood writers'—counterpart to Zeitlin's shop, attracting with its lively talk and its legendary backroom orange wine the likes of Saroyan, Cain, Faulkner, Fitzgerald, Erskine Caldwell, Fenton, West, Jo Pagano, A. I. Bezzerides, Tully, and Fante. "Jake," McWilliams wrote, "drew the swells and big names, whereas Stanley's stores served as a clubhouse for the garrulous wise guys and writers on their way up."[9]

If it was Mencken who gave Fante a literary start, McWilliams who offered friendship and encouragement, Rose who provided him a proletarian writers' "salon," and Bukowski who rescued him from obscurity fifty years after his career began, it is also the case that Fante, inadvertently, rescued the young Bukowski back in 1940—gave the twenty-year-old drifter who hung around the downtown library before the war a sense of literary direction, a way of writing with "humor and pain" and "superb simplicity." Bukowski was eleven years Fante's junior. He was born in Andernach, Germany, in 1920, the son of an American soldier stationed in Germany in World War I and a German mother. The family settled in America when he was three, moving after a short time to Los Angeles, where Bukowski attended Los Angeles High School and for a time Los Angeles City College just before World War II (as Fante sporadically attended Long Beach

City College a few years earlier). He worked a variety of jobs over the next few decades (including a twelve-year stint at various post office branches in Los Angeles, giving him the material for his first novel, *Post Office*, in 1971), traveled back and forth across the country several times, and began writing poetry and short fiction, achieving in the 1960s a reputation as an underground poet in mimeographed journals and small publications like the *Free Press* and *Open City*. He also began his lifelong drinking habit. His alcoholic binges in the 1940s and 1950s with Jane Cooney Baker became the source of his self-constructed "barfly" myth, the material of his 1989 movie script and the subsequent novel *Hollywood*, about the making of that film.

He was fifty-one when *Post Office*, featuring the semiautobiographical persona Henry Chinaski, appeared in 1971. Chinaski was to be the recurring fictional self in all but the last of his novels. He is the autobiographical protagonist in *Factotum* (1975), *Women* (1978), *Ham on Rye* (1982), and *Hollywood* (1989). A final novel, *Pulp*, completed just before his death from leukemia in 1994, abandons the Chinaski mask in favor of a raunchy, violent, parodic, noirish detective hero, Nick Delane (whose name clearly is an echo of Mickey Spillane). *Post Office* establishes the persona of the drink-sodden, working, and womanizing protagonist engaged in a series of episodic, picaresque, and chance encounters in a comic-absurdist Los Angeles compounded of petty bureaucratic civil servants, con men, and lost and lonely women. Chinaski as postal employee is a fool and comic bungler, but also a man capable of outwitting his dim-witted bosses, the mad dogs he confronts on his route, and the housewives and old maids who stand on curbs waiting for mail. His comic irony, directed so often, like Fante's, inward, at the self, is what distinguishes Bukowski's voice from those of Hemingway and Henry Miller, the writers with whom he is most often compared in terms of their direct, immediate, and colloquial styles. One can see some parallel with Miller in the aggressive freedom and celebration of sex and the body his works exhibit, but Bukowski's work, in its comic absurdity, has little of the weight of either Miller or Hemingway. In his personal, self-mocking manner, his flights of self-aggrandizement followed by periods of self-condemnation, he is far closer to the writer he most admired, Fante.

Like Fante (and like Miller) he draws directly on the materials of his life—heightened almost to the point of surrealism. *Post Office* deals, comically and painfully, with his dozen years in the postal service, *Women* with his obsessive womanizing and drinking. Set in the 1970s when Chinaski/Bukowski is in his fifties, the latter novel includes the entrance and exit of some twenty women. The Chinaski persona is now a well-known poet, but rather than talk about any writing he is doing, he focuses his narrative on his sexual conquests, which he justifies as "research" for the writing. The sex is often violent, assaultive, and cruel; it is often, as well, it should be added, initiated by the woman, and periodically Chinaski, as a result of his drinking, is not up to the act. The two later Chinaski novels explore the past: *Factotum* looks back on a series of menial jobs during the 1940s and *Ham on Rye* on the earlier period of his youth in the 1920s and 1930s. A kind of bildungsroman, *Ham on Rye* explores the emergence of the Chinaski/Bukowski personality out of an abusive childhood, one that conditioned lifelong fear and self-condemnation but also habits of endurance and toughness.

Bukowski's appeal to his fans today derives, above all, from his direct, autobiographical, improvisatory mode, qualities that comprise, according to one of his strongest admirers, Gerald Locklin, "the dominant mode in Southern California."[10] Bukowski's poetry and prose fiction have been translated into several languages and have attracted a huge following, particularly in Germany, his birthplace. Published in this country by Black Sparrow and City Lights, his works, both poetry and prose, have enjoyed large audiences, especially on college campuses in Southern California, notably at California State University, Long Beach, where Locklin teaches and where Bukowski gave readings more than once. Locklin, himself one of the country's most prolific poets, views Bukowski's poetry as "the product of a movement toward the spoken idiom that is at least as old as Wordsworth's Preface to the second edition of *Lyrical Ballads*." (31) This is true, but as Locklin acknowledges, the line of descent from Wordsworth's Preface to Bukowski is so tangled that one is tempted to look closer at hand for more direct antecedents. The 1950s New York school of poets and the Beats—less Ginsberg to be sure than the rapid-fire, semiautomatic writing of Kerouac—provide closer linkages.

Like Kerouac, too—and unlike Ginsberg—Bukowski grinds no political axes. World War II, postwar McCarthyism and the HUAC investigations, and the anti–Vietnam War movement are hardly registered by Bukowski, whose protagonist is more interested in downing a bottle of gin, finding a woman to share his bed, and betting at the racetrack. His direct, "in your face" manner, though, won him lots of readers, among them John Martin, who gave him a sinecure and a publishing home. By the late eighties Bukowski was Black Sparrow's top-selling author. Fante, who came to Black Sparrow through Bukowski, was, and is, a close second in sales.

IV

Raymond Chandler's *Farewell, My Lovely* opens with Marlowe looking for a missing husband. "It was one of those mixed blocks over on Central Avenue that are not yet all negro." Almost immediately he is shoved into a bar by a giant hoodlum named Moose Molloy, just out of prison and looking for his old girlfriend Velma Valenti who sang there when it had been a white bar in a white neighborhood. The point of view is Marlowe's as he enters the bar:

> The chanting at the crap table stopped dead and the light over it jerked out. There was a sudden silence as heavy as a waterlogged boat. Eyes looked at us, chestnut-colored eyes, set in faces that ranged from gray to deep black. Heads turned slowly and the eyes in them glistened and stared in the dead alien silence of another race.[11]

Moose apparently can't understand the change in the skin color of the bar's patrons. When moments earlier he pushed Marlowe through the swinging doors, he saw a young black man and tossed him out, explaining to the detective, "A dinge. I just thrown him out. You seen me throw him out?" "It's that kind of place," Marlowe responds, "What did you expect?" (3)

What *did* he expect? Long before 1940 Central Avenue had, in fact, become the geographic center of black Los Angeles, a north-south axis cutting through the district known as Watts, center of its commercial and night life. But then Moose has been in prison.

There were African Americans among Los Angeles's earliest settlers, but their numbers increased in the 1880s and 1890s, again in the 1920s, and most dramatically in the 1940s, when they came to work in defense plants, despite the industry's early hostility to black workers. In segregated Los Angeles, where, before the war, they worked as railroad porters, farmers, construction workers, and day laborers, blacks settled in or near downtown, in the Temple Street area, not far from Fante's Bunker Hill, in the Budlong neighborhood to the south near Adams Boulevard, and farther south and east in Watts, an area then given over largely to sugar beet fields and livestock raising. By 1920 about 40 percent of Los Angeles's black population lived in and around Watts, within a few blocks of Central Avenue. When Watts was annexed to Los Angeles in 1926, essentially as a move to dilute and control the black vote, Los Angeles was no less a Jim Crow city than the places in the South from which most of the black migrants came, the result both of the Klan's resurgence nationally and the presence of so many white southerners who had migrated to Southern California in earlier decades. During the World War II years more than three hundred thousand blacks (approximately ten times the number who were in Los Angeles before the war) migrated into the city, settling largely in Watts and South Central.

From the 1920s to the 1940s Central Avenue, Watts's main commercial corridor, was a kind of Harlem West, a linear strip lined with R&B and jazz clubs, record stores and recording studios, and breakfast and after-hours clubs. Jazz spots like Club Alabam, Memo, Downbeat, Bird in a Basket, and the Dunbar Hotel were packed with mixed black and white audiences. Bands like Louis Armstrong's, Jimmy Lunceford's, Duke Ellington's, and Count Basie's performed on Central on their western tours, and in the forties virtually every major East Coast bop musician played on Central—Thelonious Monk, Charlie Parker, Dexter Gordon, Charles Mingus, Hampton Hawes, and dozens of others. In his splendid book *West Coast Jazz* Ted Gioia notes that while standard jazz histories stress the movement of jazz upriver from New Orleans to Chicago, "just as early jazz came from the Crescent City to California."[12] Jazz, though, was only one part of the avenue's musical and entertainment scene, which extended in the 1940s to gospel, vaudeville, dance, and stand-up comedy.

Black Los Angeles appears only sporadically in fiction before the 1940s. Louisiana-born Arna Bontemps, who grew up in Los Angeles before moving to New York in the 1920s to participate in the Harlem

Renaissance, described the horse and cattle country of 1920s Mud-town in his novel *God Sends Sundays* (1931), the story of a rakish black jockey, Little Augie, who makes a lot of money and spends it lavishly on women, liquor, and cars. With Countee Cullen he adapted the novel for the Broadway play *St. Louis Woman* in 1946. Dorothy Baker's 1938 novel, *Young Man with a Horn*, offers a picture of urbanized Central Avenue in the thirties focused on the black jazz clubs along the avenue.

In two novels written in the forties, *If He Hollers Let Him Go* (1945) and *Lonely Crusade* (1947), Chester Himes offered the most painful witness to the migration of blacks into wartime Los Angeles to work in the defense industry. Best known for his Harlem cycle of police novels written in the fifties and sixties featuring the raffish detectives Coffin Ed Johnson and Grave Digger Jones (*Cotton Comes to Harlem* among them), Himes wrote his two Los Angeles novels before the Harlem novels and before his long expatriation in Europe. He was born in 1909 in Jefferson City, Missouri, and attended Ohio State University until he was thrown out for allegedly carrying on with drunken classmates at a Columbus whorehouse. The son of middle-class parents (his father taught at a small college), he was divided in his youth by a desire to make good in white society and a self-conscious rebellious streak in which he affected a tough black street hustler image. He was arrested more than once for theft, then sentenced to twenty years in Ohio State Penitentiary for armed robbery after breaking into the house of a wealthy white family. He had served more than seven years of that sentence when he was paroled in 1936. In prison he became a writer, channeling his hot-tempered violent side into fiction, publishing prison stories in *Esquire* and other magazines. As it would later alter Malcolm X, prison changed him, reshaped his consciousness. After his parole he worked as a bellhop, waiter, Works Progress Administration (WPA) construction worker, and a contributor to the Cleveland WPA Guide. He was writing all the time.

He migrated with his wife to Los Angeles in 1941 with a letter of introduction from Langston Hughes, hoping to sell the stories he had been writing to the movies. Unable to find work in the racist studio system, he spent the next three years in the equally racist environment of Southern California's defense industry. The Japanese attack on Pearl Harbor intensified West Coast nativism and xenophobia.

Japanese Americans were rounded up and placed in internment camps, Mexican Americans were victims of brutal beatings in downtown Los Angeles, and discrimination against blacks—in housing and jobs— reached a sickening peak. The protagonists of Himes's two Los Angeles novels are defense plant workers who are almost psychotically torn apart by the hatred and hostility they face daily. Like Richard Wright's Bigger Thomas (*Native Son*, 1940), Himes's protagonists are reduced to a state of alternating fear and anger, helpless panic and explosive, uncontrollable rage. The racism they experience in Los Angeles is as brutal as anything they experienced in the South or the Midwest. Himes, who worked, he claimed, twenty-three jobs in Los Angeles between 1941 and 1944, including a stint in a naval shipyard in San Pedro, wrote in his autobiography:

> Los Angeles hurt me racially as much as any city I have ever known—much more than I can remember from the South. It was the lynching hypocrisy that hurt me. Black people were treated much the same as they were in an industrial city of the South. They were Jim-Crowed in housing, in employment, in public accommodations, such as hotels and restaurants. During the filming of *Cabin in the Sky* starring Esther Waters, Bill "Bojangles" Robinson, and Lena Horne, the black actors were refused service in the MGM commissary where everyone ate. The difference was that the white people of Los Angeles seemed to be saying, "Nigger, ain't we good to you?"
>
> The only thing that surprised me about the race riots in Watts in 1965 was that they waited so long to happen. We are a very patient people.[13]

Like Himes himself, Bob Jones, the protagonist in *If He Hollers Let Him Go*, has come west from Ohio after Pearl Harbor, finding himself in a defense plant, as a "leaderman" (supervisor of a black team). He is beaten and demoted for striking back at the brutality of his white superiors and then in the novel's key scene, tempted and terrorized by a white woman, Madge, a blowzy Texas blond co-worker, who tries to seduce him in a closed compartment on an unfinished ship. Fear overpowers his desire for the woman. He panics and tries to get out. She screams rape, and the navy police break the door down. He is beaten senseless. The vignette is played with the same sense of inevitability as anything in Richard Wright's South or Chicago. All three players—Jones, Madge, and the military police—are acting out preassigned racial and gender roles: once the white female cries rape, there is no way for the black man to protest his innocence. He is a victim because he is black and male, not because of anything he has done. All he can do is run, which he does blindly and madly through the streets of Los Angeles. He travels by car all over the city until he is finally picked up by the police, a wholly broken man, and given the option of going to jail or serving in the army.

Lee Gordon in *Lonely Crusade* is another version of the black hero reduced to emotional cripple by racism. An educated black with a degree from a Los Angeles college, he is hired as a union organizer at Comstock Aircraft, his job to recruit black workers. The union has been infiltrated by Communists. A black Communist organizer named McGregor tries to buy Gordon's loyalty by setting him up with a white lover, a Communist (in name at least) named Jackie Forks. Himes is again playing on the stereotyped black male and white female sexual magnetism, with its neurotic blend of desire and fear. In this aggressively anti-Communist novel, the Communists are represented as ruthless power mongers whose union activities have nothing to do with racial, or even economic, justice. McGregor is revealed as a double agent paid by the capitalist owners to spy on the union, and by the Communists for doing the same thing. Himes's treatment of the red scare, written just as HUAC was investigating Hollywood, anticipates, as Mike Davis points out, "the emergence of an anti-Communist *noir* in the Korean War years," figured in B films like *Stakeout on 101* and Mickey Spillane's "sado-McCarthyite thrillers."[14]

A half century after Himes's wartime Los Angeles novels, Walter Mosley, from the perspective of the 1990s, looked back at black Los Angeles from the 1940s to the 1960s in his Easy Rawlins crime novels. The second of the novels, *A Red Death*, takes place in 1953, just after the time represented in Himes's *Lonely Crusade*, carrying forward into the Cold War era an account, though a far different account, of the anti-Red hysteria central to Himes's novel. The Korean War has come to an end, the Eisenhower fifties have begun, and the hunt for Reds has become the government's dominant obsession.

Mosley, who was clearly influenced by Himes (more by the Harlem detective novels than the Los Angeles novels), situates his reluctant detective hero in a racist and red-baiting Los Angeles. In return for release from a back-tax felony rap imposed by a racist, corrupt IRS official ("Some people make an awful lot of noise about equality and freedom, but when it comes to paying their debt, they sing a different song"[15]), Easy Rawlins is coerced by an FBI agent to do surveillance on a Communist labor organizer, "one of those communist kind of Jews" (48), operating in the black ghetto.

Easy here, as in the other novels in the series, must negotiate the ambiguous territory between his own community and his very survival, which depends on some cooperation with the white power structure. Unlike Himes's representation of the Communist organizer as self-serving power broker, Mosley's Communist is a wholly sympathetic figure, Chaim Wenzler, who spends most of his energies distributing clothing to the poor in Watts. If Himes was guilty of demonizing his Communists, Mosley is guilty of sentimentalizing his. Easy is torn between performing the surveillance that will keep him out of prison and his emerging friendship with, and loyalty to, Wenzler, who fought in the Polish underground during the war and most of whose family were killed by the Nazis. Wenzler tells Easy he works in the ghetto "because Negroes in America have the same life as the Jew in Poland. Ridiculed, segregated. We were hung and burned for just being alive." (91) Black and Jewish history merge here; Jim Crow America and international anti-Semitism are two faces of the same evil. Mosley, the son of a black father who had migrated from the South and a Jewish mother, and who grew up in South Central Los Angeles, carries a dual heritage that allows him to see the relationship between Holocaust history and the violence done to blacks in America.

That violence comes to Easy Rawlins most often in the form of power-wielding whites who thrust themselves into the black community demanding information. Mosley's Watts of the forties and fifties was an insular community, an enclosed enclave of blacks, most of them recent migrants from Texas and other southern states. People knew one another, shared a language, a culture, a familiar way of relating to one another. In Mosley's reconstruction, postwar Watts has a small-town southern atmosphere. An essential difference, in fact, between the fiction of Mosley and Himes is that Mosley, as insider, constitutes his black Los Angeles as a community—one that is constantly threatened from without but which nonetheless has its solidarity—whereas Himes's protagonists are outsiders who exist without community, without participation in a group life to lend them support. Both Bob Jones and Lee Gordon are existential loners living on the margins of a city from which they are wholly alienated. The awareness of the power whites have over them and won't hesitate to use is constantly on their minds, and there is no black community to fall back on.

Another difference between Himes's and Mosley's fiction is that Himes was writing directly out of a life he was at that time living and suffering, whereas Mosley was reconstituting, resurrecting a time and place in history. His is an act of historical and cultural reconstruction. Watts has changed enormously since the postwar years, and Mosley in his more recent novels has been chronicling the changes as the series has advanced into the 1960s with A *Little Yellow Dog* (1996). Watts is no longer an exclusively black community but a mixed neighborhood of blacks, Mexican Americans, and Asians, as the conflagrations of 1965 and 1992 have reminded us. It is still though, an essentially invisible enclave, terra incognita to most of the city's whites.

## V

East of Watts, across the Los Angeles River, lies the large Mexican barrio. East Los Angeles, particularly the neighborhood called Boyle Heights, once a Jewish enclave, has become since the 1920s chiefly a Mexican zone. Mexican Americans, the most populous group in both the city and county (about 40 percent compared to about 38 percent whites), have been inhabiting other regions of the basin as well—notably South Central, the neighborhood around MacArthur Park, Long Beach, and parts of suburbanized Orange County and the San Fernando Valley.

Despite their numbers, Mexican Americans have figured only marginally in Anglo fiction about the city. When Mexican-American characters do appear, they tend to do so as exotic elements or as undifferentiated members of a large working class. Raymund Paredes has observed that although

people of Mexican ancestry constitute a larger proportion
of the city's population than at any other time in this
century . . . Anglo residents continue to acknowledge the
presence of Mexican Americans only grudgingly. . . . As
much as ever, Mexican-American culture seems curiously
disconnected from general Anglo perceptions of the city,
literary or not.[16]

During the last few decades, however, partly as a consequence of
the national civil rights movement, the Chicano rights movement in
Los Angeles, and, more generally, the increasing identity-awareness
of Mexican Americans, some significant Mexican-American novels
set in Los Angeles—the city with the highest number of Mexicans
outside of Mexico—have appeared. Among them have been Oscar
Zeta Acosta's *The Revolt of the Cockroach People* (1973), Ron Arias's
*The Road to Tamazunchale* (1975), and Thomas Sanchez's *Zoot-Suit
Murders* (1978).[17] All three, though grounded in the real life of the
city's Mexican-American community, cross conventional, generic
boundaries: Acosta between fiction, personal memoir, and reportage;
Arias between realism and the "magic realism" that has been the
fictional realm of Latin American writers like Borges, Márquez, and
Fuentes; Sanchez between fiction and history. A fourth Chicano novel,
Danny Santiago's *Famous All Over Town* (1983), while not rooted in
a particular historical event, tells with convincing detail the story of
a boy coming of age in the East Los Angeles barrio.

Acosta, a friend of Hunter Thompson, entered literature as a character, appearing as the three-hundred-pound Dr. Gonzo, Samoan
lawyer and cultural outlaw, in *Fear and Loathing in Las Vegas* (1971).
A year later, Acosta, a poverty lawyer in Oakland, encouraged by
Thompson, published his first novel, *The Autobiography of a Brown
Buffalo*, set in the Bay Area. The following year he published his fictionalized memoir of his involvement in the Chicano protest movement in downtown Los Angeles at the end of the sixties, *The Revolt
of the Cockroach People*. Just as the buffalo in the title of the first work
metaphorically links Mexican-American life in California to the fate
of the slaughtered animal, the cockroach metaphor of his Los Angeles novel is a reference to the degradation of the Latino—the hated
insect underfoot in Anglo society. Five years after the Watts rebellion

and in the surrounding context of the anti–Vietnam War protests, Chicano activists rose up in Los Angeles. The city's indifference, and its hostility, to its submerged Latino population gave rise to the cockroach people's revolt that Acosta, as witness and participant, chronicles.

The style of Acosta's Los Angeles book is what Thompson called "gonzo journalism": excessive, heightened, manic personal journalism in which the reporter is also the principal actor, directly involved in what he records. The line between spectator and performer blurs, as does that between recorded events and fictional reconstruction in Acosta's drugged-out, sometimes hallucinatory encounters with both the contents of his consciousness and the events on the streets of the city. The vision is violent and apocalyptic, his manic style echoing what he sees as the sickness, the psychosis, of the city itself. "As his own literary creation," Paredes (in the essay cited above) has written, "Acosta embodies the very excesses and paradoxes that give Los Angeles its distinctiveness: quite simply Los Angeles never drew the attention of a writer so much like itself." (243–44)

The events are those surrounding the Chicano Moratorium of 1970, but shaped and filtered by the subjective consciousness of the participant-observer. We get the assassination in Los Angeles of Robert Kennedy, supporter of Chicano rights and friend of Chicano activist César Chávez; the boycotting of schools that fail to provide Mexican history for their Mexican-American students; the picketing of an affluent Wilshire Boulevard cathedral that ignores the plight of poor Mexican Catholics on the Eastside; Acosta's attempt to win the acquittal of arrested Chicano activists; the grisly witnessing of an autopsy on a Mexican youth who allegedly hanged himself in prison but was most likely beaten to death; and the death of Ruben Salazar (called in the novel Roland Zanzibar), a Los Angeles Times reporter and television commentator who was killed during the riot by a gas projectile fired by a sheriff's deputy into a bar. Acosta takes part in the bombing of the downtown Hall of Justice — the work's climactic conflagration — after which he leaves the city for San Francisco. (The real-life Acosta disappeared from sight a year after the novel was published.) In the aftermath of the riot much of East Los Angeles is in flames, a napalmed Vietnam:

> Whittier Boulevard is burning. Tooner Flats is going up in
> flames. Smoke, huge columns of black smoke looming over

the buildings. . . . Here a police van was overturned, its engine smoking. There a cop car, flames shooting out the windows. Cops marching forward with gas masks down the middle of the debris. An ordinary day in Saigon, Haiphong, Quang Tri and Tooner Flats.[18]

The image of the city in flames, familiar not only from apocalyptic renderings of the city from Nathanael West to the present but also more immediately from the Watts riots five years earlier, stands here as representation of rage against a city that has, since the Anglo conquest prospered at the expense of its large but submerged Mexican-American population.

One expression of the alienation of the Mexican American in Los Angeles is the violent, rebellious stance of the *vato loco* (crazy guy), descendant of the "pachuco," the "zoot suiter" of the 1940s and 1950s, who has since evolved into the "tagger." Gang initiation has allowed the tagger, Acosta writes (in a shift to second person that signals his empathy for the graffitist), "to put your mark, your initial, your sign, your badge, your *placa* on your turf with the name and initial of your gang:. . . . Quatro Flats, Barrio Nuevo, The Jokers. . . . " (91) Danny Santiago's 1983 novel, *Famous All Over Town*, is the portrait of one such tagger, Rudy "Chato" Medina, who grows up in the poor Latino neighborhood of Lincoln Heights, lying just east of the river. The novel covers several months of Danny's boyhood in the early sixties. Structured as a series of chronological episodes (each a short chapter), the narrative traces Chato's gang involvement leading to a joyride in a stolen car, a friend's death, Juvenile Hall detention, and, at the end, the family's eviction from the neighborhood when a government-business conspiracy takes the land to build a Southern Pacific rail line, razing the neighborhood and dispossessing its tenants. Chato's father moves in with his mistress; his mother returns to Mexico. The collapse of the family is linked to the destruction of the neighbor-hood. Chato, on his own, goes on to become "famous all over town" as a graffiti artist, inscribing, until he is arrested, his nickname all over East Los Angeles. As rogue hero Chato has something of J. D. Salinger's Holden Caulfield and Twain's Huckleberry Finn in him: the young hero as rebel, as outsider making his mark on and against the establishment grain.

The novel was initially well received. Santiago was hailed as the

Chicano author of a promising first novel. In fact, Santiago was really an Irish-American writer named Daniel James. A former Communist, James left the party in 1948 but was called before HUAC in 1951. Following his blacklisting, James moved to Lincoln Heights in East Los Angeles with his wife and became active in youth activities in the neighborhood, including the formation of theater groups. He began writing stories about the neighborhood from a Latino perspective in the sixties, some of them, like the award-winning story "The Somebody" (featured in Martha Foley's Best Stories of 1971), dealing with Chato Medina and ultimately winding up in the novel. His decision to use a Hispanic pseudonym, he claimed, was both to free his writer's block (to get away from the rational, doctrinaire mindset of his Communist years) and to lend some authority to his Mexican-American fiction. He persuaded a reluctant John Gregory Dunne to help him publish his fiction under the Santiago pseudonym. Then, in 1984, a year after the novel was published, Dunne, in a *New York Review of Books* article (August 16), "outed" Santiago, revealing that the author was really his old friend Daniel James. In the ensuing, and meaningless, controversy over whether *Famous All Over* Town is or is not a Chicano novel, James/Santiago had the support of such influential Mexican-American writers as Richard Rodríguez and Thomas Sánchez. Nonetheless, the reputation of the book suffered. To some the writing of the book was an act of betrayal. A highly praised novel was dismissed as a hoax, a pretense. The facts that (1) all authors employ fictional personae in their works (some across race and gender bounds), (2) many use pseudonyms, and (3) James was no outsider to the Latino community, but a man who lived inside the community and knew it intimately, did not placate some of the critics. The result was that an engaging, funny, vibrant novel about Chicano life in contemporary Los Angeles failed, out of misplaced political correctness, to get the recognition it deserved.[19]

Ron Arias's Los Angeles Mexican-American novel *The Road to Tamazunchale* is in its blend of realism and magic realism a very different kind of book from Santiago's gritty, street-wise novel. On one level (the realist level) it is set, essentially, in the barrio apartment of the eighty-year-old dying hero, Fausto Tejada—with excursions into other regions of the city. On another, richer level its locale is the mind and imagination of Fausto as he roams through history (his own and his culture's) and geography (Mexico and Peru). In the manner of Latin American magic realist fiction, marvelous events intrude on life and are accepted and acted on as ordinary: a flute-playing Peruvian shepherd appears with his flock of alpaca on the freeway; a drowned Mexican migrant is found in a riverbed (and only the children know that the riverbed is dry), then resuscitated, bathed, shaved, and taken as a consort by an old woman; a cloud hovers over Los Angeles, dumping snow.

As the title suggests, the novel is a journey—Fausto's final journey toward a mythical Peru, toward another world, *the* other world. Appropriate to the sense of Los Angeles as migrant city, and to the massive influx of Mexicans into Los Angeles, the story is about migration between worlds, crossings into strange places. Intertextually, the journey is linked to mythic heroic and mock-heroic journeys drawn from sources ranging from Cervantes to Márquez. The novel reverberates with echoes of other times, other places. Different planes of reality are overlaid on one another. The lines between illusion and reality, mortality and immortality, collapse, as do the boundaries between cultures and characters, who are aware of themselves as characters and capable of merging into one another: Fausto's niece and helper merges with Ana, the guide to the Amazonian valley. In a play within a play, performed for the benefit of *mojados* (wetbacks) rescued by the voyagers, the novel's characters play themselves. In one episode they wander onto a movie set in Elysian Park, where they are told they are in the wrong movie. Fausto, his skin dark as an Indian, dressed in his wife's cape and carrying as lance a garden hoe (comic allusion to Cervantes), is told by an actress: "Wrong period. We're doing seventeenth century. And that's out definitely. We're not shooting Indians."[20]

In focusing his novel on the final voyage of an old man, Arias situates his protagonist at the opposite stage of life from Santiago's young wanderer/tagger. Santiago's protagonist in *Famous All Over Town* is more like John Fante's self-advertising Italian-American writer-as-hero Arturo Bandini in *Ask the Dust* than the protagonists of other Chicano novels set in Los Angeles; both Santiago's and Fante's bildungsromans tell of young men coming of age on the wrong side of the city—on the unglamorous, un-Hollywood, down-and-out side. As novels about the poor and marginalized inhabitants of the city, *Famous All*

*Over Town* and *Ask the Dust*—together with the novels of Chester Himes, Walter Mosley, Oscar Zeta Acosta, Ron Arias, and Charles Bukowski—remind us that Los Angeles is more than Hollywood, the Westside, the coast, or the canyons that Hollywood and hard-boiled novelists, as well as media merchants, spin doctors, and latter-day boosters, have invoked as the locus of Southern California life.

# 8

# BLACK DAHLIAS AND ZOOT SUITS

## The Recovery of History

The future always looks good in the golden land, because no one remembers the past. Here is where the hot wind blows and the old ways do not seem relevant. . . . Here is the last stop for all those who come from somewhere else, for all those who drifted away from the cold and the past and the old ways. Here is where they are trying to find a new life style, trying to find it in the only places they know to look: the movies and the newspapers.

JOAN DIDION, "SOME DREAMERS OF THE GOLDEN DREAM"

The past is never dead. It's not even past.

WILLIAM FAULKNER, REQUIEM FOR A NUN

I

The Los Angeles detective story since Raymond Chandler and Ross Macdonald gave it definition has rested on the unearthing of crimes committed in the past to find sources of present infirmity. In a recent transformation of this narrative line novelists and filmmakers have increasingly been either drawing their material from actual, recorded crimes in the city's history or creating original fictions that invoke the noir aura of Los Angeles in the 1930s, 1940s, or 1950s. The reconstruction of the city's dark history has been a conspicuous feature in Los Angeles narrative since the 1970s. The novels and films that constitute this act of historic reconstruction cross a number of boundaries: fact and fiction, past and present, documented act and imaginative reenactment. The resurrection (for reasons that are in part nostalgic) of the Cain-Chandler noir ambiance has fused with and, more significantly, served the more serious purpose of cultural history: history that posits past crime not as individual events but as acts implicated in the larger context of power and hegemony in the city's development.

Film provides some of the better-known examples of these tendencies. *Chinatown*, which focuses on the Owens River water grab, was perhaps the first in the line of noirish film reconstructions of the city's past, spawning such other films as its disappointing sequel, *The Two Jakes, Mulholland Falls, L.A. Confidential* (based on the James Ellroy novel), and *Devil in a Blue Dress* (based on the Walter Mosley novel). Among the novelists Mosley and Ellroy have been the most prominent explorers of the criminal underside of Los Angeles from the postwar to the cold war eras, Mosley in his ongoing Easy Rawlins cycle, Ellroy in his cycle of "rogue cop" LAPD novels that make up the L.A. Quartet.

In this collective historical reenactment, two crimes of the 1940s have stood out as conspicuous occasions: the "Black Dahlia" murder of 1947 and the "Sleepy Lagoon" murder of 1942, which engendered the wartime "Zoot Suit" riots in downtown Los Angeles the following year. The Black Dahlia case gave both John Gregory Dunne in his novel *True Confessions* (1978) and James Ellroy in *The Black Dahlia* (1988, the first of the Quartet novels) openings for the exploration of the larger fields of politics, crime, corruption, and paranoia in postwar Los Angeles. The Sleepy Lagoon murder and Zoot Suit riots provided the novelist Thomas Sánchez in *Zoot-Suit Murders* (1978) and the playwright Luis Valdez in *Zoot Suit* (1978) narrative angles to look back on the hysterical, inflammatory war years of the city, when racism directed at Mexican Americans was intensified. In these years the young male Chicano, expressing his disaffiliation with the dominant culture by enacting the defiant role of "zoot suiter," or pachuco, became the target for the city's displaced fears of both internal and foreign subversion. The Mexican American, like the Japanese American, became the collective embodiment of disloyalty and un-Americanism. As meditations on history and politics during the transformative 1940s, the fictional reconstructions of the Black Dahlia case and Zoot Suit riots take us through and beyond those events, placing them in the larger ground of the decade's cultural apprehensions and fears. The crimes in this sense are the "texts" onto which the "contexts" of history have been grafted, or to put it differently, the "pretexts" for telling larger stories; the crimes serve as occasions to investigate broader issues in local and national history. In works of fiction the headlined events become symbolic events that reveal not simply what happened but why, and culpability is not narrowed to a specific individual, or even group, but spread across the culture.

II

The Black Dahlia case offers a clear instance of the historic event rendered by the novelist as symbolic event. On January 15, 1947, the nude body of a twenty-two-year-old female was found in an empty lot at the corner of Thirty-ninth and Norton streets in Los Angeles's Leimert Park district. She had been tortured (cigarette burns on her breasts), skillfully bisected at the waist, and eviscerated. The grisly murder made daily headlines in all three of the city's newspapers and set off one of the biggest manhunts in Los Angeles police history. The January 16 issue of the *Los Angeles Times*, which in its treatment was the least sensational of the newspapers' coverage, contained a page two story headlined "Girl Victim of Sex Fiend Found Slain," accompanied by a large photograph of police combing the empty lot for clues. Over the next ten days the paper covered the investigation led by police Captain Jack Donohue and Lieutenants Harry Hanson and

F. A. Brown. Through fingerprints that matched those of a girl arrested a few years earlier for underage drinking, she was identified as Elizabeth Short, a migrant from Medford, Massachusetts. Some of her personal effects turned up in a post office—letters, photos, and a birth certificate enclosed in an envelope with a message pieced together from letters cut from magazines: "Here is Dahlia's belongings. Letter to follow." No letter followed. Her nickname, "the Black Dahlia," came from a reporter who learned from a bartender that she was called that because of her penchant for wearing black and her thick, luxuriant black hair. (The film *The Blue Dahlia*, based on a Raymond Chandler script about the murder of a woman, starring Alan Ladd and Veronica Lake, had come out the year before.)

Her trail through Southern California was traced. She left home at seventeen and lived in, among other places, Santa Barbara, where she worked in the PX at Camp Cook, Hollywood, where she shared an apartment with other girls on North Cherokee Avenue (blocks away from Tod Hackett's apartment house in *The Day of the Locust*), and San Diego, where she worked in a movie theater, lived with the theater owner, had affairs with several servicemen, and took up with a salesman named "Red" Manly. On January 10 Manly drove her to Los Angeles, dropping her off at the downtown Biltmore Hotel where she told him she was to meet her sister. The trail ended there. Manly, the prime suspect, had an alibi for the time between January 10 and 15, from the date of her disappearance to the discovery of her body. Those five days were never accounted for. As many as two hundred policemen were assigned to the case at different times. Hundreds of suspects were questioned. Dozens of others came forward either claiming they knew who the killer was or confessing to the murder. It was as if all the deracinated dream victims from West's Hollywood had come out to take part in a masquerade. A *Life Magazine* story on March 24, 1947, reported that "hundreds of psychopaths, kibbitzers, tipsters [gave] false leads in the week after the body was discovered." Many people offered confessions, the story went on. People were naming enemies—men who deserted women, tenants they wanted to evict.[1] Although the news coverage died down after a time as lead after lead failed to produce a killer or account for the missing days, the Black Dahlia case has remained active in the collective memory of the city. (People who were living in Los Angeles as adults in 1947 remember where they were when the case broke—as people remember where they were when John F. Kennedy was assassinated.)

As a mythic Los Angeles female who seemed to step directly out of a Raymond Chandler or James M. Cain novel, Elizabeth Short played two roles: the dark, seductive mystery woman and the innocent Hollywood hopeful who drifted to the coast seeking stardom only to be betrayed by the Dream. In this latter guise she is the archetypal Hollywood victim, incarnation of the falsity of the promise offered by the fan magazines and the movies themselves—Cain's Cora Smith, McCoy's Gloria Beatty and Dorothy Trotter, the Graham brothers' Dorothy Irving. Sleek and attractive in her black outfits and with her thick black hair, she got a few bit parts in movies. Darker envisionings have her as a prostitute working out of bars in San Diego and Hollywood, a nude model, and a performer in pornographic movies. She may have been all of these things: young naif and femme fatale, dream victim and juvenile delinquent in over her head.

As the violated, defiled, mutilated woman, she suggests a deeper cultural interpretation: by-product of the misogyny resulting from the power and independence women were gaining in the war years. The Black Dahlia murder can be read in cultural terms as the consequence of male rage against the war-liberated woman, the attempt of the male to leave his mark on the woman, to reclaim her as his property and reassert his power. The defiled woman appears frequently in fiction and film during and after the war. One finds her in fiction even before America's entrance in the war—as Carmen Sternwood, for instance, in Chandler's *The Big Sleep* of 1939, the young woman drugged and forced to pose for nude photos. Male anxiety over women's sexual independence expresses itself repeatedly in films of the forties. In George Marshall's 1946 film, *The Blue Dahlia*, a returning vet discovers his wife has been exercising her independence by hanging around with a sleazy nightclub owner. She is subsequently murdered, and the husband, who didn't kill her, must find the real killer to clear himself. Similarly, in the Academy Award-winning film of 1946, William Wyler's *The Best Years of Our Lives*, a returning air corps gunner discovers his wife has become sexually promiscuous while he was overseas.

Still other films of the mid-forties provide a gloss on male sexual anxieties. James M. Cain's three Los Angeles novels, each with its murderous femme fatale, appeared on-screen in quick succession: Billy Wilder's *Double Indemnity* with Barbara Stanwyck in 1944, Tay Garnett's *The Postman Always Rings Twice* with Lana Turner in 1945, and Michael Curtiz's noir version of a non-noir novel, *Mildred Pierce*, with Joan Crawford in 1946. That year, 1946, Lewis Milestone's film about a homicidal woman, *The Strange Love of Martha Ivers* with Barbara Stanwyck, appeared, as did other films about ambitious, strong-willed women, among them Howard Hawks's version of Chandler's *The Big Sleep* that paired two sisters, the strong, independent woman (Lauren Bacall) and the victim/predator (Martha Vickers). In January 1947, when the Dahlia story broke in headlines, the advertised new movie titles of the year included—with a kind of bizarre appropriateness—*The Strange Woman* with Hedy Lamar, *Duel in the Sun* with Jennifer Jones (a Selznick film banned by the Catholic Legion of Decency), *The Wicked Lady* with Virginia Lockwood, and the film bearing the most Dahlia-suggestive title of all, *The Time, the Place, and the Girl.*

Sexual apprehension and the consequent revenge against women have been incorporated into noir resurrections of the last few decades. The violated and mutilated woman is almost a leitmotiv in recent fiction and film. She appears as Evelyn Mulwray in *Chinatown*, a woman sexually violated by her father and then shot through the eye trying to escape with the daughter who is the product of the incest. In Lee Tamahori's 1995 *Mulholland Falls* a woman (and mistress of a police detective) is thrown from a plane because she knows too much about the military's atomic radiation experiments on American soldiers. Her crushed remains—a mound of body parts lying on the desert floor—are found just after the detective (Nick Nolte) and his anti-racketeering team have tossed a gangster from the top of a cliff on Mulholland Drive—a place they call "Mulholland Falls."

The defiled, disfigured woman appears repeatedly in James Ellroy's LAPD novels—as the Black Dahlia and in other incarnations—and in those of his contemporary in the police procedural genre, Michael Connelly, whose detective hero Hieronymous "Harry" Bosch is haunted to the point of madness by the memory of his mother's brutal slaying when he was eleven. Bosch goes to the edge in *The Concrete Blonde* (1994), where he has to investigate the serial killings of eleven prostitutes, strippers, and porno-film performers—the work of the "Dollmaker" killer and his copycat who grotesquely "doll up" their victims in makeup. He goes over the edge in his next novel, *The Last Coyote* (1995), where, his house destroyed in the Northridge earthquake and his girlfriend gone, he has to revisit the 1961 unsolved case of his mother's murder. The brutally slain woman appears repeatedly in Walter Mosley's fiction as well. Connelly, Mosley, and Ellroy reveal, each in his own way, that past violence—often rendered as the defilement of the female—has present consequences; releasing history releases monsters—but also answers about who we are today and where we are rooted.

This historical shaping of the present is central to Dunne's reworking of the Black Dahlia story, *True Confessions*—a title that suggests, if anything, that there are also false confessions.[2] The novel is framed by a conversation—essentially a mutual confession—in 1975, twenty-eight years after the Dahlia murder, between two brothers, Tom and Desmond Spellacy, one a retired cop, the other a priest who has exiled himself to a small desert parish in Twenty-Nine Palms. Each was implicated in the events surrounding the 1947 murder and mutilation of Lois Fazenda, the Elizabeth Short figure, nicknamed the "Virgin Tramp" in the novel. Des has summoned Tommy to the desert to tell him he is dying of heart disease and to confess the moral failures that prompted his self-exile. The novel becomes, after the frame narrative, the memory piece of each brother as he recalls the weeks surrounding the discovery of the body. On one level the novel is about Tommy's investigation of the Virgin Tramp killing; on another it is about the relationship between the two brothers as each has been implicated in the case, "soiled Tommy" and "sanctimonious Des," Irish kids from Boyle Heights where the available career paths led either to the police or to the priesthood.

Both brothers are in the business of taking confessions, true and false, one from the police station, the other from the confessional box. After the newspaper headlines report the discovery of the Virgin Tramp corpse, dozens of people come forward to confess. The police station fills with "parents and pederasts, lesbians and whores, cab drivers and bus drivers, bartenders and waitresses, pimps and policemen and children with stray articles of clothing, all claiming some knowledge of the unidentified woman from the corner of 39th and Norton."[3]

The Spellacy brothers are linked to the Virgin Tramp through Jack Amsterdam, a millionaire building contractor and gangster who runs prostitution, phony green card, and building fund rackets in the city. Tom has served as "bagman" for Amsterdam's prostitution ring, and Des has channeled church building funds to Amsterdam, who has been, with Des's knowledge, skimming off the top. Des, furthermore, knew Lois Fazenda but kept quiet about it, having met her when he, Amsterdam, and Dan Campion, another Irish millionaire with ties to the police and the church, picked her up in a car driving home from the Del Mar racetrack in San Diego. The encounter parallels the Red Manly involvement with Elizabeth Short; in the novel it leads to Fazenda's becoming Amsterdam's mistress and then one of the prostitutes he passes around as favors. Sanctimonious Des, meanwhile, has risen to become chancellor and adviser to Cardinal Hugh Danaher, head of 1.2 million Southern California Catholics, and possibly the next cardinal because he is able to make himself useful both to church leaders and crooked businessmen.

What both brothers know, and what constitutes the essential link between them—between, in larger terms, church and state, clerical and secular worlds—is that one has to make payoffs to get payoffs, do favors to get favors. Tommy acknowledges the "golden rule" for policemen and prelates alike: "You treat people right and they treat you right and you can retire in very nice shape" (5). Early in the novel Tom secretly removes the dead body of a priest, a heart attack victim, from the bed of one of Amsterdam's prostitutes—this one of the favors that get passed around. More than the revisiting of a murder or even the story of two brothers, the novel is an exploration of the intricate web of graft, corruption, and influence peddling that exists across the city's power lines connecting and entangling the realms of crime and sin, public corruption and personal failings. Church and state represent rival, competing, yet mirroring sites of moral failure and criminal culpability in the city's history.

As for the reenactment of the Dahlia crime itself, Dunne adds some grisly details that exacerbate its ritualistic ambiance: a votive candle has been placed in Lois Fazenda's vagina and a rose tattoo shows above her pubic hair. Tommy recalls discovering the body: "She was naked as a jaybird, both halves. There was no blood, not a drop. Just this pale green body cut in two" (6). Dunne changes the time of the murder to spring, giving Tommy and his partner, Crotty, a chance to talk about the Hollywood Stars Pacific Coast League baseball team while they eat sweet and sour pork, on the cuff, in the upstairs room of Wo Fat's in Chinatown. Between sweet and sour pork and baseball talk the two cops do some investigating, though, finding out a number of things: that Fazenda had been posing for nude photos, that she was one of Amsterdam's prostitutes, and that she was involved in his phony green card scheme. And ultimately Tommy does solve the murder.

He finds the killer not by using logic or police investigatory methods but by employing the illogical, nonlinear thinking of his crazy wife when she is at home on a furlough from the state mental hospital. It's a question, to Tommy, of following the bouncing ball, of looking at things from different angles, finding that place where apparently random lines cross. The killer turns out to be a barber named Harold Pugh, who was killed when his car hit a telephone pole while he was speeding in the neighborhood of the crime at 5:00 on the morning the corpse was discovered.

Finding the actual Dahlia killer means little, however. Dunne in this revisionist crime narrative challenges the notion of individual culpability; guilt extends beyond the act of a single person to society itself. Tommy knows this and frames Amsterdam for the murder, an act of both revenge and justice, a way of both evening the score with Amsterdam and placing the crime, and responsibility for it, in the larger context of urban greed, corruption, brutality, and sexual exploitation. Amsterdam dies of cancer before his trial comes up, but this, too, is unimportant: guilt has been traced to its real source, where Tommy, along with the reader, knows it should be traced. Framing Amsterdam, though, has its consequences for both Tommy and Des. Before he dies Amsterdam implicates both men. No one escapes as culpability is spread among all those who have been a part of the corruption of both the secular and the sacred city.

James Ellroy's 1987 novelistic revisiting of the Elizabeth Short case, *The Black Dahlia*, was influenced, Ellroy has acknowledged, by Dunne's novel ten years earlier. On a deeper level, as I have indicated in chapter 5, the novel is rooted in Ellroy's obsession with the Dahlia case and its linkage in his mind to the sex murder of his mother, eleven years after Elizabeth Short's murder. In Ellroy's novel the Black Dahlia, Elizabeth, or Betty, Short, is cast as the sexual obsession of two men, Lee Blanchard and Bucky Bleichert, homicide detective partners, who if not brothers in fact are figurative brothers. Ellroy has transformed Dunne's cop/priest brotherhood into two rogue cops, each driven to the point of insanity by an insane murder and mutilation. Investigating a murder and finding a killer become, as they do in Dunne's novel, a probing into the secrets of both the divided self and the hidden city, each contained in the secret of the girl herself. The investigation becomes the occasion for Ellroy's exploration of the dark places in the two men, their necrophilic shadow sides, as each obsessively pursues the trail of a dead girl.[4]

In Ellroy's involuted, psychological, Jekyll and Hyde plot, the two partners fuse into a single figure, Blanchard, after his death, becoming Bleichert's doppelgänger, the ghostly double who takes over his partner's soul. Bleichert is transformed into a man as compulsively driven as his dead partner had been in finding the Dahlia killer and the solution to the deeper mysteries she represents. For Bleichert the search for the answers about a murder becomes also the search for answers about the self. Police and personal investigation become one and the same. What he finds is his own necrophilia: he has fallen in love with the Dahlia, "everyone's favorite dead girl."[5]

His sexually obsessed quest carries him to three women, each fused in his mind, each a variation of the other two: the violated and dead Betty Short, whom he has seen only as a mutilated corpse and on-screen in a pornographic movie; the violated but alive Kay Lake, victim of a sadistic pimp and drug dealer; and the rich-girl Dahlia lookalike Madeleine Sprague, who had met Short in a lesbian bar where the runaway girl had been cadging drinks. Madeleine, victim of a stepfather's sexual indulgence, is, like Elizabeth Short, cast by Ellroy both as victim and as performative female, a woman who constructs a series of identities and roles, becoming what she needs to be to entice, please, or deceive the men—and women—around her.

Bleichert pursues Madeleine Sprague as sexual surrogate for the Dahlia and the link to her killing. In the conclusion to the novel Madeleine provides the linkage. The solution lies deep in Sprague family history, in the patriarch Emmet Sprague's conspiracy with the film director Mack Sennett in a multimillion-dollar scheme to build shoddy, substandard houses on the side of Mount Lee—the Hollywoodland tract. One of the dilapidated shacks built by Sprague and Sennett on the hill beneath the sign turns out to be the slaughter-house of Elizabeth Short. But before the twisted family history re-veals itself as a gothic history of hidden identity, quasi-incest, deceit, and madness, Bleichert has been engaged in his own kind of mad-ness, turning Madeleine into the dead woman, encouraging her to dress and act like the Dahlia. Making love to Madeleine is his way of making love to Elizabeth Short:

> We were making love, both of us close to peaking. My hand slipped off the bed rail and hit the light switch on the wall, illuminating Betty Short beneath me. For a few seconds I believed it was her, and I called out for Lee and Kay to help me. . . . I knew it would never be that good with just plain Madeleine; when the brass girl whispered, "I knew she'd get to you sooner or later," I dry sobbed that all my pillow stories were lies and poured out the nonstop true story of Lee and Kay and Bucky, straight through to Mr. Fire's fix on the dead girl and his jump off the face of the earth. . . . (192)

Ellroy's novel transforms the bizarre text of the Black Dahlia mur-der into an even more bizarre literary text. His fictional reconstruc-tion, overloaded with gothic trappings, necrophilic and incestuous fantasies, and character fusion and confusion, is, it would seem, the attempt to mix his own dark history with the city's. While Chandler and Macdonald offered stories that hinged on false, mistaken, and in-vented identities and that conjoined the mysteries of self and city, Ell-roy's work has more turns and transformations than his forebears in the Los Angeles detective story could have concocted. All boundaries between selves collapse in Ellroy's nightmare tale. Even the living and dead fuse. Bucky Bleichert becomes one with his dead partner, and three violated women fuse, collapse, in Bleichert's psychosexual imaginings, into a single figure: Kay Lake and Madeleine Sprague become the reincarnated Betty Short, risen, like one of Poe's beau-tiful dead women, from the grave.

When she realizes that she is playing the part of the Dahlia in her lovemaking with Bleichert, Kay Lake tells him: "I'll never be a school-teacher from Sioux Falls, South Dakota, but I'll be Betty or anyone else you want me to be." (192) Betty Short, the Hollywood dream seeker from New England, the mutilated dead girl everyone in the novel either wants to become or possess, makes only one movie in Hollywood: a lesbian movie shot against a prop left over from a Mack Sennett film. And the dead Mack Sennett has bequeathed, in Ellroy's version, not only the movie prop but also the condemned shack in the Hollywoodland tract that becomes the scene of mutilation and murder. As in the film *Chinatown,* the violation and defilement of the woman function as the carnal equivalent to the greed-driven, opportunistic violation of the land itself. Los Angeles has been willed into existence not by utopian dreamers, as the booster myth had it, but by ruthless and corrupt opportunists. The violated woman serves as emblem, or synecdoche, of the violated landscape.

Both James Ellroy's *The Black Dahlia* and John Gregory Dunne's *True Confessions* situate the reconstruction of the Dahlia case in the context of postwar Los Angeles ambition and greed. Dunne's story of two brothers, cop and priest, is rendered as a cautionary fable about transgression: about crossing the line between opportunism and corruption. Making deals with the powerful, easing the flow of money, Des Spellacy is complicit with the corruption of church and state; making himself useful to the parish, he makes himself culpable of moral failure, if not criminal guilt. Real culpability in Dunne's novel spreads beyond the "actual" murderer to all the major characters in the story. Des does his penance in the desert, and when, in the mutual confession between the brothers that ends the novel, Tommy acknowledges his part in Des's fall, the dying Des replies, "You were my salvation, Tommy. . . . You made me remember something I forgot. Or tried to forget is more like it." (340) Ellroy in *The Black Dahlia* ten years later recast the story less as a fable about guilt, sin, and redemption than about sexual obsession, misogyny, paranoia, and confusion, and in doing so, resurrected, or at least came closer to invoking, the psychological noir thrillers of the 1940s. More complex, psychologically, than any novel or film that came out of the forties, and darker by far, it nonetheless recalls its antecedents in the morally ambiguous world engendered by the hard-boiled and tough-guy writers and postwar film noir.

## III

Thomas Sánchez's *Zoot-Suit Murders* and Luis Valdez's *Zoot Suit* reconstruct, in very different narrative ways, the wartime Anglo/Mexican-American conflict in downtown Los Angeles a few years before the Black Dahlia murder. The hostility between Anglos and Mexicans in the city did not, of course, begin during the war. It was present from the beginning in Los Angeles, a fact that Valdez makes far clearer than does Sánchez. Sánchez's melodramatic reworking of the 1943 riots does little to place the events in the larger historical framework of Los Angeles race relations; Valdez, by contrast, in his stage version does more to situate the riots historically. We know, from Valdez, how the riots and persecution grew out of long-held and deeply rooted Anglo racism. Sánchez narrows the scope of the events to a conspiracy theory explanation: the Mexican community preyed on during the war by outside forces from both the left and the right. As a sign of this narrowing, he collapses the Sleepy Lagoon murder and the downtown and barrio Zoot Suit riots into a single ongoing event, substituting in his fictional version the murder of two FBI investigators in the barrio for the earlier Sleepy Lagoon murder, which allows him to explain the events of the novel entirely in terms of wartime fears of subversion.

In fact, the two events were separate, the former (the murder of a Mexican gang member a year earlier) helping to fuel and justify the racial fear and hatred that went into the latter. Carey McWilliams, writing five years after the riots in *North from Mexico* (1948), has given a detailed account of the events. On August 1, 1942, Henry Leyvas, a member of the barrio's Thirty-eighth Street Gang, took his girlfriend for a drive to a small reservoir in East Los Angeles (called the "Sleepy Lagoon" and used as a swimming hole) near the Williams' Ranch, owned by a Mexican family. Threatened by a rival gang, the couple left. They returned later with other youths and attempted to crash a party at the ranch. The next day José Díaz was discovered unconscious on the rocky slopes of the reservoir. He died the next day. There were no gun or knife wounds. He apparently had been beaten with a stick or club, but the autopsy report indicated he might have fallen down the slope or even been in a car accident. Some three hundred Mexican youths were arrested; twenty-four were indicted for murder. Despite the efforts of the Sleepy Lagoon Defense Committee, twelve were convicted of second-degree murder, another five of assault. They were remanded to San Quentin where they remained until their convictions were overturned in October 1944 by an appellate court and the judge reprimanded for blatant violations of the rights of the defendants.

The press leaped on the Sleepy Lagoon episode as an example of Mexican-American barbarism. Japanese Americans had been removed to internment camps, and in their place Mexican Americans became the convenient scapegoat, providing an internal enemy onto which the fear of subversion and anti-Americanism could be vented. All three dailies—the *Times*, the *Examiner*, and the *Daily News*—stirred the anti-Mexican sentiment, reminding readers that Mexicans were inherently violent, an inborn racial trait stemming from their Indian bloodlines. According to some versions played out in the press and the courthouse, the barrio Mexicans were the dupes of America's enemies—the prey of Japanese spies, of fascist organizations like the Sinarquista group that spread from Franco's Spain to Latin America and then to the Los Angeles barrio, or of Communist agents hiding behind utopian cults like the pseudoscientific, quasi-religious San Francisco-based Mankind United.

Mankind United, concocted by Arthur Bell in 1934 to combat the "Hidden Rulers" of capitalism, promised joiners full employment, pensions, paid vacations, and houses equipped with radio, television, air-conditioning, and swimming pools. All this would come to pass when the requisite number of members (200 million) signed up and agreed to surrender all their worldly possessions. Arriving on the scene during the depression, Mankind United was one more—albeit the most bizarre (Bell claimed to have a ray gun to use against the "Hidden Rulers")—in a line of utopian schemes flourishing in Southern California. In 1943, the year of the riots, Bell was tried for promoting activities that interfered with the war effort, but a new utopian scheme he concocted, Christ's Church of the Golden Rule, persisted until 1950.

Sánchez's conspiracy-theory version of the wartime East Los Angeles riots constructs a barrio that is infiltrated by Mankind United and the Sinarquistas. His protagonist, Nathan Younger, a social worker who organizes baseball teams for Mexican boys, is also a paid informer for the government assigned to penetrate an allegedly Communist-front group called Mankind Incorporated (i.e., Mankind United). His investigation leads him to discover that the barrio is being invaded by subversive groups coming from both the right and the left; both the fifth column Sinarquistas and the communistic Mankind Incorporated have been preying on barrio poverty and exclusion to foment un-American activities.

Significantly, given the 1940s male anxieties about female independence and power, the agent of Mankind Incorporated in the barrio is represented as a woman, a frail, asthmatic redhead named Kathleen LaRue. LaRue lectures Nathan on the "Sponsors'" plan to combat the "Hidden Rulers" (Roosevelt, Churchill, Hitler, and Mussolini—heirs to their capitalist forebears, Rockefeller, Morgan, and Hearst) through its International Legion of Vigilantes.[6] It is LaRue who has killed the two FBI men, providing an odd twist to the violated, disfigured woman theme that runs through so much Los Angeles crime fiction: here the woman is cast both as terrorist, as agent provocateur, and as brainwashed automaton, as female victim wholly under the spell of the Voice of Mankind Incorporated. Late in the novel, "The Voice" himself arrives in Los Angeles for an appearance at Shrine Auditorium and promptly orders LaRue to kill Younger. Unfortunately Younger by now has fallen in love with the frail LaRue; fortunately he squeezes the trigger first.

Younger, as a multiple agent, is torn by conflicting loyalties—Sánchez's way of dramatizing the warring factions in the barrio. He is drawn erotically, if not ideologically, to LaRue, patriotically to his anti-Communist, anti-Mankind Incorporated government surveillance work and to the war effort (underscored by letters he receives from his brother on an aircraft carrier in the Pacific), and loyally to the Mexican boys in his charge who are being manipulated with heroin imported by the right-wing Sinarquistas. Having come close to being assassinated by agents of Mankind Incorporated, he also barely gets away with his life in a Sinarquista-led Mexican ambush to which he has been drawn in the Hollywood Hills just beneath the crumbling Hollywoodland sign. As it was for Ellroy in *The Black Dahlia*, the iconic sign and the housing development beneath it on the slopes of Mount Lee function as an emblem of the dream betrayed, the place where a bucolic, rustic, promise-laden Southern

California, the Southern California of the city boosters, comes into contact with violence and defeated hope.[7]

In an appropriation of Hollywood "local color" Younger regularly meets his government contact, a Senator Kinney, in a box seat at Gilmore Field, where they watch the minor league Hollywood Stars baseball team play. (One is reminded here of Dunne's two cops talking Hollywood Stars baseball in *True Confessions*.) In one scene at the ball park the senator gives Younger a gun stuffed in a bag of popcorn. The hopes of the Stars are pinned on one pitcher, a Mexican named Angel, apparently an iron-armed pitcher, who is on the mound every time Younger and Kinney are in the stands. When Angel is sharp, the Stars win; when he is not, they lose. The focus here on a Mexican pitcher is suggestive both of the breaking of the color line in baseball (which came in the minor before the major leagues) and the two men's desire for the integration, or assimilation, of the Mexican American, a goal that is undercut by extremists on both sides.

When it comes to the riots themselves, Sánchez provides only the sketchiest coverage and causation. Having folded the Diaz killing and arrests of the previous year into the killing of two FBI agents, he focuses on Younger's attempt to unveil the various conspiracies that have precipitated the violence. In fact, the riots were precipitated less by international conspiracies (the version of the press and some politicians) than by hostile, racist servicemen who invaded the barrio and nearby downtown Los Angeles, which since the 1930s was becoming a principal shopping and entertainment center for Mexican Americans, particularly along Broadway going south from the Plaza.

It was on Broadway, on June 3, that two hundred sailors, arriving in taxicabs from the Chavez Ravine Naval Armory, indiscriminately began beating zoot suiters, revenge for the alleged beating of several sailors the previous night. Over the following week sailors, marines, soldiers, and civilians descended on Broadway and the barrio, beating and stripping anyone wearing a zoot suit, which became a badge of rebellion and subversion.[8] The pachuco in his zoot suit represented to the servicemen the leisure to sit out the war, act out his inborn violent nature, and enjoy a sexually charged relationship with the "loose" Chicana.[9] The police did little but watch at a safe distance and perform "mop-up" operations, arresting beaten zoot suiters and leaving the disciplining of the servicemen to the shore patrol and military police. There is little evidence that the Mexicans fought back, but on June 6 the headline in the *Daily News* read "44 Zooters Jailed for Attack on Sailors." The next day the *Times* had this head: "Zoot Suiters Learn a Lesson in Fight with Servicemen." Hearst's *Examiner* was even more inflammatory in its headline: "Zooters Threaten L.A. Police." The riots, Carey McWilliams wrote, were almost "staged" by the city's newspapers. In a city known for its media events, this was, perhaps, the defining case. The racism that made the attacks on the Mexican youth possible, and so easily defensible, moreover, was not, McWilliams concluded, "an unexpected rupture in Anglo-Hispanic relations but the logical end-product of a hundred years of neglect and discrimination."[10]

By ignoring the historic and contemporary sources of Anglo/ Mexican tensions in Los Angeles and focusing instead on the political appropriation of the barrio by organized subversive groups, each seeking to undermine the war effort, Sánchez's treatment is reductive. In his revisiting of the events culpability is displaced onto conspiracy theory. The result is a confused mélange of pseudohistory and romantic melodrama. Another problem with Sánchez's book is that the opposing ideologies are never really differentiated: the reader can't untangle the differences among them. All the groups—fascists, Communists, and the government—converge in an indistinct blur. The novel suffers the same weakness as Chester Himes's 1947 *Lonely Crusade*, in which distinctions among the various ideological factions— labor unionists, Communists, and capitalists—in postwar industrial Los Angeles dissolve into a kind of they're-all-against-us paranoia.

By contrast, Luis Valdez's brilliant stage representation of these same events, *Zoot Suit*, produced the same year as Valdez's novel, 1978, offers a compelling, persuasive rendering of the events, one that keeps an eye on both what actually happened in 1942 and 1943 and the complex racial and class realities of Los Angeles that provide the political and historical context. Valdez, born to a migrant farmworker family in Delano in 1940, has been active in Chicano politics since the 1960s. He was the founder of El Teatro Campesino (Farm Workers' Theater) in 1965, writing and performing in plays for César Chávez's striking farmworkers in Delano and, since 1971, San Juan Bautista, where he established a permanent home for his theater company. *Zoot Suit*, a coproduction of El Teatro Campesino and Los Angeles's

Center Theater Group of the Mark Taper Forum, marked his entrance into mainstream theater. It ran for a full eleven months in Los Angeles, following its July 30 opening. Another production opened in New York in 1981 but closed after four weeks. A film version based on the Center Theater Group production appeared in 1992. Since then Valdez has been active in television and film writing and wrote the script of the popular film *La Bamba* (based on the life of rock star Ritchie Valens) in 1987.

*Zoot Suit* opens on a bare stage backed by a huge newspaper blow-up with the June 3, 1943, *Herald Express* headline: ZOOT-SUITER HORDES INVADE LOS ANGELES. US NAVY AND MARINES CALLED IN. From a slit cut in the newspaper backdrop by a switch-blade, the figure of El Pachuco in his zoot suit emerges. He is the embodiment of the pachuco spirit in the play, a mythical figure representing both the defiant Mexican zooter and the dark side of Henry Reyna, leader of the Thirty-eighth Street Gang, a young man torn between *pachucismo* and the assimilationist desire to join the military. In the play's representation he is one of four arrested and imprisoned after the Sleepy Lagoon trial. The play is, in the words of El Pachuco, who introduces it, "a construct of reality and fantasy," a complex choreography that moves between actual events—the night at Sleepy Lagoon, the arrests, the trial, the San Quentin imprisonment, the reversal of the verdict, the riots of the following year—and a heightened or symbolic realism that carries the drama beyond specific event into the broader arena of historic and wartime racism. Overlaying the action is the voice of the El Pachuco figure who hovers about the stage, commenting on the action and speaking directly to Reyna as his inner voice, his pachuco voice. We get, for instance, this interior dialogue when Reyna tells El Pachuco he has decided to join the Navy:

Henry: I'm supposed to join the Navy tomorrow.
Pachuco: Stupid move, Carnal.
Henry: I've got to do something.
Pachuco: Then Hang Tough. Nobody's forcing you to
    do shit.
Henry: I'm forcing me, ese—ME, you understand?
Pachuco: Muy patriotic, eh?

Henry: Yeah.

Pachuco: Off to fight for your country.

Henry: Why not?

Pachuco: Because this ain't your country. Look what's
happening all around you. The Japs have sewed
up the Pacific. Rommell is kicking ass in Egypt
and the Mayor of L.A. has declared all-out war
on Chicanos. On you. Te curas?[11]

In one of his incarnations El Pachuco, invoking pre-Columbian history in the New World, emerges as an Aztec god, rising in a loincloth
from the beaten and stripped body of a Mexican youth during the
riots.

El Pachuco is the commanding voice in the play, its Chicano conscience and consciousness, but not the play's only voice. Valdez's play
is a collage of versions, voices, interpretations. Resisting the conspiracy explanation of Sánchez, which places culpability on outside political groups operating in the barrio, Valdez offers a multivoiced history that forces the viewer to reexamine the events in terms of deeply
rooted, pervasive, and continual racial assumptions, assumptions that
link Los Angeles history to its present. Reconstructing a particular
time in the city's history, it transcends that time in its reach, expressing, at least by implication, a long history of anti-Mexican hostility
that erupts viciously in the war years. Among the voices that express
the city's hysterical racism are those of the trial judge (who overrules
virtually every objection raised by the defense attorney), the police,
and the press. According to the press's version, gang warfare in the
barrio either has been directed by Japanese from inside the internment camps or is simply the product of a Mexican racial predisposi-
tion to violence. Speaking directly to the jury in the murder trial, the
Press, which representationally functions as prosecutor, argues—*in
a murder case*—that the Sleepy Lagoon murder is itself of no real
consequence; the real issue is the collective, inborn criminality of
Mexicans:

The city of Los Angeles is caught in the midst of the biggest,
most terrifying crime wave in its history. . . . We are not only
dealing with the violent death of one Jose Williams in a
drunken barrio brawl. We are dealing with the threat to our

children, our families, our homes. Set these pachucos free
and you shall unleash the forces of anarchy and destruction
in our society. . . . Others just like them must be watching
us at this very moment. What nefarious schemes can they
be hatching in their twisted minds? Rape, drugs, assault,
more violence? (61–62)

The Press is not after the killer of an unknown Mexican, but the
prosecution of pachucismo itself, which it represents as the chief
threat to American civilization. The zoot suit, as outrageous parody
version of the Anglo business suit, represents to the press and the prosecution an affront to native civility, the ultimate emblem of rebellion; the "drape shape" is the garment of un-Americanism. In the play's
rendering the killer of Díaz (or Williams) is shown to be the ritual-
ized figure of El Pachuco himself, the abstract representation of Chicano malehood, angry defiance, and resistance.

In moving between realism and ritual, fact and symbol, Valdez
makes visible the complex political issues surrounding the events of
1942 and 1943. The destiny of Henry Reyna and the other convicted
young men is tied directly to Los Angeles's anti-Mexican hostility—
hostility long predating the war but peaking during the hysteria of
the nativist war years and the fear of subversion. Climaxing the play's
multivoiced texture is its open-ended projections about the future.
The ending projects Reyna, as representative Chicano, into three possible futures. The Anglo version (expressed as "factual" account by
the Press) is that Henry Reyna would be arrested for theft, become a
drug addict, and die an early death. El Pachuco, by contrast, offers
two other possible futures: that Henry would die in the war, a Con-
gressional Medal of Honor winner, or that he would marry and raise
college-educated children proud of their Chicano heritage. Valdez
ends the play by refusing as foregone conclusions either Anglo stereotyping or a sentimental celebration of the Mexican-American future.
The future of the Chicano remains open.

## IV

Paradoxically, the literature of a place so wholeheartedly given to future possibilities has demonstrated over the past few decades a recurring concern for the reconstruction of its past. The invocation of his-

tory in Los Angeles literature, though, is more than compensatory day-dream, more than a corrective to an absent history. From the begin-ning of Anglo settlement in the basin in the 1880s the myth of new-ness was set, contrapuntally, against an equally potent myth of history. Helen Hunt Jackson inscribed the myth of a heroic Spanish/Mexican/ Indian past in the first significant novel about the region, *Ramona*, in 1884; and following her lead the early city boosters—Charles Fletcher Lummis, George Wharton James, Steven McGroarty, and others—sought to yoke the romance of the old missions to the vision of a new paradise. However much they may have distorted the his-tory of Spanish California, they succeeded in constructing a regional myth that proved a marketable item for tourism and migration.

Even after the booster myth was satirized, ridiculed, and under-mined by debunking journalists and hard-boiled novelists in the 1920s and 1930s, it persisted. The Ramona Pageant and the Mission Play continued, Leo Carrillo, on horseback, kept riding at the head of the yearly parade on Santa Barbara's State Street, and mission revival ar-chitecture found a place everywhere on the landscape. In the thir-ties whole towns were taking on the red-tile-roof, white-stucco-wall look, and in the fifties and sixties architects like Cliff May were de-signing the ubiquitous California ranch house, with its low-slung "hacienda" look for new suburban tracts.

Los Angeles fiction has been no less concerned with forging ties to the past. Mystery tales, by definition, are tales of historic recon-struction: the detective's reconstruction of what happened in the past and who done it. In the Los Angeles reworking of the traditional story the detective uncovers crimes committed by men or women who are ordinarily migrants, and extraordinarily rich, having gotten so by com-ing into the land and exploiting its water, oil, real estate, and cheap labor force. The victims are the have-nots—the Black Dahlias of Dunne and Ellroy, the barrio Chicanos of Sánchez and Valdez, the parched-land farmers of Towne. The search for answers to historic crime opens out onto the mystery of the city itself, a trail leading back to the "primal" crimes of city builders, represented fictionally in men like Guy Sternwood, Jack Amsterdam, Emmett Sprague, and Noah Cross.

*Chinatown*'s gumshoe, Jake Gittes, whose work is normally con-fined to snooping on cheating husbands and wives, finds himself enmeshed in the biggest scandal in the city's history. Robert Towne has read his Raymond Chandler, his Carey McWilliams, and his Morrow Mayo (one of the first to cry foul back in 1933), and although his updated version of the water grab distorts the chain and chronology of events (setting it in the 1930s for one thing), the film offers a glimpse into the big thinking that built a city on stolen water. When, near the end of the film, Gittes confronts Noah Cross and asks him how many millions he has, what he could possibly want that he can't already buy, why he is doing what he is doing, Cross, a half-smile pulled across his face as if the answer should be obvious, responds: "Why the future, Mr. Gittes, the future." The future of Los Angeles, Towne's screenplay asserts, has been built on crimes of the past. This may be the message, implicit or explicit, in all these noirish resurrections of Los Angeles's past. Reimagining the past has been a recurring concern of present-day Los Angeles writers; imagining its future, the subject of the following chapter, has been another.

# 9

# ENDINGS AND BEGINNINGS

*Surviving Apocalypse*

Whatever else California was, good or bad, it was charged with human hope. It was linked imaginatively with the most compelling of American myths, the pursuit of happiness. When that intensity of expectation was thwarted or only partially fulfilled . . . it could backfire into restlessness and bitterness. . . . As a hope in defiance of facts, as a longing which could ennoble and encourage but which could turn and devour itself, the symbolic value of California endured . . . a legacy of the Gold Rush.

KEVIN STARR, *AMERICANS AND THE CALIFORNIA DREAM*, 1860–1915

Finally, it was the city that held us, the city they said had no center, that all of us had come to from all over America because this was the place to find dreams and pleasure and love.

CAROLYN SEE, *GOLDEN DAYS*

L.A.'s fine in the long run . . . you get to choose who you want to be and how you want to live.

ANN GOODE IN ALAN RUDOLPH'S FILM, *WELCOME TO L.A.*

I

In *The Ecology of Fear* Mike Davis reports that "at least 138 novels and films since 1909" deal with the destruction of the city. The destroying agents have been both natural and man-made (or the two in conjunction): earthquake, fire, and flood, atomic attack, extraterrestrial or other-race invasion (the former often as metonymic displacement of the latter). The destruction of Los Angeles by atomic or nuclear explosion dominates Davis's taxonomy (49 times), followed by earthquake (28), and then alien hordes and monsters. What is more significant than the frequency of the city's imagined destruction, though, according to Davis, is "the pleasure such apocalypses provide to readers and movie audiences." The entire world, he says, "seems to be rooting for L.A. to slide into the Pacific or be swallowed up by the San Andreas Fault."[1] In citing dozens of novels and films over the past ninety years that "celebrate" the city's destruction, he reminds us of how long the template for urban disaster has been in place in fiction and film about Los Angeles; apocalyptic renderings have been there almost as long as there have been novels about Los Angeles.

Many of these literary acts of destruction, he claims persuasively, have been generated by racial anxieties in California: white fear of darker-skinned people. His initiating example is Homer Lea's hysterical racist novel about the Japanese invasion and occupation of California, *The Valor of Ignorance* (1909). Lea's work, he indicates, is the beginning of a long line of xenophobic fictions, couched often enough in Bible Belt fundamentalist, kooky religious, or Aryan supremacist terms. Outside the realm of fiction, Los Angeles has had a long xenophobic prophet-of-doom tradition. An early-twentieth-century exemplar was the Reverend "Fighting" Bob Schuler, the target of whose rantings was Los Angeles as city of sin (leveled largely at the predominantly Jewish film industry but also at Catholics and at big business) that would suffer the Almighty's wrath in apocalyptic destruction. More recently there has been the American Nazi Andrew Macdonald who wrote *The Turner Diaries* (1978), an ugly futuristic fantasy based on a purportedly "real" diary kept by a martyr to the white cause, about Aryan soldiers, survivalists, fighting a guerrilla war in Los Angeles to rid the city of Jews and blacks.

While Anglo-Saxon racism has been a significant presence in doomsday renderings of Los Angeles, xenophobic literature is far from a local phenomenon. Davis documents the national strain, but he may be overstating his case by locating the racial ground so prominently in Los Angeles. Contemporary racism may well be linked to local fears about the surge of immigrants into the city in the last few decades, but xenophobia has been a common enough response in all immigrant cities. American literature from the middle of the nineteenth to the early twentieth century—a period coinciding with massive waves of European immigration, the first from northern and western Europe, the second from southern and eastern Europe—is replete with sometimes hysterical expressions of literary nativism.[2] Anti-Semitic, anti-Catholic, and anti-"yellow horde" fiction has a long national history. Los Angeles is not exceptional here, although alien/other-race invasion renderings take on an added dimension when applied to a booster city promoted in the early days to prospective migrants both as a white Protestant enclave (the future home, as Lummis put it, of the "Saxon homemaker") and as the place of the miraculous cure—a marketing strategy that drew a considerable number of sick and infirm migrants and encouraged as well a local susceptibility to healers, psychics, medical quacks, and doomsday prophets.

Disaster fiction in Los Angeles goes beyond the invasion mode, though, and there are a number of reasons—and not all of them racial—for apocalyptic fiction's taking sturdy root in Los Angeles. For one thing, although doomsday literature was not invented in Los Angeles but migrated west (in stages, as an urban form, from London through New York and Chicago), it established itself in a city that was positioned literally at the edge of the continent, a place where an unstable physical geography collided with an unstable human geography of displaced migrants and inflated expectation. Since the 1920s Los Angeles offered itself to novelists as the locus of uprooted midwesterners looking for the quick fix. Among them were religious fundamentalists, desperate health seekers, and movieland castoffs adrift in a place where, their own dreams betrayed, they read the daily headlines of violent crime, municipal and corporate corruption, and Hollywood scandal, all of which fed a loathing for the city that deceived them. "Corn-belt fundamentalism," Davis writes, "with its traditional yeoman antipathy to the 'evil city,' collided head-on with the libertine culture of the Hollywood movie colony in an urban *kultur-*

*kampf.* Each side would resort to doomsday imagery to damn and excoriate the other." (305)

Hollywood movies have been complicit with fiction in these disaster imaginings. The old booster city was the site of Armageddon in films ranging from the 1953 *War of the Worlds* (where the space invaders migrate to Los Angeles) to *Earthquake* (1974, inspired by the 1971 quake and featuring some theater seats that vibrated), *Blade Runner* (1982, with its replicants running wild among the vaguely Asian proletarian hordes), and *Escape from L.A.* (1997, with its largely Hispanic island-city concentration camp of misfits, loonies, and subversives). In Ridley Scott's dystopian *Blade Runner*, the twenty-first-century city is run by genetic engineers operating from the top of a towering pyramid (analog to Fritz Lang's mise-en-scène for *Metropolis)* while the masses crowd the derelict streets below under a persistent mist of acid rain. In Scott's scenario (based on a Philip Dick story set in San Francisco, not Los Angeles) even the violated or disfigured woman, so prominent in noir fiction and film, shows up: the beautiful heroine Rachel is not human at all but a replicant, a genetically engineered product. Joel Coen and Ethan Coen's Nathanael West send-up, *Barton Fink,* similarly, fuses the victimized woman theme with a Hollywood disaster scenario. Fink, a New York playwright who wants only to write "the theater of the common man" (an Arthur Miller or perhaps Clifford Odets stand-in?) is shanghaied, like Carl Van Vechten's Spider Boy, in a Hollywood inhabited by the usual Jewish producer and publicity man stereotypes. But also in residence is a William Faulkner look-alike named Bill Maher, an alcoholic, cynical, self-destructive screenwriter who refuses to stay sober in Hollywood. When Maher's beautiful mistress turns up with a slashed throat in Fink's hotel room bed next to a typewriter with blank pages in its roller, the point seems to be that the beautiful violated woman is metaphor, or metonymy, for Fink's creative impotence in Hollywood. What follows in the surrealistic blitz (with its Salvador Dali-like images of dripping wallpaper and melting walls) is a hotel fire (echo of the "Burning of Los Angeles" canvas in West's novel) and the demonic laughter of Fink's neighbor, the good-natured Ben Meadows, a closeted serial killer (played with manic charm by John Goodman). The Coen brothers are playing here with a number of themes that have been around for a long time in local fiction.

As Los Angeles emerged as America's most conspicuous city—film, media, and pop music capital; nerve center of its war and space industries; and troublesome zone of so many unassimilated, ghettoized immigrants (legal and illegal) who constitute cities within the city — it became the most conspicuous national site for disaster scenarios on screen and in print. The metropolitan city that Davis claims has "500 gated subdivisions, 2,000 street gangs, 4,000 mini-malls, 20,000 sweatshops, and 10,000 homeless residents" (354) has become target, repository, and scapegoat for national foreboding, the place where the worst fears about the future could be placed. The destruction of Los Angeles by bomb, earthquake, fire, riot, or tsunami operates as a recurring metaphor for anxieties about the fate and future of the nation.[3]

Geographic determinism, which Davis acknowledges but downplays, makes the city both an obvious and inevitable choice for doomsday renderings. The land itself, lying on a major fault line, given to periodic quakes as well as annual cycles of fire, flood, and mud slide, offers itself to such dark visions. The hot, dry Santa Ana winds, meanwhile, product of the confluence of desert, mountain, and coastal basin, not only contribute to the annual (fall) fires in the hills and mountains, but inflame the nerves of local residents as well, intensifying the dark imaginings.

The eco-disaster in Los Angeles fiction characteristically works in conjunction with human failure, serving in some of the novels as a kind of cosmic wake-up call to man's destructive interventions on the fragile landscape. This theme of nature's response to man's greed is prominent in Ross Macdonald's crime fiction. Even earlier, in Myron Brinig's *The Flutter of an Eyelid* (1933), the Big One comes as the answer of an angry God to Southern California Babylon, dumping the whole coast, "swiftly, relentlessly, into the Pacific Ocean,"[4] a prophesy that anticipates Curt Gentry's 1986 scenario in *The Last Days of the Late Great State of California* and John Carpenter's 1996 film *Escape from L.A.*

Even when not envisioned as the site of apocalypse, the constructed Los Angeles has been the recurring locus of the violent ending. That hard-boiled, brutal fiction has taken so strong a hold in a region so given to hyper-inflated dreaming should be no surprise, even if we omit geographic determinism from the equation. From the 1920s to the present the dominant theme in Los Angeles fiction has been the betrayal of hope and the collapse of dreams. Writing against the optimistic booster literature produced just before and after the turn of the century, the city's novelists constructed a counterfable about loss. The principal local genres—the hard-boiled crime story, the tough-guy detective tale, and the Hollywood novel, as well as recent ethnic fiction—each in its way, envisioned the city as the place where dreams founder against the edge of the continent. The end, when it doesn't come from earthquake, nuclear bomb, or fiery conflagration, comes most often, as I have indicated in earlier chapters, as fatal automobile accident, murder, or suicide.

If, though, the major body of Los Angeles fiction has pointed to violent endings, there has been in the last few decades (since the 1960s) something of a countertrend in several recent survivor's tale novels, which take for their subjects not only disaster but also the coping with disaster—the living through, surviving, and enduring disaster. The city might offer the prospect of doom, but in some contemporary works urban disaster has provided the occasion for the reaffirmation of self in the capacity to endure. The place of endings thus can become the place of beginnings—at least as some recent writers have asserted. Over against the ironic pseudoaffirmation of Alison Lurie's *The Nowhere City*, or the dark, nihilistic vision of Joan Didion's *Play It as It Lays*, there have been novels, a significant number of them by women, about people who find as they come to the end of the line and continent reasons for going on, mandates to affirm the demands of self, community, and spirit. Novels like Christopher Isherwood's *A Single Man* (1964), Kate Braverman's *Palm Latitudes* (1998), Cynthia Kadohata's *In the Heart of the Valley of Love* (1992), and, most strikingly, Carolyn See's *Golden Days* (1987) and *Making History* (1991) are such works. They do not represent a cyclic return to the old booster optimism, the pendulum swung back. Far from it. But they do offer affirmations of the strength of the human spirit in the face of millennial doom-saying and ecological and man-made disaster.

## II

In three significant novels featuring Mexican Americans in present-day Los Angeles—Kate Braverman's *Palm Latitudes*, John Rechy's *The Miraculous Day of Amalia Gomez* (1991), and T. Coraghessan Boyle's *Tortilla Curtain* (1995)—disaster is not rendered as sudden destruction but is woven into the fabric of everyday living as their characters strive to endure poverty, prejudice, and marginalization. Rechy, who is part Chicano, focuses his novel on a single day in the life of a Mexican-American woman. It is a day of reckoning for her, a day that begins with her seeing a white cross flash in the sky and ends with her assault by a thief who puts a gun to her head and, just before dying from a police bullet, begs Amalia to bless him. Scattered through the day are the painful memories that she has carried to this present: the discovery that the man she has been living with has been sexually assaulting her daughter, that her younger son has become a homosexual prostitute, and that her firstborn son has committed suicide (or has been killed by guards) in prison. Against such a horrific past, the extraordinary conclusion, played against blinding lights from cameras, police spotlights, and pistol shots, makes it "the miraculous day," the day that will give her the strength and faith to survive.

Boyle's bicultural novel pits an Anglo couple, Delaney and Kyra Mossbacher—he an environmental writer and amateur naturalist, she a successful real estate agent—against an alter ego Mexican couple, Candida and Ameriga Rincon, illegal immigrants who are holed up in the canyon behind the Mossbacher's Topanga Canyon house. While the Mexican couple fights off starvation and flooding in the canyon, their Anglo counterparts, "white flight" migrants to the rustic, "good life" California neighborhood, live behind high walls in a gated tract called Arroyo Blanco (i.e., White Canyon). The entire novel is about walls, fences, and dangerous crossings—from the coyote-led Mexican border crossing of the Rincons to their crossing, or penetrating, the walls of the guarded white world. From its opening pages, where a freak accident first links the two couples, to their proximity as "neighbors"—the couples occupying opposite sides of the wall that separates safe suburbia from dangerous wilderness (haves from have-nots)—the novel advances, satirically and comically, the story of cultural misunderstanding and Anglo terror as Delaney Mossbacher's liberal leanings are put to the test. His dilemma: how to square these leanings with the perceived threat to the world he has built posed by homeless Mexicans in his backyard.[5]

Braverman's more sustained narrative, *Palm Latitudes*, is the most interesting and ambitious of these recent novels about Mexican-

American survival. Braverman's expansive, feminist Chicana novel, borrowing in its treatment the Latin American magic realism of Márquez and Fuentes, traces the personal histories, the stories, of three Mexican-American women: Marta Ortega, born in Los Angeles of a Spanish father and Indian mother (and occupying the same house on Flores Street in the Echo Park area for more than half a century); Gloria Hernandez, her neighbor, an immigrant and abused housewife; and Francesca Ramos, La Puta de la Luna (Whore of the Moon), who winds up a streetwalker in Echo Park after being abandoned by a rich Mexican lover. Each, as she tells her story, emerges less as a character than as a voice, a lyrical assertion of female qualities (linked to the lunar, the nonlinear, the tropical zones, and the Spanish language) and an outcry against male qualities (linked to *machismo*, the linear city, and the English language).

Throughout the novel Braverman sets what she calls the "personal geography" of the women against the "angles and linear evolution" of the city. Personal geography is linked to neighborhood geography, to the streets surrounding Echo Park, which stands initially as a kind of free zone existing in opposition to the sharp angles of the postmodern Anglo city. It is represented as a multiethnic enclave of people with a "mixture of blood and gods and alphabets." Echo Park, lying east of Hollywood, west of downtown, beneath the hills that rise above Sunset Boulevard, and just below the Chavez Ravine barrio that was razed to make way for Dodger Stadium, has been central to the history of Los Angeles. Although this history is not part of Braverman's fictional province, it was the site of the city's first local oil boom (Doheny's strike in 1892) and a few decades later the location of Aimee Semple McPherson's Angelus Temple, which has been in continuous operation since the twenties. For Braverman the palm-lined park with its lake at the center is the nexus of the city, the site of silent communication among the three women, and a place where messages are implicit in natural things, in "letters strewn in leaves, sentences strung between branches." (348)

The natural world is the domain of Marta, a semimystical woman whose life is devoted to planting and nurturing flowers, digging, as we see her first from Gloria's eyes, down to "the submerged regions beneath the surface . . . as if she expected to uncover the pulse of the universe." (152) Marta has magically transformed her landscape of poverty into a lush garden and engendered, by two husbands, two luxuriant, eccentric daughters (Angelina and Orqueidia—Angel and Orchid), perverted extensions of her love for beauty. She has created them as rare, exotic plants. Like their mother they are unable to sustain marriages (which mean linearity and regularity), but unlike the plants of their mother's garden, they become rootless wanderers, constantly transplanting themselves in the search for the perfect life, the perfect man, the perfect wardrobe, returning home (their high heels sinking into Marta's garden) when things don't work out.

Generational conflict here is a sign of urban transformation from neighborhood and community to postmodern fragmentation and instability. The high-heeled, footloose daughters of a deeply rooted mother are the symptoms of a city entering a period of decay, with Echo Park as its epicenter. The neighborhood stability that has sustained Marta collapses. Flores Street experiences a series of human and environmental disasters: the woman across the street has murdered her husband; the sun is a ball of fire, and Santa Ana winds rip up Marta's plants and spew dust over everything; the gay couple next door, her only friends, one dying of AIDS, move away; and a tree mysteriously uproots itself, defying gravity by rising from the ground, an act, Marta concludes, of suicide. Marta, who reads events cosmically, senses that the apocalypse has come, "less startling and durable than predicted. Perhaps Flores Street was merely living on in altered form, ash after the conflagration, ash waiting for the sea breeze to take the dust they had become into the air, into oblivion, nothingness." (275) In her vision there are no endings: nothing dies, but everything alters. Nurtured herself by the plants she has nurtured, she knows, mystically, the permanence and numinous quality of all natural forms. Her voice is transcendent, optimistic, resilient. She will endure, go on in an altered state, living, finally, on a bench in Echo Park, where Francesca, La Puta, nearby, leans against a palm tree, waiting for customers.

Braverman's three Latina women, whether they survive or fail in the doomed city, represent alternate versions of Chicana life in contemporary Los Angeles. Despite the flaws of the book—its sometimes overwrought prose (a too-self-conscious striving for "high style") and its reductive view of Mexican-American males (all her Chicanos are ignorant, unfeeling *machos*; the only sympathetic males are the Anglo gay couple)—the novel is an impressive achievement.

## III

Four novels from the 1960s and just after—Isherwood's *A Single Man*, Lurie's *The Nowhere City*, Pynchon's *The Crying of Lot 49*, and Didion's *Play It as It Lays*—each dealing with an Anglo protagonist, converge on the gesture of the newcomer, the migrant, to lay claim to the city, to know it and find in it a sense of place, perhaps a home. The four writers were themselves migrants. Isherwood, though, was no newcomer to the city when he wrote his novel, having, like his countryman Aldous Huxley, spent the last half of his life in Southern California. He left England in the mid-1930s, lived in Berlin for four years, then settled in Los Angeles in 1939, at the age of thirty-five, just at the time his Berlin stories (*Goodbye to Berlin*) were appearing—stories that made him a literary celebrity and became the basis for the John Van Druten play, *I Am a Camera* (in 1951), and later the stage musical *Cabaret*. In Los Angeles he lived on the coast in Santa Monica, worked periodically as a screenwriter, taught college, and was a member of the Vedanta Society in Hollywood. Lurie, born in Chicago and living in upstate New York, spent little time in Los Angeles—enough, though, to gather material for her Los Angeles satire, a book that can be read, depending on who reads it, as either hate mail or ironic love letter to the city. Pynchon, who lives in New York, and whose superb essay on the 1965 riots has been cited in an earlier chapter, tells the story in *The Crying of Lot 49* of a woman seeking to know a city that remains cryptic, encoded, and ultimately unknowable. Didion, a native of Sacramento and a University of California, Berkeley, graduate, lived for a time in Los Angeles with her husband, John Gregory Dunne, where she produced, among other works, the splendid essays collected in *Slouching Towards Bethlehem* and *The White Album*.

Isherwood's *A Single Man* represents a single day in the life of a single man—a fifty-eight-year-old gay British expatriate, a professor of English at a local state college who lives at the beach (a cottage in Santa Monica Canyon) and travels cross town to his teaching job. The single day is the scaffolding for the novel, providing, as it does for Rechy in *The Miraculous Day of Amalia Gomez*, the structure that supports its narrator's meditations on life, death, and loss, rendered in interior monologues, daydreams, and conversation. The events of the day—a class taught, a hospital visit to a dying friend, a drive into the hills, a midnight swim in the Pacific—function both as trigger and counterpoint to George's reflections. Throughout the day he is tormented by a sense of loss—the loss of his youth and vitality, the loss of a simpler, more bucolic city he remembers before the postwar development mania (the same loss Marta Ortega in *Palm Latitudes* feels in the angular city), and the loss he most sorely feels, that of his lover, Jim, who has died in a car crash.

The landscape both shapes and takes on the colors of George's moods; smog blankets the San Gabriel Mountains and high-rise development lines the freeways. In a reminiscent mood he returns, on his way home from the college, to the Santa Monica Mountains where he used to hike with Jim, finding, in place of the primitive nature he enjoyed, heavy traffic on mountain roads and shoddy housing tracts clogging Mulholland Drive. Looking down into the valley from the crest on Mulholland (like Philip Marlowe looking down from Guy Sternwood's patio to the ruined landscape below), he reflects like a biblical prophet on the city's doom engendered by man's greed. If Cuban missiles haven't brought on the Armageddon, he muses, runaway suburbanization will. The developers have "eaten up wide pastures and ranchlands and the last stretches of orange grove; sucked out the surrounding lakes and sapped the forest of the high mountains . . . no need for rockets to wreck it . . . or a huge earthquake to crack it off and dump it in the Pacific. It will die of over-extension."[6] For the aging, overrefined Englishman, carrying his memories of Cotswold villages, the ravaging of the Southern California landscape is the analog to the apocalypse.

Significantly, the novel he teaches that day is Huxley's Hollywood fantasy, *After Many a Summer Dies the Swan,* about a man who lives in an ersatz medieval castle, owns a celebrity, Forest Lawn-like cemetery, and seeks obsessively the secret to eternal life. His students, though, haven't read the book, so he tells them with a good deal of wit and charm the myth of Tithonus. George knows, of course, that he can have neither eternal life nor youth, but in bed that night, having been put there by his young student Kenny Potts after their drunken late-night swim in the Pacific, he realizes that life is far from over, that he is alive *now* and this will have to do. Speaking to himself in the third person, as if the self is a character he has created, he asks: *"But George is getting old. Won't it soon be too late?"* And answers: "Never use those words to George. He won't listen. . . . Damn the future. . . . George clings only to Now. It is Now that he must find another Jim. Now that he must love. Now that he must live . . . " (154). Small affirmation, perhaps, but still affirmation, and one that is in keeping with the California life that George has chosen. He will neither retire, go back to England, nor give up his beach house; he may even find an end to his loneliness and grief. This belief in the possibilities of the renewal of self in a place where friends are dying or dead, in a landscape perched at the edge of the ocean—up against hills capable of crushing him in an earthquake, or bursting into flame, or pouring down tsunamis of mud—is enough for him to go on. Like Marta, the aging Chicana in Braverman's novel, George is rooted to a landscape, a home territory in an unstable land that offers both terror and beauty.

Alison Lurie's double-edged satire on the Westside hip people, *The Nowhere City*, plays the belief in personal regeneration as comic irony. The decision of her migrant heroine, Katherine Cattleman, to remain in a live-for-the-now, live-for-the-moment sixties Los Angeles is not the purposeful existential choice of a self-reflective and fully aware character (Isherwood's George) but that of a woman for whom going Californian means a good guru, a new wardrobe, new makeup, and a commitment to self-makeover. You can take Los Angeles on its own terms, as Katherine does, or leave it and go back East, as her husband Paul does. The chief irony of the novel is that Paul is a historian, a bookish, Harvard-trained scholar who has been lured to Los Angeles to write the history of a Santa Monica research firm (perhaps the Rand Corporation) only to find that the firm has no interest whatever in history; it simply likes the idea of having a historian on its staff. Near the end of the novel Paul writes a letter to a New England friend:

> The basic thing about L.A, he explained, was that it lacked the dimension of time. As Katherine had first pointed out to him, there were no seasons there, no days of the week, no night and day; beyond that there was (or was supposed to be) no youth or age. But worst, and most frightening, there was no past or future—only an eternal dizzying present. In effect the city had banned historians as Plato had poets from his Republic.[7]

At this point Paul is ready to go home, having had his early-on fling with the 1960s "L.A. Woman," Ceci, the sexually uninhibited, liberated female (who keeps the lights on during sex, not like Katherine), waitress by night, abstract expressionist painter by day. Katherine's early days, meanwhile, have been marked by continuous misery, migraines, and a distinct hatred for the hedonistic city.

The Cattlemans live in a West Los Angeles bungalow in a neighborhood called Vista Garden—with no vista and no garden. Lurie, following the line laid out by West, plays on the architectural masquerades—an initial source of fascination for Paul and of contempt for Katherine (who has kept her New England heirlooms in storage). The stucco houses come in "ice cream" colors, and the whole neighborhood, in which houses are constantly being razed and rebuilt, has the appearance of a movie set. Houses look like pagodas and gas stations, and gas stations look like lighthouses. A drive-in milk bar is topped by a giant plaster cow. Katherine tells a friend that coming in from the airport she passed a twenty-foot-high revolving cement donut. Like the enormous hole in the donut, Los Angeles is for her a huge advertisement for nothing.

The newly arrived Katherine is registering on the early pages of the novel the familiar, and properly Bostonian, derision for the centerless, seemingly improvised and instant city with its masquerade architecture and its plaster cows and donuts hovering above the traffic. It is the same kind of architectural derision that West's New England artist Tod Hackett expressed in *The Day of the Locust* a quarter of a century earlier. Gauging, and deriding, the built landscape of the city by eastern canons of taste has been a standard, and long-clichéd, feature in the city's ongoing fictional representation. The real issue is that Los Angeles, as one critic put it, belongs "to an entirely different urban code."[8] One can't assess the West Coast city in the language of urbanism learned in the East.

For Lurie, though, as East Coast writer, decoding Los Angeles entails the piling of one, then another image of urban disarray into a mountain of chaos. She does this largely through comic incongruities: smog against palm trees, flowers so big as to appear artificial, a French chateau crawling along a street on the back of a truck, crowds at the beach almost naked against Merry Christmas signs, store windows decorated with painted snow and icicles, and sunbathers lounging beside empty swimming pools. Glory Green, the Hollywood starlet, lives in a house in the Hollywood Hills that contains a ten-foot artificial Christmas tree sprayed "pale pinkish blonde" to match her hair. A prowler lurks the grounds, then runs off in terror when he sees her face caked with cosmetic mud and her hair wrapped in toilet paper.

All of this is funny, if not new (not, that is, since West), and all of it preamble to Katherine's own heady conversion from contemptuous outsider to celebratory insider, from headachy recluse to chic new age woman. She goes native with a vengeance. The conversion comes about after a liberating affair with her psychiatrist, Isadore Einman— a hip Beverly Hills avatar of the Ever-present Now. Nothing really counts in Los Angeles, neither the past nor the future, he tells her, so one can do anything. "If there's no schedule, then you are free to work out your own schedule. A place like this, Los Angeles, actually it's a great opportunity." (173) To be appreciated, the novel insinuates through its guru figure, Los Angeles must be decoupled both from a sense of history and an ordered sense of place, notions that derive from the East.

In the key conversion scene Katherine, fresh from sex with Iz, stops in an upscale Beverly Hills boutique and tries on tight yellow capri pants and a pink top. Wearing sunglasses, she approaches the mirror; what she thinks is another customer coming up behind her is actually her own reflection. She has been, she believes, transformed, made new. At the end of the novel, a disgruntled Paul, who has had enough of hedonism in the antihistorical city, leaves for Boston to look for a job. On his return to retrieve Katherine, he meets her at a Hollywood party (celebrating the reunion of Iz and his mistress, the starlet Glory Green), spotting her in the crowd wearing her yellow pants. Her hair has been dyed ash blond. She tells him she has decided to stay. "You know what's the matter with you, Paul," she admonishes. "You're always thinking about what happened before now or what might possibly happen some time later. You're squeezed between the past and the future; you're not living." (318)

So much for history. So much for the angst of Isherwood's George, who cannot and will not let go of the past. Playing against one of the dominant themes in Los Angeles fiction—the inescapability of history—Lurie offers the quick fix to historical conditioning. One wonders whether to take Lurie's novel as unadulterated satire by an eastern writer who truly hated Los Angeles—and loved to hate it, the way Woody Allen hates it—or a quasi-feminist tract about a woman who comes out from under the domination of an overintellectualizing, patronizing nerd of a husband (albeit capable of his own California fling). Lurie has it both ways, and that is the point of the novel.

Pynchon's postmodernist take on a woman's search for the meaning of Los Angeles, *The Crying of Lot 49*, could not in tone, structure, and density be more different from Lurie's book, and yet in offering the city as a network of signs, or free-roaming signifiers that elude meaning, Pynchon's book has an odd connection to Lurie's, which offers a catalog of visual images that bear no relation to Katherine's Bostonian sense of reality (sunbathing beside an empty swimming pool, for instance).[9] With Pynchon, though, the broad satirical stroke gives way to an involuted, labyrinthine comedy resting on the border between insanity (paranoia and delusion in a world of self-referential signs) and conspiracy (the possibility that the signs *do* point to threatening realities outside the self). The city, called by Pynchon San Narcisco, is an arena of signs that point both inward, narcissistically, to the self and outward to a mysterious other world, a world beneath the "real" world, that Oedipa Maas (her name suggesting her role as seeker) has to penetrate. She has come to the city as executrix of the will of a mysterious billionaire financier/developer, Pierce Inverarity, her onetime lover. Inverarity has transformed the city into an industrial and technological behemoth. His legacy is not only Los Angeles (which suggests he is something of a latter-day Harrison Gray Otis, Harry Chandler, or perhaps Howard Hughes), but America itself. Oedipa's quest is to understand what he has built and bequeathed, with "his need to possess, to alter the land, to bring new skylines, personal antagonisms, growth rates into being."[10]

Oedipa, who sees the city for the first time from the freeway and pictures it as printed circuit (unreadable, though offering the promise of communication), stays in a motel called Echo Court. Everything in the novel bounces back on itself, bringing to mind what Inverarity had once told her: "Keep it bouncing, that's the secret, keep it bouncing." (134) At the end of the novel Oedipa Maas, as urban detective, has come to the end of the line. The quest for answers leads her to the very edge of the ocean, where so many Los Angeles characters have come to the end. A dead telephone in her hand, she stands "between the public telephone booth and the rented car, in the night, her isolation complete, and tried to face toward the sea. But she had lost her bearings." (134)

No character in Los Angeles fiction, though, has lost her bearings the way Maria Wyeth has in Didion's *Play It as It Lays*. Everything has come to nothing for her. Narrated essentially as a memory piece by Maria from a mental hospital in Nevada following her breakdown, the novel is a "white book" with more white space than print—87 chapters, some only a paragraph, in 218 pages—the typographical equivalent to the fragmentation, the discontinuity, of her life. A sometime Hollywood actress, sometime model, she is separated from her director husband and her brain-damaged daughter, forced by her husband, Carter, into having an abortion, and witness—one could say accomplice—to the suicide of a friend, an alcoholic, homosexual producer named BZ, who dies in her arms. After his death she says to herself: "I know what 'nothing' means, and keep on playing. Why, BZ would say, Why not, I say."[11] Nothing matters—including survival or suicide—in this novel that goes beyond existentialism into pure nihilism.

Maria's life has been reduced to pointless rounds of barbiturate-laced sexual encounters, movement across freeways with no destination, nightmares of stopped-up plumbing, and television news bytes of children found in abandoned refrigerators, houses sliding into canyons, and evangelists preaching that eight million people will perish in an earthquake on a Friday afternoon in March. Her only moments of solace come in daydreams about herself, Carter, and their daughter, Kate, restored to a happy family. She takes to freeway driving as ritual, a way of playing it as it lays. Habitually, she gets on the freeway at ten in the morning, crisscrossing the concrete landscape, carrying her lunch so she won't have to stop, and making complicated lane changes in a futile effort to give her life some meaning.

> Once she was on the freeway and had maneuvered her way
> to a fast lane she turned on the radio at high volume and she
> drove. She drove the San Diego to the Harbor, the Harbor up
> to the Hollywood, the Hollywood to the Golden State, the
> Santa Monica, the Santa Ana, the Pasadena, the Ventura. . . .
> Again and again, she returned to an intricate stretch just

south of the interchange where successful passage from
the Hollywood onto the Harbor required a diagonal move
across four lanes of traffic. On the afternoon she finally did
it without once braking or once losing the beat on the radio
she was exhilarated, and that night she slept dreamlessly. (14)

Elsewhere, in the essay collection *The White Album,* Didion has
written of freeway driving as a form of "secular communion"—the
only one we have, she says—requiring "total surrender, a concentration so intense as to seem a kind of narcosis, a rapture of the freeway." In this rapture "the mind goes free. The rhythm takes over. . . .
The exhilaration is in doing it."[12] For Maria the ability to cross four
lanes of traffic without braking or missing a beat on the radio constitutes a victory. The past is blotted out and the future holds nothing;
the freeway, as present encounter, is all there is, offering the paradox
of endless mobility without destination. This is the only ground to
"play it as it lays." The freeway is an environment, a place, not a passage to somewhere. Reyner Banham, the British architectural critic
who spent time in Los Angeles in the 1960s, named the freeway as
one of the distinct zones of the city: "Autopia" is one of the four ecologies in his *Los Angeles: The Architecture of Four Ecologies.* The freeway, he wrote, is "a single comprehensive place, a coherent state of
mind, a complete way of life, the fourth ecology of the Angeleno."[13]
   Much of the action—such as it is—in Didion's novel takes place
not on the urban freeway but on the highway between Los Angeles
and Silver Wells, Nevada, where Maria was born. The town she remembers is gone, like everything else. It has become, appropriate to
her state of mind, a nuclear test site. The desert is a wasteland lit-
tered with ghost towns, cinderblock motels, gas stations, trailer courts,
abandoned talc mines, Pentecostal churches, beer bars, and an occasional hot spring. From the early booster celebrants of the rejuve-
nating power of the Mojave through Norman Mailer's desert as fun
zone for a bored Hollywood crowd to Didion's wasteland, the California desert has gone from a potent symbol of regeneration to one
of utter ruin.
   In *The Nowhere City* and *Play It as It Lays* Alison Lurie and Joan
Didion offer opposing fictional versions of the destiny of the 1960s
Los Angeles woman. For Lurie's Katherine Cattleman Los Angeles

winds up ironically as the place of new beginnings, a future away from the strictures of New England; for Didion's Maria Wyeth the city marks the end of the line. What both women share, though, is the need for erasure of the past. Katherine, the New England migrant, after an initial period of misery in the "dizzying present" of Los Angeles, gleefully joins the Westside Now Generation, leaving behind both history and husband; Paul, the professional historian, returns to Boston, where, presumably, history counts. Maria Wyeth, the Los Angeles woman bereft of husband, daughter, and career, and haunted by the past, suffers misery that no new wardrobe will assuage. There is no new California beginning for her, only the hope of getting by each day by finding ways to ease the pain of memory. Driving the freeways without destination, as ritual exercise, is one way of regaining some control. In one sense she is a reincarnation of James M. Cain's Mildred Pierce, for whom fast driving across the Southern California landscape provided a sense of control over one's life, but Mildred was always heading somewhere—toward a future destination she believed could be reached. Maria Wyeth's aimless movement across the freeways suggests a closer parallel to Gloria Beatty's movement across the dance floor in Horace McCoy's *They Shoot Horses, Don't They?* It is movement, Gloria knows with painful existential awareness, that is only a round of endless motion without progress; one ends up in the same place, but exhausted.

## IV

Mobility, geographic and social, has always been one of the great enticements of Los Angeles, the city promoted from the beginning as the locus of regeneration and self-transformation. Beginning with Paul Cain, James M. Cain, and Horace McCoy in the 1930s and extending to the 1960s and 1970s of Thomas Pynchon and Joan Didion, though, Los Angeles fiction has undermined this faith in progress, mobility, and regeneration; the California highway ends up as a cul-de-sac, turning back on itself, offering only the illusion of a future. In Cynthia Kadohata's *In the Heart of the Valley of Love* and two recent novels by the Los Angeles-born Carolyn See, *Golden Days* and *Making History*, each the tale of a survivor, the story gets turned around again. Kadohata's and See's female protagonists move in, and across, a landscape of disaster in which they manage to find not only courage and hope but even occasions for celebration.

Kadohata's novel is set in a postapocalyptic Los Angeles of 2052. The city has not dropped into the ocean or become an island as it did in Brinig's *The Flutter of an Eyelid* or the film *Escape from L.A.*, but while not literally cut off from the continent, it may as well have been. After the apocalypse, it has become an unreal city, a nightmare zone of mob violence, roving gangs, police brutality, and rigid class polarization. The rich minority live in "Richtown" on the Westside, and the masses of poor survivors are scattered about the inner city. Air pollution has made the stars invisible, and rationed gas is obtainable only by black-marketed "creds." The novel is both a postapocalyptic imagining of the city and a projection into the future of present-day Los Angeles, a heightened vision of late-twentieth-century reality.

There is little conventional "plot" in the novel, which is constructed as a series of scenes and episodes that appear randomly ordered, suggesting fragmentation, disjunction, and the reduction of life to the diurnal—the day-by-day battle just to survive in an urban wasteland of homelessness, inexplicable arrests, and marauding, well-armed gangs. While the young female narrator, Francie, has wildly mixed ethnic parentage—Japanese, Chinese, and black—race conflict plays little part in the book, which was published, coincidentally, on the eve of the 1992 Watts riots. Warfare is class based; the déclassé warring masses are of all races. Francie at nineteen, forced to leave her aunt's home after her aunt's lover has been arrested, gets involved with a college newspaper, hanging out with a crowd of former gang members, outcasts, an editor who is dying of cancer, and the man who is to become her lover, Mark. With Mark's love, though, and an occasional blue sky, Francie experiences joy. Los Angeles is "surprising and violent but full of hidden savage beauties."[14] With love comes the will to accept and cope. The novel ends with Francie and Mark hiding in an arroyo from armed marauders. It is not a happy or redemptive ending; they know nothing will change. But the doomed city is also "the valley of love," and this must be enough. In this oddly, perhaps ambivalently, affirmative novel we are left with Francie's final judgment: "Los Angeles was the only home either of us had ever known, and maybe this would be the only love we would ever know. For these reasons, I knew I would never leave Los Angeles. I could not." (225)

The same conviction that affirmation can grow out of catastrophe —
indeed that the value of life and love are *born* of tragedy and loss —
is the central theme in See's recent "yea-saying" novels, *Golden Days*
and *Making History*, the first her apocalyptic stop-worrying-and-enjoy-
the-bomb novel, the second, and stronger of the two, the story of a
family's grappling with catastrophe and finding through it a path to
illumination, insight, and reintegration. Both are about white and
affluent people living in the hills and canyons at the very edge of the
continent (Topanga Canyon in *Golden Days* and Pacific Palisades
in *Making History*) — the ambiguous coastal zone that represents both
the locus of the California "good life" up against nature and the place
of violent endings for so many Los Angeles protagonists since Cain
and McCoy. Buoyed by love, friendship, and family, See's characters
find at the edge the strength to go beyond tragedy, beyond last acts
into new beginnings.

On one level *Golden Days* is a feminist, men-and-their-missiles,
bomb-as-phallus novel about an impending and finally arriving nuclear doomsday on the Southern California coast and on another the
tale of willed affirmation of life lived on the edge of doom. See's protagonist, Edith Langley, repeatedly invokes the spirit of Ronald Reagan, Caspar Weinberger, and Alexander Haig as the wielders of male
power that will bring on the apocalypse. Offered as a "domestic"
equivalent to the phallocentric political power the president and his
men have, Edith tells the story, as exemplum, of a single day in the
life of an "ordinary" man, a day in which he betrays both his wife and
his mistress. Beyond the radical feminist positioning of its narrator,
the novel is a celebration of life in a city where survival depends on
the art of improvisation. For Edith improvisation goes well. Like See
herself, Edith is a product of Los Angeles. She returns to the city in
1980, a twice-divorced single mother without apparent skills, and set-
tles in a rented cottage in Topanga Canyon. The postmodern city
she finds is one where people no longer "make" anything. Instead
they make themselves:

> . . . there were few what you'd call *businesses*. No raincoat
> makers. No soup manufacturers. Yes, there were sweatshops
> in downtown LA. And I remember a ceramics factory out
> in Glendale, but they soon went out of business. What you
> really have out here is the *intangible*. When you drove you

saw buildings, often windowless. They were either cable
television stations or movie studios . . . or death factories
where they made missiles, or think tanks where they
thought them up. . . . I ended up doing something, it
seems to me, everyone in Los Angeles did then: I made
myself up half hour by half hour.[15]

*Golden Days* is about Edith's making herself up in Los Angeles,
becoming in turn a gem expert, a financial columnist and consultant, and owner of the Third Women's Bank. Two relationships are
central to her transformation—with Lorna, her friend from L.A. State
College in the fifties, and with Skip, a financial consultant and Pacific
Rim investor, who becomes her live-in companion and lover. Lorna,
a several-times-divorced woman, is a disciple of the San Francisco-
based prophet Lion Boyce (who operates EST-like "seminars" catering to yuppies with his you-can-do-anything-you-want message), who
becomes herself, in this version of Southern California makeovers, a
prophetess and healer, a new age Sister Aimee without Christianity.
As celebrity performer, she preaches the California gospel of living
in the Now and living bravely in the face of doomsday fear (the fear
of the bomb, that is, which hovers over the entire novel). Calling herself Lorna Villanelle, she manages to perform some miraculous heal-
ings that the skeptical Edith, until her own conversion, dismisses as
pure illusion.

When the holocaust comes, Edith and Skip, fortified by love and
their advocacy of Lorna's living-in-the-Now philosophy, decide not
to flee Topanga Canyon, the place where they feel so rooted. Together with Edith's daughter and a few friends, they make their pil-
grimage on foot to the ocean where they form a community with
other survivors who have refused to leave. The ocean, the symbolic
site of California endings, is also, in Edith's revelatory vision, the place
of beginnings. That they are alive—and alive to sensations of joy—
is the miracle with which the novel closes: "There will be those who
say the end came. . . . But I say there was a race of hardy laughers,
mystics, crazies, who knew their real homes, or who had been drawn
to this gold coast for years, and they lived through the destroying light,
and on, into Light ages." (195–96)

Such are the "golden days" of the title, a title not without irony.

Heightening the irony is the snobbish and condescending tone of Edith, who reveals only contempt for the "stupid ones," the inlanders who don't make their final, brave stand on the beach and who can't spend their final days before the evacuation dining with the right people at Spago. It remains for the superior people—Edith, her daughter, Skip, some of their neighbors—to survive the holocaust and rebuild society on a matriarchal, pacifist, eco-sensitive model.

See's next and more satisfyingly realized novel, *Making History*, also deals with a family living through disaster: here not nuclear holocaust but the devastating trauma of successive, fatal automobile accidents along the coast, one killing a boy named Robin, the boyfriend of Jerry Bridges's stepdaughter Whitney, the second killing both Whitney and her infant stepbrother, Josh. It is a case of history repeating itself—like Cain's postman ringing twice—the second time with devastating effect on Jerry Bridges and his wife, Wynn. The coastal highway crash has, since the time of Cain and Chandler, been a recurring metaphor for Southern California endings; See is tapping into a long tradition of writing about the city. Even when it has not been the site of a fatal accident, the highway at the edge of the continent has repeatedly been appropriated as an image that evokes the sense of being at the end of the line, as for instance in Didion's *Play It as It Lays* and Pynchon's *The Crying of Lot 49*. In *Making History*, though, See complicates the metaphoric use of the coastal highway: it is the site both of the disastrous ending and the potential new beginning. Disaster becomes the *occasion* for Jerry and Wynn Bridges to learn the lesson of living fully in the present, just as the nuclear disaster furnishes Edith Langley with the mystical illumination of her "golden days."

See reworks some of the material of the earlier novel in *Making History*, but she reworks it into a richer, more deeply felt, and complex narrative (told by at least a half dozen alternating voices). The similarities between the two suggest the earlier novel as preparation for the latter. Jerry Bridges, the Pacific Rim financier-developer is a more fully developed Skip from *Golden Days*, and Thea, the psychic, functions much the way the prophet Lorna Villanelle does in the earlier novel: spiritual guide and mystical presence who awakens the characters to an affirmation of life lived in the present. While Thea has little direct contact with the Bridges family (a chance meeting with Jerry halfway up Ayers Rock in Australia, a single consultation with daughter Whitney), her presence hovers over the novel, as does that of the dead boy Robin, whose voice from beyond the grave, as cosmic utterance, frames the novel.

The novel also scales down the antimale tone of *Golden Days*. Edith Langley in the earlier novel would have, before meeting Skip, imagined finding a good man not hard but impossible. She puts the destruction of the world clearly on men's shoulders—not only those of the cold warrior triumvirate of Reagan, Weinberger, and Haig, but *all* men. The struggling single mom rages about male destructiveness on levels both local and global: penis as missile and premature ejaculation as the sexual equivalent to nuclear betrayal. In an interview after the later novel, *Making History*, came out, See said the new book is "both a love letter and apology to the 97% of the men who *don't* intend to blow up the world."[16]

*Making History's* Jerry Bridges, like Skip in *Golden Days*, has no intention of blowing up the world—just making it "better" by pouring billions of dollars into investments in Asia, reshaping the Far East into the image of America. As consummate postmodern, Pacific Rim-oriented California capitalist, Jerry is both an idealist and materialist, democrat and empire builder, a man who equates Asian investment with the perfection of the world. He is the New World explorer, his reach extending beyond the well-traveled territories of Japan, Australia, and Hong Kong to newer frontiers for development like Papua New Guinea, Indonesia, and Irian Jaya: "If the worlds across the sea were inchoate, unformed, then *fix* them." The resulting New Asia would be like America, but better, "not just a hotel or a factory, but a twenty-first-century city-state. . . . a new world—and a better one."[17] This is one way of making history—taking the plunge into the future, taking risks, extending the boundaries of self, going west to appropriate the East.

In the life-affirming finale, narrated by the dead Robin from high above the scene, we view Jerry Bridges's drive home to Pacific Palisades through a heavy rain along Pacific Coast Highway—the highway he had avoided since the accident that killed his son and stepdaughter. Unable to pull off the freeway in the heavy traffic to take the Lincoln Avenue off-ramp and avoid the highway, he finds himself, tears in his eyes, near the site of the accident.

He thought, in anguish, that it was just as well. He couldn't
avoid driving over where Whitney and Josh had died forever.
Pull off the scab again! Pull it off! The torn flesh was there,
the gaping wound was there. Nothing could cover it.
Nothing ever could. (269–70)

While Jerry drives the last few miles home, the narrator cuts to Wynn,
who gets up for the first time from the bed where she has lain since
the accident. She "splashed cold water on her face and combed her
hair. And went down to the den with Tina, the first time she'd done
that in months. And turned on the light." (275) Both Wynn and Jerry
are making the first, tentative steps toward healing, allowing the
prophetess Thea's advocacy of the value of the present moment to
enter their lives. Robin's playful voice, meanwhile, reiterates the lesson, channeling it down from high above the canyon to Jerry through
"some leftover Indians [he conjures] from up in the dark canyon":
"This is a beautiful world just the way it is, they breathed, waving
their waterproof baskets. Don't worry too much about it. You don't
have to fix it up *too* much." (274–75) Jerry's vision had been precisely
that: to fix the world, to make it perfect; random violence has taught
him it can never be that. He knows, too, that he can, like Wynn, begin
the task of healing the soul and celebrating what he does have in the
present day. See's multivocal narrative, rendered in voices speaking
from this and the other side of the grave, indicates a world of interconnected human relationships that transcend the global, neo-colonial
ventures that Jerry Bridges has so obsessively pursued.

## V

See's *Golden Days* and *Making History*, together with Braverman's
*Palm Latitudes* and Kadohata's *In the Heart of the Valley of Love*, can
be read as works that synthesize the dialectical opposition that has
shaped writing about Los Angeles since the beginning: the boosted
and bloated place of new beginnings and the fated site of disastrous
endings, America's Utopia and Dystopia. The protagonists of the Los
Angeles novel have been for the most part migrants, men and women
who have come to the city seeking freedom, opportunity, and the fresh
start in a region at continent's edge, where one's past is presumed to

be irrelevant and every day is a first day. From America's beginning, mobility has been inscribed in the national myth as the analog to freedom; the open road has been the signifier of selfhood—self-discovery, self-renewal, and regeneration. But the burden of the greater number of Los Angeles novels has been to reveal that movement into and through the deceptively open, fluid landscape at the end of the land doesn't easily translate into freedom and that history, what one has brought to the present from another place, is an inescapable condition of the present.

The Southern California highway as cul-de-sac has, as I have indicated in various places, been a recurring image. The 1930s protagonists of James M. Cain, George Hallas, and Horace McCoy—and a generation later Joan Didion—find that at land's end movement—on the highway or dance floor—is circular and aimless. At the end of the continent, one runs out of room. The vision is claustrophobic. Raymond Chandler's and Ross Macdonald's criminals have fled the scenes of their crimes and moved, as migrants, into high-walled sanctuaries in the hills or against the ocean, only to have their sanctuaries invaded by the detective who knows, and discloses, their histories, destroying their escape routes. The Hollywood protagonists of Nathanael West, Budd Schulberg, F. Scott Fitzgerald, and Aldous Huxley, similarly, learn that the road comes to an end. The culturally diverse voices of such writers as Walter Mosley, Luis Valdez, John Rechy, Cynthia Kodahata, Kate Braverman, and Carolyn See, however, suggest that there may be heretofore unseen streets that lead into the city, to neighborhoods that survive because they are sustained by a sense of community and connection.

Such writers have carried a sense of the city of disaster into the urban present but portray in their works characters who discover the courage, the resilience, to go on. In Carolyn See's fiction the apocalyptic event becomes the opportunity for a new beginning, the occasion for discovering and celebrating life in the present. Edith Langley, in See's *Golden Days*, returns to Los Angeles in a battered Volkswagen, two kids in the back, and learns that surviving, succeeding, and celebrating mean making your life up, "half hour by half hour." Jerry Bridges, in *Making History*, has created his perfect Pacific Palisades life—perfect house against the ocean, perfect wife, perfect children—but time, history, and chance intrude on the future-oriented Pacific

Rim financier's life in the form of the fatal car crash at the continent's rim—an event that returns her novel, in one sense at least, to James M. Cain's 1930s fables. Jerry and Wynn Bridges must remake their lives in the aftermath of tragic knowledge. Acknowledging and coming to terms with time and history is one of the essential themes in Los Angeles fiction, and See's *Making History* is one of its essential contemporary accounts. The city built by its founders on the promise of a utopian future took its essential literary identity in the decades since the 1930s—in hard-boiled crime and tough-guy detective stories, Hollywood novels, and apocalyptic fictions—as the place resting dangerously on the edge of the continent, the place that forces one to look back to sources and origins.

# NOTES

## Chapter 1

1. Frank Norris, "An Opening for Novelists: Great Opportunities for Fiction Writers in San Francisco," *The Wave* 16 (22 May 1897), 7.
2. Horace Bell, *Reminiscences of a Ranger*, quoted in Gordon DeMarco, *A Short History of Los Angeles* (San Francisco: Lexicos, 1988), 30.
3. Horace Bell, *Reminiscences*, quoted in Carey McWilliams, *Southern California: An Island on the Land* (1946; rpt. Salt Lake City: Peregrine Smith, 1973), 92.
4. McWilliams, *Southern California*, 118.
5. Mike Davis, *City of Quartz: Excavating the Future of Los Angeles* (London: Verso, 1990), 119.
6. Arna Bontemps, *God Sends Sundays* (New York, Harcourt, Brace, 1931), 160.
7. Don Ryan, *Angel's Flight* (New York: Boni and Liveright, 1927), 62.
8. Nathanael West, *The Day of the Locust* (1939; rpt. New York: New Directions, 1962), 60.
9. Joan Didion, "Some Dreamers of the Golden Dream," in *Slouching toward Bethlehem* (New York: Simon and Schuster Pocket Books, 1981), 20.
10. James M. Cain, "Paradise." Reprinted from *American Mercury* (March 1933) in *Sixty Years of Journalism by James M. Cain*, ed. Ray Hoopes (Bowling Green, Ohio: Bowling Green State University Press, 1988), 166.
11. Quoted in "Homes and Housing," in *Los Angeles: Preface to a Master Plan*, ed. George W. Robbins and Deming L. Tilton (Los Angeles: Pacific Southwest Academy, 1941) 196.

12. William Faulkner, "Golden Land," in *Collected Stories of William Faulkner* (New York: Random House, 1950), 721.

13. Gavin Lambert, *The Slide Area* (New York: Ballantine, 1951), 8.

14. Joan Didion, "Los Angeles Notebook" in *Slouching toward Bethlehem* (1968; rpt. New York: Washington Square Press, 1981), 220.

## Chapter 2

1. Before the Spanish conquest there were an estimated 300,000 Indians in California living in semipermanent villages along the shore, in the low mountains, in the desert, and on offshore islands. There was no Indian Nation in California; the Indian population, perhaps 8,000 years old, lived in small tribelets and belonged to some 100 language groups. Because they did not practice agriculture, the Spanish viewed them as primitive.

2. Kevin Starr, *Inventing the Dream: California through the Progressive Era* (New York: Oxford University Press, 1985), 89.

3. Mike Davis, *City of Quartz: Excavating the Future of Los Angeles* (London: Verso, 1990), 27.

4. Carey McWilliams, *Southern California: An Island on the Land* (1946; rpt. Salt Lake City: Peregrine Smith, 1973), 70.

5. Helen Hunt Jackson, *Ramona* (1884; rpt. New York: Grosset and Dunlap, 1912), 14.

6. Quoted in Gordon Demarco, *A Short History of Los Angeles* (San Francisco: Lexicos Press, 1988), 118.

7. Charles Fletcher Lummis, "In the Lion's Den," *Land of Sunshine* 3 (1895): 83.

8. The literature on the Owens Valley aqueduct is voluminous. Mary Austin's *The Ford* (1917) obliquely deals with it in fiction. Morrow Mayo's 1933 book, *Los Angeles* (New York: Knopf) which exposes the aqueduct "scandal," was among the first shots fired in a nonfiction account. McWilliams's *Southern California* followed Mayo's lead in 1946. More balanced views are found in William L. Kahrl's *Water and Power: The Conflict over Los Angeles' Water Supply in the Owens Valley* (Berkeley: University of California Press, 1982) *and* Abraham Hoffman's *Vision of Villainy: Origins of the Owens Valley-Los Angeles Water Controversy* (College Station: Texas A&M University Press, 1981).

9. Charles Fletcher Lummis, "In the Lion's Den," *Land of Sunshine* 3 (1895): 81.

10. Charles Fletcher Lummis, "In the Lion's Den," *Land of Sunshine* 4 (1895): 103–6.

11. Charles Fletcher Lummis, "In the Lion's Den," *Land of Sunshine* 10 (1899): 207.

12. Charles Dudley Warner, "Race and Climate," *Land of Sunshine* 4 (1895): 106.

13. Mark Lee Luther, *The Boosters* (Indianapolis: Bobbs-Merrill, 1923), 8–9.

14. Willard Huntington Wright, "Los Angeles: The Chemically Pure," *Smart Set* (1913): 99–100.

15. Katherine Ames Taylor, *The Los Angeles Trip Book* (New York: Putnam's, 1928), 22, 31.

16. Harry Carr, *Los Angeles: A City of Dreams* (New York: Appleton-Century, 1935), 31.

17. Gill constructed a good number of magnificent buildings in Los Angeles and San Diego. The razing in 1965 of the Dodge House on Kings Road in West Hollywood (near where Theodore Dreiser, Aldous Huxley, and the architect Rudolph Schindler lived) was protested vigorously. See Esther McCoy, *Five California Architects* (1960); rpt. New York: Praeger Publications, 1975), 59–100, and Kevin Starr, *Material Dreams: Southern California through the 1920s* ( New York: Oxford University Press, 1990), 218-223.

## Chapter 3

1. Quoted in Carey McWilliams, *Southern California: An Island on the Land* (1946; rpt. Salt Lake City: Peregrine Smith, 1971), 160.

2. Carey McWilliams, "Sunlight in My Soul," in *The Aspirin Age*, ed. Isabel Leighton (New York: Simon and Schuster, 1949), 59–60.

3. The quotations, drawn from Mencken's letters, are derived from Walter Wells, "Mencken in Hollywood," *Los Angeles Times Book Review*, 7 September 1980, 3.

4. Quoted from her autobiography, *Southern Belle*, by Lawrence Clark Powell, in "Upton Sinclair's *Oil!*" *Westways Magazine* (September 1970): 17.

5. Upton Sinclair, *Oil!* (1927; rpt. Berkeley: University of California Press, 1997), 21.

6. My account, including the quotations, of the Otis-Sinclair feud is drawn from Lionel Rolfe's *In Search of Literary Los Angeles* (Los Angeles: California Classics Books, 1991), 150–52.

7. A bridge between the Hollywood novel in the 1920s and the magic or fantasy life the city offered can be found in the subliterary occultist and theosophical novels that appeared with frequency in the decade, works cited by Kevin Starr in *The Dream Endures: California Enters the 1940s* (New York: Oxford University Press, 1977), 301 ff.—for example, Ada White Taylor's *The Mystic Spell* (1925), Evelyn Whitehill's *A California Poppy* (1925), and Thomas Spivey's *The Last of the Gnostic Masters* (1926). Such works, Starr writes, "touch base with the eccentric dream life of the evangelical Theosophical Southland that would make Los Angeles ground zero of science fiction, scientology and other prophetic movements of cults, most of them animated by a sense of impending doom of apocalypse, should certain steps not be taken" (301).

8. Carl Van Vechten, *Spider Boy, a Scenario for a Moving Picture* (New York: Knopf, 1928), 100.

9. Edward Lueders, *Carl Van Vechten* (Boston: Twayne, 1965), 107; and *Carl Van Vechten and the Twenties* (Albuquerque: University of New Mexico Press, 1955).

10. Neal Gabler, *An Empire of Their Own: How the Jews Invented Hollywood* (1988; rpt. New York: Doubleday/Anchor, 1989), 2.

11. For an encyclopedic catalog of Hollywood fiction, see, for instance, Anthony Slide's *The Hollywood Novel: A Critical Guide to over 1200 Works with Film-related Themes and Characters, 1912 through 1994* (Jefferson, N.C.: McFarland, 1995). Carolyn See's *The Hollywood Novel: An Historical and Critical Study* (Ph.D. dissertation, UCLA, 1963) is a pioneer work on the subject.

12. Carey McWilliams, "Books/Writers," *Overland Monthly* (January 1928): 20.

13. Don Ryan, *Angel's Flight* (New York: Boni and Liveright, 1927), 13.

14. Brinig, Myron *The Flutter of an Eyelid* (New York: Farrar and Rinehart, 1933), 13.

15. McWilliams (in the essay cited above) tells us that a twenty-six-year-old man named Robert Browning leaped into the sea after Sister Aimee and was drowned (64).

16. Mosier appeared in an earlier draft of the novel as Ike Lazarus, a book dealer, but Los Angeles bookseller Jake Zeitlin is said to have found the portrait too close to home and forced the change. For more on this, see Kevin Starr, *The Dream Endures*, 291–92; and Lionel Rolfe, *In Search of Literary Los Angeles*, 50.

# Chapter 4

1. I examine the recent resurrection of noir crime fiction in chapter 8.
2. The 1930s "hard-boiled" narrative and the "tough-guy" detective story, the one identified largely with James M. Cain and Horace McCoy and the other with Raymond Chandler, are frequently considered together as versions or manifestations of the same genre. See, for instance, David Madden's pioneering collection of critical essays, *Tough Guy Writers of the Thirties* (Carbondale: Southern Illinois University Press, 1968), which looks to both. In this study I am treating them as separate, though related genres, each growing directly out of the crime writing that emerged in pulp magazines like *Black Mask*. The following chapter looks at Los Angeles detective fiction from Chandler to the present.
3. Mike Davis, *City of Quartz: Excavating the Future of Los Angeles* (London: Verso, 1990), 38.
4. Paul Cain, *Fast One* (1933; rpt. Carbondale: Southern Illinois University Press, 1978), 299.
5. Paul Skenazy, "Behind the Territory Ahead," in *Los Angeles in Fiction: a Collection of Original Critical Essays*, ed. David Fine (Albuquerque: University of New Mexico Press, 1984), 91.
6. *You Play the Black and the Red Turns Up* (New York: Robert M. McBride, 1938), 129.
7. Edmund Wilson, "The Boys in the Back Room," in *Classics and Commercials: A Literary Chronicle of the 1930s* (New York: Farrar, Straus and Giroux, 1950), 46.
8. Paul Skenazy, *James M. Cain* (New York: Frederick Ungar/Continuum, 1989), 21.
9. Skenazy's study of Cain provides a summary and solid assessment of Cain's work and film adaptations of his work.
10. James M. Cain, *The Postman Always Rings Twice* (New York: Knopf, 1934), 3–4.
11. James M. Cain, *Mildred Pierce* (1941; rpt. Cleveland: World, 1944), 67.
12. Horace McCoy, *They Shoot Horses, Don't They?* (1935; rpt. New York: Knopf, 1939), 76.
13. Lee Richmond, "A Time to Mourn and a Time to Dance: Horace McCoy's *They Shoot Horses, Don't They?*" *Twentieth-Century Literature* 17 (1971): 91.

Chapter 5

1.  The seven novels are *The Big Sleep* (1939), *Farewell, My Lovely* (1940), *The High Window* (1942), *The Lady in the Lake* (1943), *The Little Sister* (1949), *The Long Goodbye* (1953), and *Playback* (1958). An eighth novel, *Poodle Springs*, was completed after Chandler's death by Robert Parker, author of the Boston-based Spencer novels. Two collections of his stories have been published as *The Simple Art of Murder* (1950) and *Killer in the Rain* (1964). Parker has also written a "sequel" to *The Big Sleep* titled *Perchance to Dream* (1991).
2.  *The Life of Raymond Chandler* (New York: E. P. Dutton, 1976; rpt. New York: Penguin Books, 1979), 66–67.
3.  Frederic Jameson, "On Raymond Chandler," *Southern Review* 6 (1970): 625.
4.  *The Long Goodbye* (1953; rpt. New York: Ballantine, 1971), 89–90.
5.  *The Little Sister* (1949; rpt. New York: Ballantine, 1976), 202.
6.  *Farewell, My Lovely* (1940; rpt. New York: Ballantine, 1975), 101.
7.  Carey McWilliams, *Southern California: An Island on the Land* (1946; rpt. Salt Lake City: Peregrine Smith, 1973), 153–54. Chandler rarely deals with blacks and Mexicans in his fiction; *Farewell, My Lovely* opens with a scene in a black bar on Central Avenue.
8.  Raymond Chandler, *The Big Sleep* (1939; rpt. Ballantine, 1977), 18.
9.  Richard Lehan, "The Los Angeles Novel and the Idea of the West," in *Los Angeles in Fiction: A Collection of Essays*, 2d ed., ed. David Fine(Albuquerque: University of New Mexico Press, 1984), 36–37.
10. Ross Macdonald, *The Blue Hammer* (New York: Knopf, 1976), 98–99.
11. Ross Macdonald, "The Writer as Detective Hero," in *On Crime Writing* (Santa Barbara: Capra Press, 1987), 19.
12. Ross Macdonald, foreword to *Archer in Hollywood* (New York: Knopf, 1967), viii.
13. Ross Macdonald, *The Moving Target* (1949; rpt. in *Archer in Hollywood*), 5.
14. Jerry Spier, "The Ultimate Seacoast: Ross Macdonald's California," in *Los Angeles in Fiction, (2nd ed.)* 153.
15. Ross Macdonald, *The Underground Man* (1971; rpt. New York: Bantam Books, 1972), 26, 69.

16. Interview with John Carroll, "Ross Macdonald in Raw California," *Esquire* (June 1972): 149.

17. Charles Nicol, "The Hard-Boiled Go to Brunch," *Esquire* (October 1987): 61–65.

18. To cite all the new detectives who break the mold is not feasible here. A few examples will suffice. There is Daniel Mainwaring's [pseudonym for Geoffrey Holmes] Humphrey Campbell, who works for the Missing Person's Bureau—a strapping man but also a thinking man who drinks milk, wears white suits, and plays the accordion. Anthony Boucher [pseudonym for William Anthony Parker White, who wrote under the name E. T. Ballard in his early *Black Mask* fiction] has offered in Tony Constaine and Fergus O'Brean, the first the flashily dressed, Dartmouth-educated private eye and the second the young, brainy investigator who reads, cooks, and listens to classical music. In William Campbell Gault we have Brock "the Rock" Callaghan, an ex-Stanford All-American and L.A. Ram guard, and Joe Puma, of Indian stock. Richard Prather's stylish, gentlemanly Shell Scott drinks Bombay gin, likes rare prime rib, works out in a gym, and drives a robin's egg blue Cadillac. Timothy Harris's Thomas Kyd (named after the Elizabethan playwright) is a widower, Vietnam vet, and Berkeley graduate (but no liberal). Stuart Kaminsky's Toby Peters, in a series of parodic novels set, retrospectively, in the 1940s, is the inept, comical detective solving crimes involving real celebrity movie people (including, as reductio ad absurdum, the murder of a munchkin in *Murder on the Yellow Brick Road*, 1977). Faye Kellerman's PI heroine is an orthodox Jew. Michael Nava's detective is a gay Mexican American. Gerald Locklin's *The Case of the Missing Blue Volkswagen* (1984) is a witty parody of the genre.

19. Ernest Fontana, "Joseph Hansen's Anti-Pastoral Crime Fiction," *Clues* (Spring 1986): 89–96.

20. Joseph Hansen, *Early Graves* (New York: Mysterious Press, 1987), 36.

21. Roger Simon, *The Big Fix* (San Francisco: Straight Arrow Press, 1973), 3.

22. I am indebted here to my research assistant, Mark Laurila, for calling these connections to my attention.

23. *Detecting Women 2: A Reader's Guide and Checklist for Mystery Series Written by Women*, ed. Willetta. L. Heising (n.p., 1986), 243–44.

24. Robert Crais, *Free Fall* (1993; rpt. New York: Bantam Books, 1994), 19.

25. Walter Mosley, *A Red Death* (1991; rpt. New York: Simon and Schuster Pocket Books, 1992), 15.

26. Walter Mosley, *Devil in a Blue Dress* (New York: Norton, 1990), 9.

27. Walter Mosley, *Black Betty* (New York: Norton, 1994), 61.

28. Walter Mosley, *A Little Yellow Dog* (New York: Norton, 1996), 32.

29. Interview with Jim Impoco, "On L.A.'s Mean Streets," *U.S. News Report*, 21 August 1995, 55.

30. Robert Parker, *A Savage Place* (New York: Dell, 1981), 143.

31. Interview in *The Armchair Detective* 28, no. 3 (Summer 1995): 241.

32. While the locus of Hell in Ellroy is Los Angeles, he has written about national political and criminal life in his novel *American Tabloid* about the sixties — Hoffa, Castro, the 1960 election, The Bay of Pigs, etc.

33. James Ellroy, *White Jazz* (New York: Fawcett Gold Medal, 1992), 105.

34. James Ellroy, *My Dark Places* (New York: Vintage Books, 1996).

35. Connelly, a former *L.A. Times* police reporter has been turning out a series about police detective Harry Bosch. Among the best in the series are *The Last Coyote*, *The Concrete Blonde*, *The Poet*, and *Trunk Music*. A significant coincidence between Ellroy and Connelly is that Connelly's Bosch is the son of a murdered woman. The memory of that murder conditions Bosch's responses to present cases. The murdered, mutilated, or disfigured woman is a recurring figure in Los Angeles detective fiction, as I elaborate in chapter 8.

## Chapter 6

1. Nathanael West, *Miss Lonelyhearts and The Day of the Locust* (New York: New Directions, 1962), 178.

2. Letter to Josephine Herbst. Quoted in Jay Martin, *Nathanael West: The Art of His Life* (London: Secker and Warburg, 1971), 205.

3. *The Jazz Singer*, the first talkie, offered in 1927 a significant exception in its Jewish subject matter, but in theme it urged the drive toward secular American success. The most complete account of the Jewish roots of the American film industry is Neal Gabler's *An Empire of Their Own: How the Jews Invented Hollywood* (New York: Doubleday/Anchor, 1988). Kevin Starr takes up the issue in *The Dream Endures: California Enters the 1940s* (New York: Oxford University Press, 1977), 342 ff.

4. Aldous Huxley, *After Many a Summer Dies the Swan* (1939; rpt. New York: Harper and Row, 1965), 5.

5. Walter Wells, "Between Two Worlds: Aldous Huxley and Evelyn Waugh in Hollywood," in *Los Angeles in Fiction: A Collection of Essays*, ed. David Fine (Albuquerque: University of New Mexico Press, 1984), 200.

6. In 1948, the year Waugh published *After Many a Summer Dies the Swan*, he also published *Ape and Essence*, a futuristic, dystopian fantasy about Hollywood as postatomic necropolis inhabited by a Satanic cult of mutants and dominated by a cemetery that is plundered by grave robbers.

7. Evelyn Waugh, *The Loved One, an Anglo-American Tragedy* (New York: Vintage, 1948), 40. The "painted word" in the quotation refers to a sign in front of the building that announces that the structure is a "perfect replica of an old English manor" but made of "grade A steel."

8. Less than half the novel was finished when Fitzgerald died of a heart attack on December 20, 1940. In 1994 Matthew Bruccoli, who has spent much of his career on Fitzgerald studies, issued a critical edition of the novel as *The Love of the Lost Tycoon: A Western* (Cambridge: Cambridge University Press).

9. F. Scott Fitzgerald, *The Last Tycoon* (New York: Scribner's, 1941), 3.

10. The paths of the two men crossed when Schulberg accompanied Fitzgerald on a trip east to do a treatment of the Dartmouth Winter Carnival. Schulberg wrote a novel about the experience—the aspiring screenwriter and the drunk has-been writer—*The Disenchanted* (1950). In the late thirties Fitzgerald and Schulberg had become friends. The role of Cecelia Brady in *The Last Tycoon* derives in part from what Schulberg had told Fitzgerald about his growing up as a Hollywood insider, son of a producer. Schulberg, in turn, acknowledged that the alcoholic writer in *The Disenchanted* was based on Fitzgerald but that he drew on other Hollywood alcoholic writers as well. Fitzgerald's Pat Hobby stories, which were appearing in *Esquire* at the time he was working on his last novel, portray the screenwriter as alcoholic hack, reduced to low-paying occasional assignments, the image perhaps that Fitzgerald feared others saw of him—or perhaps he saw of himself.

11. Quoted in Gabler, *An Empire of Their Own*, 337. Gabler provides an

interesting informed account of Schulberg, left-leaning writers, and the Jewish studio heads in these years.

12. Terry Curtis Fox, "The Hollywood Novel," *Film Comment* (April 1985): 12; Schulberg's comments cited in this paragraph appeared in the *Los Angeles Times*, 3 September 1987, B1.

13. Norman Mailer, *The Deer Park* (1955; rpt. New York: G. P. Putnam's Sons, 1981), 3.

## Chapter 7

1. Thomas Pynchon, "A Journey into the Mind of Watts," *New York Times Magazine*, 12 June 1966; reprinted in *Unknown California*, ed. Jonathan Eisen and David Fine (New York: Macmillan, 1985), 295.

2. The Black Sparrow collection is composed of the seven novels: *Wait Until Spring, Bandini* (1938, 1985), *The Road to Los Angeles* (1985), *Ask the Dust* (1939, 1980), *Dreams from Bunker Hill* (1982), *Full of Life* (1952), *The Brotherhood of the Grape* (1977), and *1933 Was a Bad Year* (1985); a story collection *The Wine of Youth: Selected Stories of John Fante* (1985), containing all the magazine stories in his 1940 collection, *Dago Red*, plus seven later stories; *West of Rome* (1986), containing two novellas, *My Dog Stupid* and *The Orgy*; and two volumes of letters, *John Fante and H. L. Mencken, a Personal Correspondence, 1930–1952*, ed. Michael Moreau (1989) and *Selected Letters, 1932–1981*, ed. Seamus Cooney (1991).

3. Charles Bukowski, introduction to *Ask the Dust* (1939; rpt. Santa Rosa, Calif.: Black Sparrow Press, 1980), 6.

4. As still another sign of Fante's recognition, a conference on his work held at California State University, Long Beach, in 1994 drew several hundred participants and observers, including many from Europe. A collection of essays drawn from this conference has been published by Fairleigh Dickinson University Press. The authorized biography of Fante by Stephen Cooper has just been released by Farrar, Straus, and Giroux.

5. Don Ryan, *Angel's Flight* (New York: Boni and Liveright, 1927), 62.

6. Raymond Chandler, *The High Window* (1943); reprinted in *Raymond Chandler* [a five-novel compilation] (London: William Hinemann, 1977), 167–68.

7. Stephen Cooper, "John Fante's Eternal City," in *Los Angeles in Fic-*

*tion: A Collection of Critical Essays*, 2d ed., ed. David Fine (Albuquerque: University of New Mexico Press, 1994), 84.

8. Zeitlin, the real paterfamilias of Los Angeles bookselling, had a reputation for arrogance. He, or a character loosely based on him, is satirized, in fact lampooned, in Myron Brinig's *The Flutter of an Eyelid*. See my discussion of this novel in chapter 3.

9. Carey McWilliams, "Writers on the Western Shore," *Westways* 17, no. 11 (November 1978): 20.

10. Gerald Locklin, *Charles Bukowski: A Sure Bet* (Sudbury, Mass.: Water Row Press, 1996), 31.

11. Raymond Chandler, *Farewell, My Lovely* (1940; rpt. New York: Ballantine, 1971), 3.

12. Ted Gioia, *West Coast Jazz* (New York: Oxford University Press, 1992), 8. Two recent books have appeared, both from the University of California Press (1998): *Central Avenue Sounds: Jazz in Los Angeles*, an oral history edited by several musicians, and *California Soul: Music of African Americans in the West*, edited by Jacqueline Cogdell DjeDje and Eddie S. Matthews.

13. Chester Himes, *The Quality of Hurt: The Autobiography of Chester Himes* (Garden City, N.Y.: Doubleday, 1972), 73–74.

14. Mike Davis, *City of Quartz: Excavating the Future of Los Angeles* (London: Verso, 1990), 44.

15. Walter Mosley, *A Red Death* (1991; rpt. New York: Simon and Schuster Pocket Books, 1992), 33.

16. Raymund A. Paredes, "Los Angeles from the Barrio: Oscar Zeta Acosta's *The Revolt of the Cockroach People*," in *Los Angeles in Fiction*, 239.

17. In the last chapter of this book I look at other recent novels about Mexican-Americans in the city, novels written by non-Mexican authors, or mixed-parentage authors.

18. Oscar Zeta Acosta, *The Revolt of the Cockroach People* (1973; rpt. New York: Bantam Books, 1974), 217.

19. For discussions of the issue, see Gerald Haslam, "A Question of Authority, or Who Can Write What?" *Western American Literature* (Fall 1985): 246–50; and Jonah Raskin, "The Man Who Would Be Danny Santiago," *San Francisco Bay Guardian*, 28 November 1984, 13–14, 19.

20. Ron Arias, *The Road to Tamazunchale* (Tempe, Ariz.: Bilingual Press), 70.

Chapter 8

1. Louis Banks, "I Killed Her," *Life Magazine*, 24 March 1947: 19–24. I have drawn for this summary of the case largely on accounts in the *Los Angeles Times* (16–25 January 1947). A full-length book, *Severed: The True Story of the Black Dahlia Murder*, by John Gilmore, came out in 1994 (Los Angeles: Zanja Press).

2. Dunne, who has been a correspondent for several national magazines as well as a novelist, screenwriter, and author of several nonfiction books, including *The Studio* (1969) and *Monster: Living off the Big Screen (1998)*, collaborated with his wife, Joan Didion, on the fine film adaptation of *True Confessions*.

3. John Gregory Dunne, *True Confessions* (New York: E. P. Dutton, 1977), 72.

4. The police detective as necrophiliac is represented, less explicitly, in Otto Preminger's 1944 film, *Laura*, where the voyeuristic detective falls in love with a presumably dead woman while hanging out in her New York apartment, handling her personal effects, and gazing at her oil portrait on the wall. Of course, the woman is not really dead, and the pair go on to have a "normal" relationship.

5. James Ellroy, *The Black Dahlia* (New York: Warner Books, 1988), 184.

6. P. 57. LaRue's account is fairly consistent with the program and terminology of Mankind United, as expressed by Bell.

7. The "Hollywoodland" sign, shortened to "Hollywood" in 1945, has been as much the city's icon as the Empire State Building or Chrysler Building has been for New York in past years. It has reappeared in novel after novel and has been the city's chief screen icon — its fundamental location shot. The Nirdlinger "house of death" in James M. Cain's *Double Indemnity* was beneath the Hollywoodland sign.

8. Carey McWilliams, *North From Mexico* (1948; rpt. New York: Greenwood Press, 1968), 257. In this summary of the events of 1942 and 1943 I have drawn on McWilliam's account and from the more recent account provided in David Wyatt's *Five Fires: Race, Catastrophe, and the Shaping of California* (New York: Addison-Wesley, 1997), 169–74.

9. See Wyatt, *Five Fires*, 172 ff. Wyatt interestingly links the image of the sexually promiscuous Los Angeles Chicana to earlier images of the sexually loose Mexican woman embedded in American mythol-

ogy and expressed, for instance, in Richard Henry Dana's *Two Years before the Mast.*

10. McWilliams, *North from Mexico,* 257.

11. Luis Valdez, *Zoot Suit and Other Plays* (Houston: Arte Publico Press, 1992), 30.

## Chapter 9

1. Mike Davis, *Ecology of Fear: Los Angeles and the Imagination of Disaster* (New York: Henry Holt, 1998), 276–81.

2. See, for instance, my discussion of nativist (and Anglo-Saxonist) attacks on the Eastern European immigrant during the 1880–1920 period in *The City, the Immigrant, and American Fiction, 1880–1920* (Metuchen, N.J.: Scarecrow Press, 1977), 1–15.

3. Futuristic, postatomic novels about Los Angeles constitute a significant subgenre in local fiction. The city as nuclear waste ground has been the subject of such works, to cite only a few of the most significant examples, as Aldous Huxley's *Ape and Essence,* about a genetically damaged proletariat ruled by a fascist band in a twenty-first-century Los Angeles wasteland; Steve Erickson's poetic and surreal *Days Between Stations* and *Rubicon Beach,* the latter about a man's search for a woman and his own identity in a futuristic Los Angeles landscape of ruin; and two novels I deal with in some detail in this chapter, Cynthia Kadohata's *In the Heart of the Valley of Love* and Carolyn See's *Golden Days.*

4. Myron Brinig, *The Flutter of an Eyelid* (New York: Farrar and Rinehart, 1933) 305.

5. As a novel about borders and crossings, Diane Johnson's early satiric novel, *Burning* (1971), bears some similarity to *Tortilla Curtain,* although all the characters are white. Set in affluent hillside Bel Air, the novel focuses on neighboring families who mix it up after the fire department forces conventional Barney and Bingo Edwards to cut down the hedge that separates their yard from that of Hal Harris—new age psychotherapist who runs nude therapy sessions in his house and turns on his patients with acid—a kind of Timothy Leary send-up. The "burning" of the title refers to the 1961 Bel Air fire, which provides the comic/apocalyptic finale.

6. Christopher Isherwood, *A Single Man* (New York: Avon, 1964), 92.

7. Alison Lurie, *The Nowhere City* (1965; rpt. New York: Penguin Books, 1977), 309.

8. Graham Clarke, "'The Great Wrong Place': Los Angeles as Urban Milieu," in *The American City: Literary and Cultural Perspectives*, ed. Graham Clarke (New York: Vision Press and St. Martin's, 1988), 128.

9. The connection may be more than coincidental. Lurie and Pynchon were both at Cornell at the same time—he as an undergraduate (publishing his first story in *Epoch*, the university's literary magazine), she as the wife of a faculty member in English (and later herself as a member of the department). Pynchon's novel followed Lurie's by one year.

10. Thomas Pynchon, *The Crying of Lot 49* (1966; rpt. New York: Bantam Books, 1967), 134.

11. Joan Didion, *Play It as It Lays* (New York: Farrar, Straus and Giroux, 1970), 214.

12. Joan Didion, "Bureaucrats," in *The White Album* (1979; rpt. New York: Pocket Books, 1980), 83.

13. Reyner Banham, *Los Angeles: The Architecture of Four Ecologies* (1971; rpt. Harmondsworth: Penguin Books, 1973), 213.

14. Cynthia Kadohata, *In the Heart of the Valley of Love* (1992; rpt. Berkeley: University of California Press, 1993), 25.

15. Carolyn See, *Golden Days* (1987; rpt. Berkeley: University of California Press, 1996), 12.

16. Quoted in *Contemporary American Authors*, vol. 25 (New York: Gayle Research, 1989), 403.

17. Carolyn See, *Making History* (1991; rpt. New York: Laurel/Dell, 1992), 14–17.

# INDEX

273

anti-Catholic sentiments, 233, 234
anti-Communism, 198–99. *See also* HUAC; leftist politics
anti-Nazi films, 163
anti-Semitism, 69, 199, 233. *See also* Jews
anti-Yankee sentiments, 32–33, 34
anti-"yellow horde" fiction, 234
*Ape and Essence* (Huxley), 22
apocalyptic fiction, 22–24, **231–57**; *A Single Man*, 241–43; *Crying of Lot 49*, 246–47; disaster movies, 235; fire symbolism in, 23, 132, 202–3; geographic instability as source of, 22, 188, 234–35, 236; *The Nowhere City*, 21, 243–46, 248–49; ocean symbolism in, 23, 133; *Play It as It Lays*, 247–49; racial anxieties as source of, 233–34; survival tales in, 237, 249–57; as symbol of national anxieties, 235–36; violent endings in, 236–37. *See also The Flutter of an Eyelid*
Appleton, Victor, 63
aqueduct, 8, 37–38. *See also* water supply
Arbuckle, Fatty, 63
Arcadia, 140
*Archer in Hollywood* (R. Macdonald), 130
architecture: criticism of, 138; real compared to movie sets, 12–13, 18–19; types of, 10, 13, 19–20
architecture symbolism: in *After Many a Summer Dies the Swan*, 166–67; of houses, 96–98, 127–28, 135–36. *See also* landscape symbolism

*Argonaut* magazine, 41
Arias, Ron, 201, 204–5
Arroyo Seco, 120
*Ask the Dust* (Fante), 162, 183; LA poor in, 205–6; reissued, 182, 184; text from, 179; themes in, 22, 46, 186–89
assimilation, of Jewish immigrants, 163
Atherton, Gertrude, 43
At the Sign of the Grasshopper bookstore, 190–91
Austin, Mary, 15, 36, 38–39, 41, 44, 45
Austin, Wallace Stafford, 38
*The Autobiography of a Brown Buffalo* (Acosta), 201
automobile symbolism, 24, 95–96, 98–99, 139, 142, 248. *See also* highway symbolism
Autopia, 248

Babylon set, 18
Baker, Dorothy, 196
Baldwin, Lucky, 1
Banham, Reyner, 10, 20, 138, 181, 248
barrio, 200. *See also* Mexican Americans
*Barton Fink* (film), 66, 153, 235
Baum, Vickie, 74
beach community, 140–41
*Beggars of Life* (Tully), 84
Bel-Air, 12
Belfrage, Cedric, 75, 76, 92
Bell, Arthur, 221
Bell, Horace, 5–6
Benchley, Robert, 75
Bercovich, Sacvan, 162